PR 4144 .M63 F6 1976
Fox, Susan, 1943-
Poetic form in Blake's
  Milton
MY 29 '01

D0216058

Poetic Form in Blake's *Milton*

1. Plate 42 (Albion, Jerusalem, and the eagle of inspiration)

Poetic Form
in Blake's *Milton*

Susan Fox

Princeton University Press
Princeton, New Jersey

Copyright © 1976 by Princeton University Press
Published by Princeton University Press, Princeton, New Jersey
In the United Kingdom:
Princeton University Press, Guildford, Surrey
All Rights Reserved

Library of Congress Cataloging in Publication Data will
be found on the last printed page of this book

Publication of this book has been aided by
The Andrew W. Mellon Foundation

This book has been composed in Linotype Janson

Printed in the United States of America
by Princeton University Press, Princeton, New Jersey

All quotations of Blake are from *The Poetry and Prose
of William Blake*, edited by David V. Erdman,
commentary by Harold Bloom. Copyright © 1965 by
David V. Erdman and Harold Bloom. Reprinted
by permission of Doubleday & Company, Inc.

to Larry

Contents

List of Illustrations

All illustrations are from the D copy of *Milton*, and are reproduced by permission of the Library of Congress, Rosenwald Collection. Plate numbers do not correspond to those in the Keynes and Erdman editions of the poem, which were numbered without the full-page illuminations.

Preface

William Blake's exegetes have abundantly demonstrated the coherence of his late prophetic poems, but they have conceived that coherence primarily as a visionary one, a philosophical system into which the poetry initiates one through a series of splendid but erratic passages of great imaginative intensity. The narrative coherence of these works has had little attention; their verbal structures have been considered too esoteric or too confused to yield to any systematic rhetorical criticism. Yet Blake himself placed great emphasis on artistic form:

> I have heard many People say Give me the Ideas. It is no matter what Words you put them into & others say Give me the Design it is no matter for the Execution. These People know ⟨Enough of Artifice but⟩ Nothing of Art. Ideas cannot be Given but in their minutely Appropriate Words nor Can a Design be made without its minutely Appropriate Execution[.]¹

Furthermore, his sense of artistic form at about the time he first engraved *Milton* depended on outline, on delineating structure:

> The great and golden rule of art, as well as of life, is this: That the more distinct, sharp, and wirey the bounding line, the more perfect the work of art; and the less keen and sharp, the greater is the evidence of

¹ Public Address, *The Poetry and Prose of William Blake*, ed. David V. Erdman, commentary by Harold Bloom (Garden City, N.Y.: Doubleday, 1965), p. 565. All quotations of Blake will be from this edition.

xi

weak imitation, plagiarism, and bungling. . . . The want
of this determinate and bounding form evidences the
want of idea in the artist's mind. . . .[2]

This study, in defining the elaborate rhetorical structure of
Milton and in demonstrating the congruency of that struc-
ture with the poem's system of ideas, is an attempt to sug-
gest that the late prophecies are as profound in their poetic
structures as they are in their thematic ones.

The formal principles of the poem, its symmetry and al-
ternating perspectives and disruption of conventional time
sequence, are familiar enough in Romantic poetry. "Frost
at Midnight" and "Ode to a Nightingale" are symmetrical,
Prometheus Unbound is built of the various perspectives of
its characters, and *The Prelude* for all its apparently chron-
ological development skips back and forth in time via flash-
backs and parallel experiences and late explanations of
early phenomena. But Blake uses these familiar principles
with such radical concentration in *Milton* that they are
hardly familiar any longer. Symmetry becomes the exhaus-
tive parallelism of the poem's two contrary books; all the
perspectives of the poem are focused on a single event; that
event takes place in a single instant which takes Blake fifty
pages to describe but has no measurable duration.

As the structure of *Milton* is a distillation of many of the
formal techniques of early nineteenth-century poetry, so it
is a distillation of certain techniques of an older tradition,
that of the biblical prophecies. The poem's refracted narra-
tion, its manifold repetitions of key incidents and images,
its defiance of purely rational order in the name of suprara-
tional order link it with the visionary forms of Isaiah,
Ezekiel, Daniel, and especially Revelation. But *Milton* em-
ploys these techniques even more insistently than the
prophecies do. It abolishes conventional sequential narra-
tive altogether, and establishes a system of congruencies so
precise as to make repetition into identity.

---

[2] A Descriptive Catalogue, p. 540.

I shall not argue that Blake consciously devised the structure of *Milton* according to the principles delineated in this study. The only evidence I can detect of deliberate organization is in a single revision Blake made of the poem (see Appendix B for discussion of that revision), and that evidence is too slight to bear such an argument. Blake himself described the composition of a long poem, probably an early version of *Milton*, in a letter to Thomas Butts in 1803:

> I have written this Poem from immediate Dictation twelve or sometimes twenty or thirty lines at a time without Premeditation & even against my Will. the Time it has taken in writing was thus rendered Non Existent. & an immense Poem Exists which seems to be the Labour of a long Life all produced without Labour or Study.[3]

Whether the "eternals" who allegedly dictated that poem bothered themselves with such things as rhetorical structure we have no way of knowing; Blake had certainly trained himself in such concerns, as we can tell from his earliest lyrics. Furthermore, at least five years (probably six or seven) passed between this letter and the engraving of *Milton* in nearly its final form, and we also have no way of knowing what revisions Blake made during that period, or why he made them.

The question of conscious artistic control is particularly tantalizing when the work in point is as intricately and suggestively formed as *Milton*. It may be a question of greater psychological than literary pertinence, but that does not diminish its fascination. We do not know whether Blake

---

[3] p. 697. The art to which Blake is specifically referring here is pictorial art, but his own expansion of the reference permits us to apply this comment to literary art at least by analogy.

Anne Kostelanetz Mellor's study, *Blake's Human Form Divine* (Berkeley and Los Angeles: University of California Press, 1974), traces the development of Blake's attitudes toward outline throughout his pictorial and poetic career.

consciously chose to create a poem of two exhaustively parallel books; we do not know whether he consciously arranged their matching progressions of style, or their paired stanzas, or their patterns of reflecting images. We do not know what processes of mental association are responsible for such patterns, conscious or unconscious. We can, however, recognize that in *Milton* those patterns observe perfect decorum with the meaning of the poem.

Two major issues raised by recent Blake criticism, the relation between Blake and his epic predecessor Milton and the relation between the illuminations and the texts of Blake's poetry, have direct and powerful bearing on any understanding of *Milton*. Because the purpose of this study is to elucidate the verbal structure of the work, and because so much excellent scholarship has appeared on these subjects in the last few years, I shall limit my discussion of Blake's argument with Milton to commentary on those passages in which it is instrumental in the poem's structure, and my discussion of the illuminations largely to an appendix in which I shall describe their relation to the verbal structure. Readers who wish to pursue these issues further might consult the work of Northrop Frye, S. Foster Damon, Peter F. Fisher, Florence Sandler, Joseph Anthony Wittreich, Jr., and others on Blake's response to Milton,[4] and of

[4] Northrop Frye, *Fearful Symmetry: A Study of William Blake* (1947; rpt. Boston: Beacon, 1962), pp. 351–352; S. Foster Damon, "Blake and Milton," *The Divine Vision: Studies in the Poetry and Art of William Blake*, ed. Vivian de Sola Pinto (1957; rpt. New York: Haskell House, 1968; hereafter cited as *Divine Vision*), pp. 89–96; Harold Bloom, *Blake's Apocalypse: A Study in Poetic Argument* (1963; rpt. Garden City, N.Y.: Doubleday Anchor, 1965), pp. 78–82; Peter F. Fisher, *The Valley of Vision* (Toronto: University of Toronto Press, 1961), p. 70; Florence Sandler, "The Iconoclastic Enterprise: Blake's Critique of 'Milton's Religion,'" *Blake Studies*, 5, 1 (1972), pp. 13–57; Irene Taylor, "Say First! What Mov'd Blake?: Blake's *Comus* Designs and *Milton*," *Blake's Sublime Allegory: Essays on The Four Zoas, Milton, Jerusalem*, ed. Stuart Curran and Joseph Anthony Wittreich, Jr. (Madison: The University of Wisconsin Press, 1973; hereafter cited as *Sublime Allegory*), pp. 233–258; Harold Fisch, "Blake's Miltonic Moment," *William Blake:*

David V. Erdman, W.J.T. Mitchell, Jean H. Hagstrum, and others on the illuminations.[5]

Essays for S. Foster Damon, ed. Alvin H. Rosenfeld (Providence: Brown University Press, 1969; hereafter cited as Rosenfeld), pp. 36–56; Joseph Anthony Wittreich, Jr., "William Blake: Illustrator-Interpreter of *Paradise Regained*," *Calm of Mind: Tercentenary Essays on Paradise Regained and Samson Agonistes in Honor of John S. Diekhof*, ed. Joseph Anthony Wittreich, Jr. (Cleveland: Press of Case Western Reserve University, 1971), pp. 93–132; Wittreich, "Opening the Seals: Blake's Epics and the Milton Tradition," *Sublime Allegory*, pp. 23–58.

Of these the Sandler essay and "Opening the Seals" are the most comprehensive. The latter is the only work on the list that deals principally with the poetic rather than the conceptual relation of the two poets.

5 David V. Erdman, *The Illuminated Blake* (Garden City, N.Y.: Doubleday Anchor, 1974), pp. 216–267; W.J.T. Mitchell, "Style and Iconography in the Illustrations of Blake's *Milton*," *Blake Studies*, 6, 1 (1973), pp. 47–71; Mitchell, "Blake's Composite Art," Rosenfeld, pp. 82–91; Jean H. Hagstrum, "Blake and the Sister-Arts Tradition," Rosenfeld, pp. 82–91; Robert N. Essick, "Blake and the Traditions of Reproductive Engraving," *Blake Studies*, 5, 1 (1972), pp. 59–103. The first two of these essays deal directly with the illuminations of *Milton*, and the others argue the general relation of Blake's illuminations to his poetry.

Acknowledgments

My debts to previous Blake scholarship are too great to be adequately acknowledged in footnotes, and I am eager to record my gratitude here, especially to the works of S. Foster Damon and Northrop Frye. For their scholarship, and even more for their advice and encouragement, I am grateful to Harold Bloom, who first guided me through Blake's complexities, and David Erdman, whose generosity in sharing his knowledge is Blakean in proportion. Anthony Heilbut, Thomas R. Frosch, and Florence Sandler read my manuscript and offered invaluable suggestions.

For permission to reproduce six of Blake's illuminations of the final, D copy of *Milton* I am grateful to the Library of Congress, Rosenwald Collection.

The Queens College Word Processing Center prepared the manuscript. I appreciate the skill of Wendy DeFortuna, who typed patiently through Blake's vagaries and my own.

An early version of the argument of this study appeared in *Blake Studies*, II, 1 (1969).

Poetic Form in Blake's *Milton*

I. Contexts

Throughout his poems William Blake attempted to reform established traditions; *The Book of Thel* is a revision of pastoral idealism, *Europe* of Milton's theology, *Jerusalem* of everyone's theology. The nature of Blake's revision of conventional poetic techniques deserves particular attention, because exaggerations of his heterodoxy have encouraged even sympathetic readers to assume that his prophetic poems have no coherent structural frameworks. *The Four Zoas, Milton,* and *Jerusalem* have been considered brilliant collections of set pieces in random or at best indecipherably subjective orders; their supposed randomness has even been elevated to the ranks of their principal virtues. A close study of the individual poetic units of *Milton* and their interrelationships, however, should at least mitigate any suggestion of structural randomness charged to or against the prophetic Blake. The structure of *Milton* is unique, and forbidding in its complexity, but it is a comprehensible poetic structure nonetheless.

However unique the frameworks of Blake's late prophecies may be, their basic elements are surprisingly conventional. Blake's diction, for example, may seem perverse to a reader who likes his angels exemplary, and yet the basis of that diction is anything but perverse: as Josephine Miles has demonstrated, the language of Blake's poetry throughout his career is the familiar poetic language of the eighteenth century.[1]

---

[1] *Eras and Modes in English Poetry* (1957; rpt. Berkeley and Los Angeles: University of California, 1964), Chapter Five. Robert F. Gleckner, in "Blake's Verbal Technique" (Rosenfeld, pp. 321–332), notes that Blake uses his inherited vocabulary "towards ends quite foreign to eighteenth-century thinking," and finds this new use "a

3

Traditional though Blake's vocabulary may be, of course, he does often employ it in a startingly innovative way. Not only does he introduce extravagant, invented names (Luvah, Golgonooza, Ololon) and radically reworked conceptions (Innocence, Spectre, Eternity), he makes even the most familiar places and things ominously unfamiliar. Yet, however Blake tampers with our automatic responses to words, he relies on those responses for his effect. It is no use calling Hitler an arch-angel unless we all know what an angel is: a revered spokesman for the public and private self-conceptions of a given society. For all their mythic and ironic dimensions, Blake's redefinitions have a curious literalness. They are never arbitrary; if they seem so, that is only because society has been arbitrary in assigning values to what they signify. They never reverse or otherwise deny the established conceptions of what they indicate; they merely criticize those conceptions by exposing the limitations, usually moral or perceptual, inherent in them. A "Spectre," for example, is no less an incorporeal ghost in Blake than it would be in any Gothic novel, but it is only an incorporeal ghost as defined from eternity, whence all true definitions are derived. What is, from the standpoint of eternity, dead and invisible, happens to be, from our standpoint in Generation, the only material life. Blake is not being perverse when he calls our hard live flesh a ghost, he is being literal to his vision, which must, as all genuine poetic vision must for him, derive its perspective from eternity.

Similarly, the concept of eternity itself has an unexpected literalness in Blake's poetry. We are so used to a vague, convenient use of the word that we may find it merely quaint to hear its denizens named familiarly and without awe "the eternals," as if they were the Nixons or the sanitation workers. But Blake had a very particular idea of eternity and its inhabitants: "Many suppose that before [*Adam*] ⟨the Crea-

---

measure of his antipathy to and distance from the poetic technique he inherited" (p. 322).

tion) All was solitude & Chaos This is the most pernicious Idea that can enter the Mind as it takes away all sublimity from the Bible & Limits All Existence to Creation & to Chaos To the Time & Space fixed by the Corporeal Vegetative Eye & leaves the Man who entertains such an Idea the habitation of Unbelieving Demons *Eternity Exists and All things in Eternity Independent of Creation which was an act of Mercy. . . .*"[2] Blake does not permit us our comfortable stock responses to words of major significance. He challenges those responses to reveal the greater meaning those words imply. In his poetry "eternally" never means "for ever and ever"; it always means "in that state of existence which is neither chaos nor creation." Recognizing this expansive literalness, we may spare ourselves confusion when we read of a character's sleeping eternally or going to eternal death, only to find him wide awake or quite alive several pages or even paragraphs later; this is not the poet's absent-mindedness, but his conscious renovation of words. His characters do not die or sleep forever; they enter a state of what seems like death or sleep to those left awake in eternity. By this kind of redefinition Blake makes familiar expressions like "Surrey" or "eternity" as raw and vulnerable and resoundingly suggestive as "Oothoon" or "Los."

The meter of Blake's later works also represents a reordering of convention. Blake's septenary is unusual in a tradition that has adopted pentameter as its standard, but it is a perfectly natural vehicle for a poet who loved the Bible's long-lined eloquence and the ballads with their seven-beat units. The fourteener does change, to be sure, during the course of Blake's career, and the regular, identifiable ballad rhythms of the early illuminated prophecies have been hammered into an entirely new and scarcely recognizable metrical invention by the time of the composition of the *Jerusalem*. But the hammering is a process, a traceable development not entirely unlike the development of

[2] "A Vision of the Last Judgment," p. 552.

Milton's iambic pentameter from its simplicity in the sonnets through its ornate involutions in *Paradise Lost* to its spare and ringing quiet in *Paradise Regained*.[3]

Blake's reworkings of traditional diction and meter are dramatically innovative, but they cannot in themselves account for the confusion or the genius attributed to the artistry of his late prophecies. Either confusion or genius must be charged instead to the structural principles to which diction and meter are subservient. A study of those principles in *Milton* should suggest both the coherence and the originality of Blake's prophetic art.

Two particular structural principles seem to me to grow in influence throughout Blake's career until they culminate in *Milton*: the principle of simultaneity, by which the duration of the entire action of the poem is defined as a single unmeasurable instant, and the principle of multiple perspectives, by which every facet of that action is analyzed from the point of view (or points of view) of every major character. A brief sketch of the developments of these two principles in Blake's poetry may clarify both their increasing importance in the course of his thought and art, and their dominant influence on the composition of *Milton*. Because multiple perspective is the more widespread of the two principles in Blake's work, and the more nearly conventional, let us begin with it.

Even in the *Songs of Innocence*, published in 1789, Blake is clearly playing perspectives off each other. The chimney sweeps may take comfort in sweet dreams of death, but the reader cannot be less appalled at their plight for that dark relief. There has been extensive critical debate over the de-

---

[3] Alicia Ostriker traces that process of Blake's developing prosody in *Vision and Verse in William Blake* (Madison and Milwaukee: University of Wisconsin, 1965). John Hollander considers the prosody further in "Blake and the Metrical Contract," *From Sensibility to Romanticism: Essays Presented to Frederick A. Pottle*, ed. Frederick W. Hilles and Harold Bloom (New York: Oxford, 1965). See also Kathleen Raine, "A Note on Blake's 'Unfettered Verse'" (Rosenfeld, pp. 383–392).

gree, even over the existence, of irony in the Songs; but there can be no debate that the perspective of Innocence, which can speak to the lamb and the emmet as equals and which fears no harm of wild beasts, is not the perspective of the adult reader. In the tension between the two perspectives lies the greatest significance of the poems. "The Lamb" is a great poem only when it is endowed with the nostalgia or the bitterness or the pain of loss or the wise re-creation of one who has long since ceased to converse with livestock; otherwise it is nursery patter.

Blake's use of perspective in the *Songs of Innocence,* and in the *Songs of Experience* printed five years later, is perfectly conventional in everything except, perhaps, the emphasis he places on it. Tension between perspectives forms a major part of the substance of *The Book of Thel,* dated the same year as the *Songs of Innocence,*[4] and again there is nothing conspicuously original in Blake's conception of that tension. But in *Thel,* for the first time in Blake's poetry, multiple perspective is a governing principle of the structure of the poem. *Thel* has four numbered parts. The first three, pastoral in diction and biblical in rhythm, are set in the Vales of Har, a garden of Innocence in which flowers and clouds and the earth itself chat encouragingly with the heroine. Thel has begun to have inklings of mortality; she finds no comfort for her anxiety in the Vales, but fears to enter any other reality. By the fourth part she has been persuaded to set aside her fears. She passes to the grave, the edge of Experience, and hears from beyond it a dreadful lamentation of existence there. As the perspective of the poem shifts from Innocence to Experience, so does its language: pastoral diction gives way to apocalyptic, lilies and lambs and gentle breezes to "fibrous roots" and poisons and

[4] Because of discrepancies in the script styles of the plates, it is possible that the poem was not completed until at least 1791, that plate 6 is a revision of an earlier plate (see David V. Erdman's textual notes to his edition of *The Poetry and Prose of William Blake* [Garden City, N.Y.: Doubleday, 1965], p. 713).

"a whirlpool fierce." This new perspective is too much for
Thel; she flees shrieking back to the Vales of Har. The sub-
stance of her anxiety is the same regardless of perspective:
it was mortality she feared in the Vales, and it is mortality
that frightens her in the grim prophecy of Experience.
From Innocence, though, mortality seems merely a matter
of fading gently away. From Experience, it seems a matter
of torment and betrayal. The structural pivot of the poem
is the transition between the two perspectives, between the
lamb and the whirlpool.

Oothoon, in *Visions of the Daughters of Albion* (1793),
is not frightened by new perspective; she embraces it. In
the first two plates of the poem she passes from Innocence
through Experience to a confident new vision of reality that
subsumes both. The remaining six plates, however, see her
enslaved by the limited perspectives of Theotormon, her
lover, and Bromion, her defiler. The whole poem may be
seen as a dialectic between her comprehensive perspective
and their fragmented perspectives. Theotormon is a kind
of parody of false Innocence; he rejects what reminds him
of loss or evil, and spends his hours moping (much as Thel
moped) that he cannot be strong and good. Bromion is a
parody of the limitations of Experience, tyrannical and
mystifying and committed to the existence of the evils Theo-
tormon laments. Oothoon, having known both their states,
transcends both. Innocence and Experience are always lim-
ited, and limiting, states in Blake's poetry: it is little more
viable only to fear tigers than it is not to fear them at all. In
Oothoon's comprehensive vision we see the beginnings of
an alternative to these limitations.

In Blake's early poems one's perspective may be mea-
sured roughly by the criterion of childhood. The only true
Innocent is a child who can know no other perspective. Ex-
perience is the next developmental state, beginning symbol-
ically with puberty and entrance into social obligation.
Those who can accurately recognize both these states may
enter into Oothoon's comprehensive perspective, which

critics call Organized Innocence. The three states may be conceived linearly, as a personal progression from early childhood to true maturity.

After *Visions of the Daughters of Albion*, Blake measures perspective not by this limited personal criterion of biographical development, but by the objective, comprehensive criterion of what he calls eternity. One's state of being, the magnitude of one's perspective, is defined in the later poems not by one's earliest and simplest perspective, but by the vastest and most sophisticated perspective possible. The linear progression from Innocence through Experience to Organized Innocence gives way to a series of concentric circles initiated at a center point without extent or duration, Eden. From Eden, which opens inward into eternity, perspective is charted outwards in three realms of diminishing vision, Beulah (described as Innocence had been described), Generation (which incorporates the earlier Experience), and Ulro (a kind of lethal extension of the limitations of Beulah and Generation). The mythic implications of this new cosmology have been vigorously analyzed by Damon, Frye, Bloom, and others, and we shall have cause to consider them again in a later chapter. What is pertinent to our present argument is the relationship of this series of perspectives to the composition of Blake's prophecies. Innocence / Experience, the linear, personal axis of vision, has ceased to be effective by *America*. In *Europe* (1794), the Eden / Ulro axis, identified as the line from a fairy's perception to a mortal tyrant's, has formed. The major significance of that shift to the development of Blake's prophetic art is that the emerging, more complex, less personal system allows the poet great new freedom in elaborating the range of perspectives that is the basis of his vision. The difference between Innocence and Experience is simple, dramatic, and absolute—a quantum distinction in individual understanding. The difference between Eden and Beulah, or between any two states on the Eden / Ulro axis, is a matter of gradation at points so subtle as to be indistinct—a universal principle of perception constantly in flux. The greater complexity of vision suggested by the shift in references of perspective is reflected in a greater complexity of poetic structure. We may see these developing complexities especially clearly in *Europe*, which seems to me a prototype of the structure of *Milton*.

Europe is a sequence of three parts, an introduction, the Preludium, and the Prophecy, each of which provides at least one major perspective on the action of the poem. The first offers an eternal perspective; the second adds one that is cosmic but not eternal; the third amplifies the cosmic and adds a temporal, historical perspective. All three parts, with their very different styles and substances, are about the same thing, which we may identify in its simplest expression: uprooting, the painful reversal of temporal expectation which can reveal to the willing eye a whole new order of reality.

In the introductory stanzas a fairy, who has established his proto-Edenic vision by ridiculing mortal limitations on perception, laughs at the whimpering of plucked wildflowers. He knows that one must look for "each eternal flower," and thus can only be amused by the suffering of the temporal aspect of the being. In the Preludium we focus on a single plucked flower, the nameless shadowy female who laments her uprooting: "My roots are brandish'd in the heavens. my fruits in earth beneath / Surge, foam, and labour into life. . . ." She mourns the anguished cycles of mortal generation, the process by which life is wrung continuously from the resisting form of nature. There is no eternal perspective in the Preludium, nor even the comforting temporal perspective which recognizes in counted time an end to suffering. The shadowy female is a wildflower plucked again and again without even the consolation of dying.

In the Prophecy death does exist. This longest section of the poem details a mythologized account of Christian history, specifically European history, framed by two enormously ironic sequences revealing the cosmic setting of that history. There is no time measured in the Preludium; its cycles amount to binding "the infinite with an eternal band." The cosmic level of the Prophecy is closer to the mundane; time does exist there, though not time as mortal minds count it. The inhabitants of this realm celebrate a single night which has regular duration for them, but during its course eighteen hundred years of nights pass for the mortal beings of a lower order of perception. Both the dawn of that night, and the end of that eighteen hundred years of Christian history, will be consummated in the ultimate uprooting of the poem, apocalypse.

The multiple perspectives of the poem unite in that bloody dawn. Only one, of course, the fairy's Edenic perspective, is comprehensive, but soon all the other limited, fragmentary perspectives will cease to be. Cycle will be ended for the shadowy female and for Los, history will be ended for mortal sufferers. All that remains is the uprooting —which will be agonizing, but which makes the fairy laugh.[5]

We have in *Europe* two polar perspectives, that of eternity (the fairy) and that of history (the eighteen hundred years of European tyranny), and an intermediate "cosmic" perspective which forms a spectrum between them. These perspectives will be clarified and named later in Blake's prophecies, but the process of their alignment in the structure of the poetry is already clearly established. The limitations of all non-Edenic perceptions are played ironically

[5] The fairy's laughing at the weeping flowers seemed callous; the extension of his mirth to embrace apocalypse itself seems even more unfeeling, and makes his vision seem as limited as that of Enitharmon, who does not even know that night has passed as she slept. That he does not recognize the anguish that is a feature of less than Edenic perspective reflects, however, not a flaw in him, but a flaw in that perspective. The inhabitants of Eden, as we may see more clearly in subsequent poems, do not accept error, and the anguish of fallen reality is the sign and cause of error. That is, of course, no more comforting to us than to the weeping wildflowers. Or little more.

against each other, and against the single perspective which is capable of admitting eternal truth.[6]

Europe, in which each major perspective has its own section of the poem and all three sections are about the same thing, is the first instance in Blake's poetry of a layered organization of multiple perspectives. By "layered" I mean a superimposition of congruent perspectives: the fairy, the shadowy female, Enitharmon, and the English people all witness the same event but perceive it differently; the variations in their perceptions are due only to variations in their perspectives, not to any variation in the event, which does not change; their perceptions are independent and have no mutual influence, and no developmental sequence in the plot (the birth of Orc, which is the shadowy female's uprooting in the Preludium, is the birth of apocalyptic revolution in the Prophecy). This manifold focus on a single event will be, in a much more complicated and absolute version, the basic organizational principle of the multiple perspectives of *Milton*.

Between *Europe* and *Milton* Blake's poems are linear, not layered, in organization; that is, their perspectives are ordered consecutively and responsively, even when they are perspectives on the same event. In *The Book of Urizen* (1794) and the subsequent Books of *Ahania* and *Los* (1795), Blake satirizes received notions of the first books of the Bible, and accordingly adopts their linear presentation of action. *The Four Zoas*, his first and unfinished epic poem, is an expansion of the nine-part *Urizen*. All of that great quarry of Blake's myth is a series of testimonies on the nature of a single act, the fall of Albion from eternity, from its beginning in the strife of the Zoas to its resolution in their reintegration, by witnesses to that act on all levels of reality. Those testimonies interact progressively, not merely

[6] It is because Edenic vision excludes all things outside eternity that I call it a perspective, when properly, because it comprehends all that is true, it is not a perspective at all. My denomination is paradoxical, but it has, I think, at least a rhetorical validity.

repeating or repudiating each other but also eliciting each other, and eliciting as well the series of alliances that will ultimately reverse them. Night the Ninth is to a significant extent a reflection of Night the First: each has a great feast (that of Albion in I and Los and Enitharmon in IX), a twin birth (first Tharmas and Enion, finally Los and Enitharmon), and the death of an emanation (Ahania, then Enion). This structural reflection indicates that apocalypse is simply the completion of the fall, which ends where it begun—but that completion is presented throughout the poem as a linear process.

After *Milton*, Blake returned in his last epic poem to what is basically a linear organization of perspectives, but with a strong undertow toward layering. Critics have deliberated a full definition of the four-part structure of *Jerusalem*, but without consensus. Models have been proposed for it in Ezekiel[7] and *The Four Zoas*;[8] its form has been described by Frye as "a drama in four acts: a fall, the struggle of men in a fallen world . . . , the world's redemption by a divine man . . . , and an apocalypse";[9] its four chapters have been identified with the individual Zoas,[10] and with, after an introductory chapter, the three ages of man (childhood, adolescence, maturity,[11] the three errors of the fall (misuse of body, mind, and imagination),[12] and "the progression of the successive stages of the fallen condition."[13] The only

[7] Harold Bloom, Commentary to the Erdman edition, pp. 833–834.

[8] David Wagenknecht, *Blake's Night: William Blake and the Idea of Pastoral* (Cambridge, Mass.: Belknap, 1973), p. 359.

[9] *Fearful Symmetry*, p. 357.

[10] Edward J. Rose, "The Structure of Blake's *Jerusalem*," *Bucknell Review*, II, 3 (1962–1963), pp. 35–54.

[11] Karl Kiralis, "The Theme and Structure of William Blake's *Jerusalem*," *Divine Vision*, pp. 139–162.

[12] Anne K. Mellor, "The Human Form Divine and the Structure of Blake's *Jerusalem*," SEL, XI, 4 (Autumn 1971), pp. 595–620.

[13] Henry Lesnick, "Narrative Structure and the Antithetical Vision of *Jerusalem*," *Visionary Forms Dramatic*, ed. David V. Erdman and John E. Grant (Princeton, N.J.: Princeton University Press, 1970), p. 394.

13

real consensus among critics of the structure of *Jerusalem*, and it is a shaky consensus, is that the poem is plotted progressively—but even that proposition is open to question: it is frequently noted that within the poem's apparent progression certain major elements are repeated unexpectedly and insistently. These repetitions, such as the emanation of Enitharmon from Los in both the first and the last chapters (plates 6, 17, and 86), the creation of states in the second and third (plates 31 and 73), and the various ossifyings of fallen humanity recorded throughout, may eventually prove to be cornerstones of the kind of congruity such repetitions support in *Milton*. It may be that what is now considered progressive may ultimately prove circular, that the events of *Jerusalem*, like those of *Milton*, are all the same event witnessed through various perspectives. As of now, though, we may tentatively define the arrangement of multiple perspectives in Blake's two finished epics as layered in *Milton* and linear in *Jerusalem*.[14]

The employment of multiple perspective as a structural principle began early in Blake's work and developed steadily in influence and complexity, reaching one kind of culmination in *Milton* and another in *Jerusalem*. The development of the second dominant structural principle of *Milton* is not so regular. There are only two clear earlier uses of

[14] A contrast in structure similar to the one I draw between linear and layered is suggested by Harold Bloom in "Blake's *Jerusalem*: The Bard of Sensibility and the Form of Prophecy" (Eighteenth-Century Studies, 4 [1970]; rpt. *The Ringers in the Tower: Studies in Romantic Tradition* [Chicago: University of Chicago Press, 1971, pp. 65–79]), although the more traditional terms Bloom uses seem to me too loaded with prejudicial connotations to permit accuracy: Bloom proposes that in *Jerusalem* Blake abandons "epic" for "prophetic" structure. Wittreich criticizes this assumption, insisting that "*The Four Zoas, Milton,* and *Jerusalem* possess both epic and prophetic structures" (*Sublime Allegory*, p. 49). My own belief is that the "epic" structure of *Milton* is largely illusory, that Blake uses it only as a superficial organizing device and so undermines it by the simultaneity of the events that comprise it that it ceases to function in any recognizably "epic" manner.

simultaneity in Blake, in *Europe* and *The Four Zoas*, and the second of the two is not quite legitimate. The initial disintegration of Albion's members takes four full books out of nine to describe, and the fifth through seventh books take place in the kind of cosmic limbo we have already seen in *Europe*. Time as we know it does not even begin to be counted until the end of Night the Seventh (either version), when we poor mortal vestiges of Albion's humanity are established in the natural universe. Accordingly, all the events before the counting of the providential six thousand years of Night the Eighth, or at least all events before Los finishes hammering out the forms of fallen humanity in Night the Fourth, may be said to be simultaneous, because they cannot be measured at all in hours or even eons. But that definitional simultaneity is really a quibble: things cannot happen at the same time when there is no time. Furthermore, the events of the poem, whatever their duration, are presented as continuous. It is true that the creation and the fall and the flood and the resurrection are one and the same act in *The Four Zoas*, are indistinguishable in duration as in any other factor except our perception of them. But that act is presented as a linear process with a dramatic structure, beginning–middle–end complete with peripeteia and anagnorisis, crisis climax and denouement.

If there is a precedent for *Milton*'s concentrated use of simultaneity, it is in *Europe*, in which all Christian history, eighteen hundred years by mortal count, passes during a single night on the "cosmic" level of the poem. Yet what we have here may still be more a function of perspective than of simultaneity: that nearly two millennia have the same duration as a cosmic dream implies more about ways of measuring duration than it does about any equality of what is measured. The simultaneity of Enitharmon's dream with European history is paradoxical: things cannot have the same duration in Los's perspective and Newton's because time is not the same in both. Yet there is a sense of simultaneity that does apply here. At the beginning of the Prophecy we are told, in a reworking of Milton's Nativity Ode,

> The deep of winter came;
> What time the secret child,
> Descended thro' the orient gates of the eternal day:
> War ceas'd, & all the troops like shadows fled to
>   their abodes.
>
> (3:1-4)

Then Enitharmon glories in her dominion and falls asleep. At the end of her dream,

> Yellow as leaves of Autumn the myriads of Angelic hosts,
> Fell thro' the wintry skies seeking their graves;
> Rattling their hollow bones in howling and lamentation.
>
> (13:6-8)

The troops who fall away from war before her dream and at its conclusion are the same dregs of autumn falling through the newly chilled winter skies. In the first passage, the echo of Milton suggests, the troops are dispersed by the appearance of Christ; in the second they are vanquished by the appearance of Orc, spirit of the revolutions of the late eighteenth century. By identifying the revolutions of his era with the coming of Jesus, Blake cannot mean that for us the two phenomena are simultaneous—how many generations of us were born and died between them? But he does suggest that beyond our realm of decades and centuries, in the consciousness that does not recognize calibrated duration, the two are the same and occur at the same time. For us Jesus and Orc are independent, and Milton was silly to echo the biblical prophecy of peace at Christ's birth when, over sixteen hundred years later, he had to have known how false it was. For Enitharmon, Jesus is a myth and Orc a bad dream, and the two are divided by no more than a short night's sleep. For the fairy, presumably, the two are one and they always exist and Milton was right. Simultaneity, like everything else in Blake, is largely a matter of perspective. In eternity all things are "simultaneous."

The events of *Milton* are simultaneous on all other levels of reality as well. The suggestion of simultaneity through identification of figures and actions is a major device of *Milton*, the device, in fact, by which its layering of perspectives is enforced: the various perceptions and reactions of the poem seem linear, seem to influence and elicit each other progressively, until we recognize that all of them except those that are explicitly prefatory occur simultaneously and therefore cannot be linear. Each of the two books of the poem offers a range of perspectives on its central action from Eden to Ulro and from remembered past to foretold future, but in each all perspectives focus on a single instant, the instant of the purgation and union of Milton and Ololon, the instant in which past and future are joined in the abolition of time. Even those events in the poem that are clearly antecedent to its main action, the events of the Bard's Song and the creation of Beulah, are described as the action occurs: Milton decides to descend as he hears the Bard sing (and, as we shall see, his decision is identical with his descent), and the daughters of Beulah sing their history as Ololon descends. Milton's descent is both simultaneous and identical with Ololon's descent; all the other actions of the poem, past and present, are merely component actions of that focal event.

The instant of their descents is the culmination of what Blake describes at the end of Book I as a kind of visionary moment:

> Every Time less than a pulsation of the artery
> Is equal in its period & value to Six Thousand Years.
> For in this Period the Poets Work is Done: and all the
>   Great
> Events of Time start forth & are concievd in such a
>   Period
> Within a Moment: a Pulsation of the Artery.
>
> (28:62–29:3)

The time less than a pulsation of the artery is all recorded history, the entire period of the fallen human imagination. The moment includes also the seventh thousand years, the "Day of Mourning" Los establishes in the Bard's Song, the millennium before Judgment. The action of *Milton*, on this historical scale, is the ending of mourning; it is the trigger of apocalypse, which is the consummation of the moment.

As Christian history is for Enitharmon a single night, a thousand years are for Los a single day. And as Enitharmon's dream and Christian history end simultaneously, so do Los's day and the millennium. The act that ends the millennium, the day, the moment, occurs in all its complexity on all levels of reality at the same instant. It is composite not only of the descents of Milton and Ololon, but also of the purgations of Los and Blake, the appearance of Jesus, and the renovation of Satan and Albion—all of which occur simultaneously with Milton's realization of the Bard's prophecy.

I have chosen the word "instant" as the time reference of the actions of the poem in order to distinguish that reference from Blake's broader, more inclusive conception, "moment." The events of *Milton*, I must emphasize, are not simultaneous because they all occur within that paradoxical moment which is at once seven thousand years long and as brief as a poet's sudden inspiration. They are not, that is, simultaneous because time is irrelevant to them, because they occur beyond or within the calibrations of time. They are simultaneous because each occurs at the same precise "instant" of that moment, the same minute, calibrated segment of that seven-thousand-year period that comprises fallen history. All the actions of the poem occur in the last measurable segment of the moment, the last fragment of time itself, the instant before apocalypse puts an end to time.

We have in *Milton* a nearly fifty-page analysis of what happens in Revelation as the seventh seal is opened, the seventh trump sounded, the seventh vial poured out. The

Bard's Song and the opening plates of Book II record the events leading to that instant, but the remaining plates of the poem focus exclusively on the instant itself. Such intense elaboration of the climax of fallen history permits Blake to define it not only in terms of cosmic cataclysm but also in terms of individual mortal response. In Revelation we see dozens of dozens of thousands of human beings marked for salvation or destruction; in *Milton* we see one living man struggling to comprehend the old heaven and the new. Blake's vision, in its intimacy and detail, humanizes the great moral abstractions of St. John's vision.

The complexity of *Milton* derives from its presentation of its focal event as it occurs in all its minute particulars on all levels of reality. The constantly shifting perspectives of the poem, both universal (Eden through Ulro) and individual (Albion through Blake), give that presentation the semblance of sequence. Because we hear first of Milton's descent through Ulro to Generation and then of Ololon's, we assume, trained as we are in consecutive narrative form, that Milton's descent preceded Ololon's. But Ololon seems to arrive before Milton. Are we to conclude simply that she is faster on her feet? Or are we not to conclude that our habitual conception of sequence does not apply here, that Milton's descent and Ololon's, though their inceptions and conclusions must necessarily be described one after the other, are virtually simultaneous? Similarly, the figures known in *Milton* as the Seven Angels of the Presence, the Starry Seven, are, with the completion of Milton's act, increased to "Eight Immortal Starry-Ones." Throughout the poem they are described in three conditions: seven starry (22:1, 39:3, 39:58), seven starry with an eighth as yet dark (15:1–6, 20:12–14), and eight starry (34:3–4, 35:29–30, 35:32, 35:34, 42:10). One can see by the line references that the descriptions are not consistent with any linear temporal representation of Milton's becoming the eighth bright angel. Blake skips back and forth among the conditions, not because he is absent-minded or eager to confuse, but because in so doing he can remind us again and again that what we thought of as sequence was not sequence, that the consummation of Milton's act of purgation began with the beginning of the poem and ended with the end, but that the beginning and the end are simultaneous. The angels are seven at the beginning and eight at the end and seven plus a dark eighth between, but because the beginning is the end all the descriptions apply at all parts of the poem. What determines the number of angels at any given point is the perspective through which they are perceived. The action of *Milton* seems a process only because language is linear and exposition sequential. Precedence in description no more implies precedence in occurrence in *Milton* than it does in *Paradise Lost*, which begins with the result of an act not described till half-way through the poem. The difference is that John Milton skipped back and forth in time in his poem, and Blake abolishes time in his.

Multiple perspective and simultaneity do not in themselves control the structure of *Milton*. If they were the sole ordering devices of the poem, however conscientiously and philosophically devised, they would ensure a work of the most delirious chaos. They can themselves provide no comprehensive order to the poem—indeed, they would seem to encourage randomness. If they are to be used intelligibly they must be governed by an overriding structural principle both powerful in its own right and sympathetic to their elaborate system of identifications. The principle that organizes the perspectives and repetitions of *Milton* is a framework of parallels at once general and exact.

Anyone who has responsively read *The Marriage of Heaven and Hell*, or for that matter the *Songs of Innocence and Experience*, knows that the basis of Blake's vision is a dramatic dialectic of partial truths, a progressive conflict of contrary perceptions in which "Opposition is true Friendship." The counterpoint of Innocence and Experience, of Prolific and Devourer, of Orc and the British Angel, of Los and Urizen, is the tension out of which Blake's prophetic vision is created. The effect of the dialectic on the poetry of that vision is clear in the ironies of the Songs, in the debates of the prophecies, and in the structures of the longer poems from the delineations of the parts of *Thel* and *Europe* according to antithetical perspectives to the series of shifting conflicts and alliances that comprise the nine units of *The Four Zoas*. In *Milton* the dialectic of essential contraries is not just reflected generally in the poetic design; it controls that design in its minutest as well as its most comprehensive features.

That the two books of the poem have a kind of polar correspondence has often been suggested. Frye identifies them respectively with *Paradise Lost* and *Paradise Regained*,[15] I have elsewhere compared them with "Il Penseroso" and "L'Allegro,"[16] and Bloom has found Book I a chronicle of the redemption of Experience, Book II of the redemption of Innocence.[17] But the dialectical nature of the two books goes much further than the basic correspondence of theme and imagery suggested by these paradigms. The verbal structures of both are exactly congruent in the nature and order of their parts; in their congruency they reveal the necessary mutuality of the principles, cosmic-masculine-visionary and earthly-feminine-sensuous, they embody.

As we shall see in subsequent chapters, each book has three basic sections, a prologue to its action, an account of the various aspects of the action, and an epilogue defining the effects of the action. Each prologue is built of four parts, each account of the action is a three-part narrative with a continuously shifting focus, each epilogue is a description of an intense visionary experience liberated by and concomitant with the action. The action of Book I is Milton's descent to Ololon; the action of Book II is Ololon's descent to Milton. Those descents are, as I have noted, si-

[15] *Fearful Symmetry*, p. 337.

[16] "The Structure of a Moment: Parallelism in the Two Books of Blake's *Milton*," *Blake Studies*, II, 1, pp. 21–22.

[17] Commentary, p. 834, and *Blake's Apocalypse*, p. 376.

multaneous. Together they realize the purgation of Milton, and through it the purification of Blake and of the imaginative principle, Los himself.

This system of reflecting polarities permits a familiar technique of Blake's poetry its fullest expression. Because any element of the poem will surely be repeated in a new context, often again and again, no element need be defined explicitly when it first appears. Wholesale definitions of any of Blake's essential ideas would be antagonistic to his conception of truth as an organic reality which we can perceive only through multiple perspectives. Accordingly, he rarely defines even the strangest new material when it first appears in his work. Rintrah howls in the argument to *The Marriage of Heaven and Hell* with absolutely no introduction to the startled reader, Los appears for the first time in *Europe* without so much as a hint as to what he might signify, nobody tells us why the shadowy female is shadowy, and we have to read all of *The Four Zoas*, probably more than once, to be at all confident we really know what a spectre is. Definitions are not propounded in Blake's poetry; they accrue. The poetic structure of *Milton* is the perfect milieu for accruing definitions. The Three Classes of Men, for example, are described again and again throughout the Bard's Song, and alluded to explicitly and implicitly thereafter, but our fullest understanding of them does not come until nearly the end of the poem, when Ololon cries out in terrible recognition, "are we Contraries O Milton, Thou & I" (41:35). We probably think we know the Three Classes the first time the Bard brings them up, in his very first lines, but each subsequent reference alters our conception of them, expanding their significance and our comprehension of it until Ololon consummates the definition by rendering it personal to herself and to each of us.

The technique of accruing definitions leads many readers to suppose that Blake does not fully define his basic tenets within any individual work. Thus critics explain *Milton* via *The Four Zoas* and *The Four Zoas* via *Jerusalem* in an endless attempt to isolate a single consistent system of thought. That attempt seems to me doomed by gradual but essential modifications of Blake's ideas through the course of his poems. His major tenets, to be sure, changed hardly at all, except to grow in complexity and profundity. But certain components of those tenets did change. For example, cross-references are frequently made in Blake criticism to the doctrine of states expounded in *Milton*, "A Vision of the Last Judgment," and *Jerusalem*, as if the doctrine were the same in all three. But in *Milton* we hear, "Distinguish therefore States from Individuals in those States. / States Change: but Individual Identities never change nor cease . . ." (32:22–23), whereas in the later works the idea seems reversed: "Man Passes on but States remain for Ever he passes thro them like a traveller who may as well suppose that the places he has passed thro exist no more . . . Every Thing is Eternal" ("Vision," p. 546); "As the Pilgrim passes while the Country permanent remains / So Men pass on: but States remain permanent for ever" (*Jerusalem*, 73: 44–45). Perhaps the later expressions are only a clarification, not a direct reversal, of the earlier; it may be that by "States Change" Blake meant only that they seem to change for the individuals who pass through them. But clarification or reversal, the later terms do not match the earlier. Most criticism seems to build on the *Jerusalem* formula,[18] and probably correctly, insofar as the critics are trying to isolate the clearest, most mature version of the idea. But that formula does not quite apply to *Milton*.

Attempts to explain *Milton* by other Blake poems occasionally create minor inaccuracies in interpretations of *Milton*. More damagingly, such attempts underestimate the unity and coherence of *Milton* in itself. It may take the

---

[18] See, for examples nearly thirty years apart, Thomas J. J. Altizer, *The New Apocalypse: The Radical Christian Vision of William Blake* (East Lansing, Mich.: Michigan State University Press, 1967), p. 153, and Milton O. Percival, *William Blake's Circle of Destiny* (1938; rpt. New York: Octagon, 1964), p. 236.

whole poem to define "Three Classes of Men" fully, but the full definition is there, in this poem. Elynittria may be a total stranger when she first shows up in the Bard's Song, and an identification from *Europe* may make the reader temporarily more comfortable about her, but by the end of *Milton*, even by the end of the Bard's Song, Blake will have told us everything we need to know about her in this poem.

Accruing definitions, simultaneity, multiple perspectives all are organized in *Milton* by the elaborate system of parallels that is the poem's basic framework. Michael Riffaterre's definition of any poem has thus a particular applicability to *Milton*: "so then, a poem is a verbal sequence wherein the same relations between constituents are repeated at various levels and the same story is told in several ways at the same time and at several times in the same way."[19] The levels Riffaterre means ("phonetic, phonological, syntactical, semantic, *etc.*"[20]) are largely employed less than deliberately; the uniqueness of *Milton* is that in its controlling as well as in its underlying structures it seeks to tell the same story "in several ways at the same time and at several times in the same way." "The recurrence of equivalent forms," Riffaterre interprets Roman Jakobson, "*parallelism*, is the basic relationship underlying poetry."[21] Parallelism is more than that in *Milton*; it is the theme of the poem realized concretely as its narrative structure.

[19] "Describing Poetic Structures: Two Approaches to Baudelaire's *les Chats*," *Structuralism*, ed. Jacques Ehrmann (Garden City, N.Y.: Doubleday Anchor, 1970), p. 189.
[20] *Ibid.*   [21] *Ibid.*

2. Plate 1 (frontispiece)

✹✹✹✹✹✹✹✹✹✹✹✹✹✹✹✹✹✹✹✹✹✹✹✹✹✹✹✹✹✹✹✹✹✹✹✹✹✹✹

II. Hammer

The Preface that introduces *Milton* appears only in the earliest two of the four texts of the poem Blake engraved. It begins with a prose polemic against imperfect art which, in its relentless anger, bears a subtly contradictory relationship to the text of the poem. Blake decries those whose art springs not from inspiration but from imitative exercise, warning against "a Class of Men whose delight is in Destroying." His anger is justified as a purgation of all that is false and perverted, not as an end to be desired but as a necessary means to the achievement of pure imaginations, the "Worlds of Eternity in which we live for ever."

The prose polemic declares stridently what the rest of *Milton* illustrates compassionately. That stridency may have been what led Blake to abandon the plate, for it contradicts the attitude of forgiveness and conversion that informs the poem itself. Both Preface and poem insist upon the purification of imagination, but the first counsels conflict and the second reconciliation; in the first we are to set our "foreheads against the ignorant Hirelings," whereas in the second we are to "Break the Chain / Of Jealousy" (23:37–38).

With the Preface, Blake abandoned also the shapely contrasting poem on the same plate. The polemical prose of the Preface yielded to the Jerusalem hymn, perhaps the most famous of Blake's lyrics and one of his simplest and most rousing. There is a lyric kernel to all of Blake's longer poems except the biblical parodies, a spare introductory poem which contains the basic elements of what is to follow. The longer works are amplifications of the parabolic visions in their lyric statements. The Jerusalem hymn is more urgent than other lyric kernels, less cryptic and paradoxical. It admits no equivocation:

26

I will not cease from Mental Fight,
Nor shall my Sword sleep in my hand:
Till we have built Jerusalem
In Englands green & pleasant land.

Milton itself, in all its conscious paradoxes and structural involutions, describes the process of human purification through which Jerusalem will be built anew.

Book the First opens with a two-stanza epic invocation of Blake's muses, the Daughters of Beulah, which is notable for the series of polarities it comprises. Beulah itself is a realm of both "terror & mild moony lustre," a pleasant refuge for those who need to pause from mental strife, but also a gateway into the fearful states of Generation and Ulro. The story the daughters are to tell, the story of Milton's descent, is to be recorded "in soft sexual delusions / Of varied beauty": the "married land" is the source of both sexuality and art in Blake's universe, and both are "delusions," *i.e.*, they are merely images of what in Eden would be love and truth. Delusions are only representations, but they can be redemptive if what they represent, however they distort it, is genuine, if it is the reality of Eden and not the subjective fantasy of Ulro. The "delusions" of Beulah that Blake calls for here are the only means we mortal beings have of witnessing reality.

The inspiration poets usually call for in their invocations supposedly originates in a reality beyond their own power to conceive. Blake's originates in his own mind: he summons his muses "From out the Portals of my Brain, where by your ministry / The Eternal Great Humanity Divine. planted his Paradise. . . ." Paradise yields immediately in this dense passage to its contrary, the "False Tongue" vegetated beneath Beulah, the limitations of generated life. Paradise and its threatened ravager—organizing consciousness and reductive empiricism—will be the subjects of *Milton*. The polarities of the invocation will be confirmed and amplified by the body of the poem.

A. Eden

What moved Milton to act was a prophetic song. The Bard who sings it sings among the sons of Albion in the heavens of Albion; he is an "immortal," a word Blake uses to define one who is neither eternal nor generative, who has died from Generation without fully becoming Edenic (Milton himself is an immortal, although he has "walked about in Eternity" since his death). The setting of the Bard's singing is thus ambiguous; it is the old Christian heaven transposed to Blake's cosmology, where it is rather less than heavenly, but Blake assures us that the Bard sings "at eternal tables." The setting of his song is also ambiguous. The events take place after the fall of Albion in the kind of cosmic limbo we are familiar with from *Europe*, a place where time is counted but not time as we mortal beings know it. Still, the characters involved in that action are at least vestigially eternal: the generation of Los has fallen from Eden but has not been vegetated into mortal existence, and of the generation of Los's sons, Rintrah and Palamabron have resisted being vegetated; all Eden itself descends into the limbo of the action to pass judgment on it. Thus although the Bard's Song does not take place in Eden, it does take place in the environs of Eden, and its subject is the maintenance of Edenic reality, by those who still imperfectly remember it, in the face of eternal death.

The Bard's Song epitomizes the difficulties many readers find with the organization of *Milton*. Bloom cites one major difficulty: "like *Jerusalem*, *Milton* confronts its reader with problems of continuity, and of sudden changes in perspective. The principal problem is the relationship of the Bard's Song (2:25–13:44) to the rest of the poem."[1] We can begin to resolve that problem by considering first the more local problem of the internal unity of the Song.

Of the four extant engraved copies of *Milton*, the earliest two contain forty-five plates each, including the plate of the

[1] *Commentary*, p. 823.

Preface and the Jerusalem hymn; the third omits the Preface plate and adds the plates numbered by Keynes and by Erdman 3, 4, 10, 18, and 32; the fourth, the version of the Erdman text and hence of this study, follows the third with the addition of the plate numbered 5.[2] The four late plates interpolated into the Bard's Song, plates 3, 4, 5, and 10, considerably complicate its structure. The narrative line of the Song is cogent without them—more cogent, some would argue, than with them. Frye has suggested that the clearest order of the opening plates of the Song would be 2, 7, 4, 6, 3, 8, with 5 omitted, which he mistakenly assumes to be the order of the third version of the poem.[3] But Blake did add four plates to the Bard's Song, and he did add them in the sequence reflected by the Keynes and Erdman numberings, and we ought to ask why. The main thematic contribution plates 3, 4, 5, and 10 make is to extend the scope of the Song's action beyond the Edenic family squabble otherwise described; they offer a series of reflections on that contention outside its Edenic (or more properly, its cosmic limbo) context. The main structural contribution they make seems to be confusion; they interrupt the narrative, and although polite rearrangement can minimize the interruption, it cannot dispense with it altogether. Blake apparently intended to interrupt his narrative. Plate 5 would, as Frye indicates, have to be eliminated altogether for the Song to have conventional coherence, and plate 5 was Blake's last addition, his final contribution to a coherence he seems to have preferred to the conventional.

The interpolated plates raise questions not only of the coherence of the Bard's Song but of the process of composition of *Milton* as well. David Erdman believes that plates 3, 4, and 5 were probably etched with the initial copies, bypassed in the binding of those copies, and then later reinstated.[4] The reasons for their reinstatement will probably

---

[2] Erdman, textual notes, p. 727.
[3] "Notes for a Commentary on *Milton*," *Divine Vision*, p. 130.
[4] Textual notes, p. 728.

remain mysterious. Perhaps they were part of a longer work, an ur-*Milton* which Blake mined and reworked in the years between Felpham and copy D. Perhaps they were false starts he later reappraised and found useful. They might have been incorporated for their structural resonance, but they might as reasonably have been incorporated for their thematic value. The strange and difficult form they give the Bard's Song may thus have been partly accidental. Accidental or not, that form is perfectly compatible with the meaning of the Song, and with its status in the entire poem.

We can see that compatibility in the way Blake constructed a single plate of the Song, the last one he interpolated: plate 5 in its wheelings and windings reflects the unexpected configurations of the entire Song. It seems internally disordered as it fluctuates among perspectives, and it has little immediately apparent relation to the rest of the Song. Its opening lines are cryptic both individually and in sequence:

Palamabron with the fiery Harrow in morning returning
From breathing fields. Satan fainted beneath the artillery
Christ took on Sin in the Virgins Womb, & put it off on
the Cross. . . .

Rather than explaining those lines, Blake suddenly introduces altogether different material, an amplified definition of the Three Classes of Men, with their threefold female concomitant, and a lament over fallen existence. But at the end of the plate Blake not only returns to the opening cryptogram, he returns to it by means of the intervening material—and in so doing relates it directly to the rest of the Bard's Song:

Thus they sing Creating the Three Classes among Druid
Rocks
Charles calls on Milton for Atonement. Cromwell is ready

James calls for fires in Golgonooza. for heaps of smok-
  ing ruins
In the night of prosperity and wantonness which he
  himself Created
Among the Daughters of Albion among the Rocks of the
  Druids
When Satan fainted beneath the arrows of Elynittria
And Mathematic Proportion was subdued by Living
  Proportion. . . .

(5:38-44)

Palamabron's return, Satan's faint, and Jesus' incarnation
are still not explicitly related, but a relationship is begin-
ning to emerge: Satan has been felled, we may extrapolate,
by Palamabron's return (Elynittria is Palamabron's emana-
tion, as Blake will tell us later in the poem); that act, like
the incarnation, is the subduing of mathematic by living
proportion. It is achieved on all levels of reality through the
appropriate operations of the Three Classes of Men (Bloom
identifies Milton as Reprobate, Cromwell as Redeemed, and
Charles and James as Elect[5]) and their female concomitant.
Thus plate 5 has its own internal order, and by its thematic
content it is related to the rest of the Song: it is a gloss on
plate 4, which also focuses on the operations of the Three
Classes through Satan's contentiousness and through his-
torical war, and an introduction to plate 6, which is a lam-
entation over the consequences of satanic war. The order
and propriety of plate 5 epitomize the order and propriety
of the Bard's Song as a whole.

The internal structure of the Song, however arbitrary and
perversely rugged it may seem at first, is actually a progres-
sion of four parts which reflect each other, amplifying the
poetic material as the narrative line proceeds. The first part,
lines 2:25–4:5, contains a prologue to the Song's focal ac-
tion, the myth of creation developed in *The Book of Urizen*
and *The Four Zoas;* lines 4:6–8:44 describe the action itself,

[5] Commentary, p. 825

Satan's usurpation of Palamabron's harrow and the forma-
tion of the Three Classes of Men; lines 8:45–11:27 detail the
Great Assembly which passes judgment on that action; and
finally, in lines 11:28–13:44, the contrition inspired by the
result of that judgment reveals the act's full motivation.

The action of the Bard's Song reflects biographical events
during the period in which Blake probably conceived *Mil-
ton*. Although I do believe that biographical influence has
often been overemphasized in interpretations of the Bard's
Song, I think it would be unproductive to ignore the per-
sonal dimension of the Song altogether. The power of *Mil-
ton* results in large part from the range of its applicability:
what is true of Albion in his sleep of Beulah or Ulro and of
Los in his cosmic limbo is equally true of Blake in his gar-
den, and that system of congruencies is much of the point
of the poem. Accordingly, let me sketch briefly the bio-
graphical events that may partly have inspired *Milton*. In
1800 Blake accepted the patronage of a well-known writer
and self-appointed guardian of the arts, William Hayley.
He and his wife moved to a cottage in Felpham, where
Blake was to work on artistic commissions garnered by
Hayley, and on his prophetic poems. Tensions between the
willful visionary and his protector grew as Hayley innocent-
ly and generously attempted to guide Blake's development
along conventional, profitable routes. After three years and
what must have been a bitter quarrel, Blake stormed back
to London more convinced than ever of the necessity of
maintaining his prophetic stance. His disagreement with his
mentor and the eruption of that disagreement into wrath
may be seen in the contention of Satan and Palamabron;
more important, Blake's eventual repudiation of his tem-
porary fury probably inspired the insistence on mercy and
forgiveness that is the basis of the vision of *Milton*.[6]

[6] Frye notes the hazards of strictly biographical interpretations
(*Fearful Symmetry*, pp. 325ff.), as does James Rieger (" 'The Hem
of Their Garments': The Bard's Song in *Milton*," *Sublime Allegory*,
pp. 259–280, esp. p. 260); Wittreich illustrates them by assuming a

Blake's epic introduction and the Bard's Song meet in a
line that we shall soon recognize as a frequent refrain of the
Song but that, because of Blake's ambiguous punctuation,
might as easily be the last line of the introduction as the
opening of the Song:

A Bard broke forth! all sat attentive to the awful man.

Mark well my words! they are of your eternal salvation:

Three Classes are Created by the Hammer of Los. . . .
$$(2:24-26)$$

Nowhere else in the Song is the refrain "Mark well my
words! they are of your eternal salvation" followed by a
colon; in fact, only twice is it punctuated at all, and then by
an exclamation point. It may thus be construed as Blake's
admonition before he repeats the Bard's tale. This is a tenu-
ous construction, one it would be difficult to press; the line
is clearly part of the Song, and only vaguely part of Blake's
introductory. Yet so natural is the transition that when we
first read the line, before we can recognize it as a refrain,
we have no way of knowing who speaks it. It is appropriate
to both poets—and this ambiguity is in turn appropriate
to *Milton*. Both Blake and the nameless Bard speak words
of our eternal salvation. For both, Milton is the vehicle of
that salvation.

The Bard's Song begins with six lines in which most of the
action of *The Four Zoas* is compressed:

Three Classes are Created by the Hammer of Los,
   & Woven
By Enitharmons Looms when Albion was slain upon his
   Mountains

---

stronger influence of Hayley on Blake than seems reasonable ("Domes
of Mental Pleasure: Blake's Epics and Hayley's Epic Theory," *Stud-
ies in Philology*, 69 [1972], pp. 101-129).

And in his Tent, thro envy of Living Form, even of the
    Divine Vision
And of the sports of Wisdom in the Human Imagination
Which is the Divine Body of the Lord Jesus. blessed for
    ever.
Mark well my words. they are of your eternal salvation!

(2:26–3:5)

The difference in tense in the first two lines juxtaposes the
continual creation by Los and the fatal abruptness of Al-
bion's fall. The fall itself is analyzed in two phrases that
comprehend all the causes probed extensively in *The Four
Zoas*, the emanations' treachery ("envy of Living Form")
and the Zoas' ambitions (envy "even of the Divine Vision").
We need not know the *Zoas* to recognize the source of the
tragedy; we have compressed in these phrases both the
whole cause of the original fall and the cause of the disaster
soon to be related. In a further compression, the Bard's
identifying the Human Imagination with the Divine Body
of the Lord Jesus echoes Blake's invocation, in which the
Eternal Great Humanity Divine planted paradise in the
poet's brain. The two pronouncements are not identical
(Blake's is a more tentative identification of divinity and
imagination, working through the symbolic medium of par-
adise, and a more personal one), but they are the same in
substance—as the Bard and Blake are different manifesta-
tions of the same prophetic nature. It is by echoes like this
one that Blake's poem proceeds; its meaning is revealed in
a system of correspondences frequently as subtle as this
one, correspondences evocative not only of the identities
they suggest, but of the kind of universe in which those
identities exist.

The Bard has announced the Three Classes and ex-
plained elliptically the reason for their existence. But now,
instead of defining them, he digresses in what seems an ir-
relevant history lesson. Instead of proceeding to Los's crea-

34

tion of the Classes of our generation of life, he pauses over the smith's first creation, the bound form of Urizen. He seems to forget his announced subject, to be sidetracked by his mention of the fall into an extended description of its first manifestation. That description leads in turn to what seems like a further digression:

> Terrified Los stood in the Abyss & his immortal limbs
> Grew deadly pale; he became what he beheld: for a red
> Round Globe sunk down from his Bosom into the Deep
>   in pangs
> He hoverd over it trembling & weeping. suspended it
>   shook
> The nether Abyss in tremblings. he wept over it, he
>   cherish'd it
> In deadly sickening pain: till separated into a Female
>   pale
> As the cloud that brings the snow: all the while from
>   his Back
> A blue fluid exuded in Sinews hardening in the Abyss
> Till it separated into a Male Form howling in
>   Jealousy. . . .
>
> (3:28–36)

Symbolizing the mastery in him of his feminine, weaker nature, Los gives birth. He bears the pale female "in deadly sickening pain," and as he does, thus cherishing his weaker portion, his spectre also separates from him. We shall see a dark fluid effusion again in *Milton*; this is its prototypic occurrence, an event original in *Milton* although this same division of Los and his emanation is described in two earlier poems.

The Bard seems to have forgotten the Three Classes altogether, to have been carried away by his cosmic history. From the creation of the generation of Los he moves to the creation of the next generation:

> First Orc was Born then the Shadowy Female: then All
>   Los's Family
> At last Enitharmon brought forth Satan Refusing Form,
>   in vain
> The Miller of Eternity made subservient to the Great
>   Harvest
> That he may go to his own Place Prince of the Starry
>   Wheels
> Beneath the Plow of Rintrah & the Harrow of the
>   Almighty
> In the hands of Palamabron.
>
>   (3:40–4:2)

And this generation repeats, as the verse implies, the pat-
terns of the earlier. As Urizen struggled vainly, "Refusing
all Definite Form," Satan now refuses form but is neverthe-
less subdued. One day the identification of Satan and
Urizen will be complete, when Satan goes "to his own Place
Prince of the Starry Wheels"; meanwhile it is only a pro-
jected identification, suggested in the repeated words "Re-
fusing Form" but not explicitly declared.

Despite the apparent absent-mindedness of the Bard, the
first part of his Song ends, as it began, with a reference to
the Three Classes created by Los:

>   Where the Starry Mills of Satan
> Are built beneath the Earth & Waters of the Mundane
>   Shell
> Here the Three Classes of Men take their Sexual
>   texture[.] Woven
> The Sexual is Threefold: the Human is Fourfold.
>
>   (4:2–5)

What seemed like an aimless digression after the initial in-
troduction of the concept has been, in fact, an intrinsic defi-
nition of that concept. Although we still do not know exact-

ly what the Three Classes are, we do know one major aspect of them, their relationship to their cosmic-mythic environment. All the agony of Albion's fall, of Urizen's fall, of Los's division, has culminated in the creation of mankind. Here, in the soil of this earth, under the governance of Los's sons, are men formed. Because they are created they are partial, "threefold" beings in a universe in which to be human is to be fourfold, complete, eternal. As there are three governing sons, Satan, Palamabron, and Rintrah, so there are Three Classes of Men.

We know that there are Three Classes; we know their lineage, and, by analogy, we know something of their nature. Part two of the Bard's Song (lines 4:6–8:44) defines them further by depicting their prototypes in action. The language of this section is starkly different from the concentrated mythic pronouncements of the first part; its pace is breathlessly varied. It brings us from the mythic background of the action the Bard relates directly into the action itself, and it does so by means of the fragmented perspectives Blake always employs to describe action too momentous for the immediate comprehension of a fallen, "threefold" imagination.

Plates 4, 5, and 6 move rapidly among the various aspects of the deed, accenting now a particular figure's attitude, now a historical parallel, now a lyric interpretation. The effect is cinematic, as the Bard's focus shifts abruptly among seemingly unrelated elements. He makes no connections other than subtle verbal echoes that give the passage a kind of aural unity but no apparent logical progression. This lack of conventional transitions eliminates tedious intellectual accountings, freeing the reader's imagination to make the required connections, and whatever other connections seem appropriate. The passage thus achieves a startling immediacy which both involves us in the chaotic events and permits us to recognize their ramifications. The event is at once specific and open-ended.

The Bard's account begins with an angry speech by Los which contrasts startlingly with the impersonal rhetoric of the first part of the Song. Once again a character begins to speak unannounced; as Blake's introduction yields suddenly to the Bard's Song, so Los's voice interrupts the Bard: "If you account it Wisdom when you are angry to be silent, and / Not to shew it: I do not account that Wisdom but Folly." It is four lines before the speaker is even tentatively identified, ten lines before the dramatic situation is established, and meanwhile Los and the Bard have been identified with each other by the transitionless merging of their voices. Los speaks words the angry Bard himself might speak: that "awful man" did, after all, begin his Song "Terrific among the Sons of Albion in chorus solemn & loud." We do not know at first why Los is angry, any more than we know why the Bard is angry. But we do know that both are aligned in a kind of company of wrath.

Los defines not only his own psychic stance but also his son's: "Anger me not! thou canst not drive the Harrow in pitys paths. / Thy work is Eternal Death, with Mills & Ovens & Cauldrons. / Trouble me no more. thou canst not have Eternal Life" (4:16–18). Satan is the regent of the Mundane Shell, to mortals, as Los consoles him, the only god. Master of eternal death, this our life, he still yearns for the transcendent powers of his brothers. But he may not deal in matters beyond this sphere of our visible universe. He is a being like the fallen Urizen of caves and darkness; the fiery light of eternity is denied him. His desiring it is a violation of his nature, a perversion of his Class of Men.

If Satan's distortion of nature is an abstract mythic formulation, there are plenty of contemporary English events to corroborate it. Blake was, for all his cosmic visions, ever an enemy of abstraction, ever the poet of minute particulars. Consequently, his Bard abruptly shifts focus from this titanic domestic quarrel to a warning for the people of Blake's England:

Between South Molton Street & Stratford Place:
Calvarys foot
Where the Victims were preparing for Sacrifice their
Cherubim
Around their loins pourd forth their arrows & their
bosoms beam
With all colours of precious stones, & their inmost
palaces
Resounded with preparation of animals wild & tame
(Mark well my words! Corporeal Friends are
Spiritual Enemies). . . .

(4:21–26)

The passage contains contemporary, Christian, and even
personal analogues of the mythical situation: as Satan smol-
ders in unnatural desire, so England prepares its sons for
war, so Jesus was made to suffer on the Cross, so Blake's
prophetic spirit is shackled by a Corporeal Friend—each
an incident of the false subduing the true, of the triumph
of the mundane over the eternal.

The pattern of the fifth plate from its cryptic beginning
to its partly explained conclusion has been described ear-
lier. Let us look now at the central material of the plate,
which is, like the beginning and end of it, a further defini-
tion of the Three Classes:

And this is the manner of the Daughters of Albion
in their beauty
Every one is threefold in Head & Heart & Reins, &
every one
Has three Gates into the Three Heavens of Beulah
which shine
Translucent in their Foreheads & their Bosoms &
their Loins
Surrounded with fires unapproachable: but whom
they please

39

They take up into their Heavens in intoxicating delight
For the Elect cannot be Redeemd, but Created
    continually
By Offering & Atonement in the crue[l]ties of Moral Law
Hence the three Classes of Men take their fix'd
    destinations
They are the Two Contraries & the Reasoning Negative.
(5:5-14)

There are no Three Classes of Women, because females are counterparts of males and have no truly separate existence. But in their sexuality they are triply empowered to delight and to incarnate the Three Classes of Men. Their role in that incarnation directly parallels the masculine role we have already witnessed: at the mills of Satan the Three Classes take their sexual texture (4:4), and in the "intoxicating delight" of Beulah they "take their fix'd destinations." It is a cruel creation performed at the anvils and the looms. In a transfiguration of the South Molton Street passage, now set wholly on a mythic plane, the Bard describes the scene:

While the Females prepared the Victims. the Males
    at Furnaces
And Anvils dance the dance of tears & pain: loud
    lightnings
Lash on their limbs as they turn the whirlwinds loose
    upon
The Furnaces, lamenting around the Anvils. . . .
(5:15-18)

They sing their dismay at the creatures they copy from Los's pattern in Urizen until a sudden close-up in this cosmic chronicle reveals its particular historical significance: "Charles calls on Milton for Atonement. Cromwell is ready / James calls for fires in Golgonooza" (5:39-40). Cut off from eternity by the very forms they inhabit, mortal men are not capable of Eden's mental strife, but only of the corporeal war Blake despised. Yet there is still hope—the apocalyptic hope of an end to negation, an end to falsehood: "Satan fainted beneath the arrows of Elynittria / And Mathematic Proportion was subdued by Living Proportion" (5:43-44).

From this close-up of man in history the Bard pulls back to a panorama of the inhabitants of the Mundane Shell. The song of the males at their furnaces inspires the Bard's own chant, a plate-long hymn (plate 6) that puts the previous song's close-up into perspective. Its subject is the same creation of the Three Classes, but its longer perspective cancels the frantic urgency of the act. The outcries of the males, their often-broken lines and their restless dichotomies give way to a grand and even psalm. Close by the anvils, one sees only the harsh battering of the tools; away in the cool distance, one sees only the rhythm of their wielding, "ever building, ever falling." The refrain "Loud sounds the Hammer of Los," the "lulling cadences" of Enitharmon's looms, regulate a verse of gracious vastness. The entire world is part of this creation of men, which is at once personal and universal. Golgonooza, built by Los and his consort from the moment of their separation, is both "the spiritual Four-fold London eternal," and Lambeth's Vale, where Blake began his prophetic art. That Lambeth "Dark gleams before the Furnace-mouth a heap of burning ashes" (6:17) is but the mythic fulfillment of "James calls for fires in Golgonooza. for heaps of smoking ruins," identifying Lambeth with Golgonooza by the same process of aural repetition we have noted before.

The Bard is no less anguished at this creation which is a fall from eternity than the men at their anvils, but his anguish is not their lashing torment, their repulsion, but rather a sustained biblical yearning:

When shall Jerusalem return & overspread all the Nations
Return: return to Lambeths Vale O building of human
  souls. . . .
            (6:18-19)

There may be more pain for the man who sees more devastation, but there is also more understanding. The forgers see only a single, "narrow doleful form" in their handiwork, the mortal form struck for all their victims; the Bard sees in this form Three Classes of Men: "The first, The Elect from before the foundation of the World: / The second, The Redeem'd. The Third, The Reprobate & form'd / To destruction from the mothers womb" (7:1–3). We have come even further toward a definition of the Classes.

"Follow with me my plow!" exhorts the Bard, rousing himself from his hymn back to prophetic action, and not quite incidentally identifying himself with the Reprobate Class of Rintrah the plowman. With Reprobate ardor he returns to the basic action of his Song, which he can relate, now that all its symbolic and historical ramifications are established, in simple chronological detail. Each of the many stylistically varied segments of the first plates of this second part of the Bard's Song is really but a single facet of the pattern now to be revealed. Plates 7 and 8 are vigorous and direct; their straightforwardness contrasts effectively with the mythic involutions of preceding passages, and sets off starkly the account of the act itself. The two plates record the yielding of Los, after repeated confrontations like the wearying one that opened this part of the Bard's Song, to Satan's desire to run the Harrow of the Almighty. Palamabron, fearful of appearing ungrateful for the Elect Satan's help, hides his anger and turns over the harrow. The result of this willful perversion of order is disaster. Satan and Palamabron exchange occupations for one eternal day, which lasts a thousand years. Neither is capable of his brother's task. Palamabron's horses and servants are deranged by Satan's mismanagement, and Satan's own servants are frenzied, not by torment, but by the intoxications of Palamabron's wine and songs, which are too heady for their mundane souls. Los warned Satan in his first speech, "To Mortals thy Mills seem every thing & the Harrow of Shaddai / A scheme of Human conduct invisible & incomprehensible" (4:12–13); by giving the servants of the mills a glimpse of the invisible, Palamabron has ruined them as Satan ruined his servants.

Los attempts to quiet the ensuing argument by ordering a moratorium. He puts his left sandal on his head, "Signal of solemn mourning," and with an echo of the Bard proclaims a day of mourning, presumably to last a thousand years like the day of Satan's labor at the Harrow:

> Mine is the fault! I should have remember'd that pity
>   divides the soul
> And man, unmans: follow with me my Plow. this
>   mournful day
> Must be a blank in Nature: follow with me, and
>   tomorrow again
> Resume your labours, & this day shall be a mournful
>   day. . . .
>
>   (8:19–22)

As the Bard encouraged himself to continue his tale by allying himself with the Reprobate Class, so Los, in the same words, signifies the return to wise governance by allying himself with the plowmen. The echo serves to identify the two prophets not only with the spirit of prophecy, but with each other.

The two camps, Satan's Elect and Palamabron's Redeemed, "mourn'd toward one another" through the day until Rintrah, "who is of the reprobate: of those form'd to destruction / In indignation" (8:33–34), could contain his rage no longer and flamed furious above the contenders. The war and murder that ensue climax when Enitharmon creates a space for Satan and for all those "infected" with the wrath of corporeal war. Thus she imitates the Daughters of Beulah, taking into her heavens the Elect who "cannot be Redeemed, but Created continually" (5:11). In doing so she completes the direct action of the Bard's Song, the wars among Los's sons which culminate in Satan's fall.

The first section of the Bard's Song records the fall of Urizen and his being bound into rigid form by Los; the second section records the fall of Satan and his being contained within fixed space by Enitharmon. But, we are soon to hear, "Satan is Urizen" (10:1): the Elect Prince of the Starry Wheels is the same in Los's generation or in that of his sons, and the fall of Satan is simply the fall of Urizen repeated on a lower plane of reality. The second section of the Song thus repeats the first in more detail and on a level of existence further from eternal wholeness.

As the second recapitulates the first, the third section, 8:45–11:27, recapitulates the first and second. Each recapitulation extends the action, the fall of Urizen/Satan, further into the desolations of Generation. In part three we see the judgment of the eternals on Satan's error, a judgment that results in further consolidation of that error. Satan, like Urizen before him, grows opaque and solipsistic; the emanation of Enitharmon from Los, begun in part one (3:28–34) and extended in part two (8:40–41), is confirmed in part three (11:2–5).

The judgment of part three begins when Palamabron, resisting wrath, calls "down a Great Solemn Assembly,"

> That he who will not defend Truth, may be compelled to
> Defend a Lie, that he may be snared & caught & taken
> And all Eden descended into Palamabrons tent
> Among Albions Druids & Bards, in the caves beneath
> Albions
> Death Couch, in the caverns of death, in the corner of
> the Atlantic.
>
> (8:46–9:3)

The descent of all Eden into the limbo beneath Albion's Couch is the immediate result of Satan's act, an ominous descent which will be reflected in the judgment itself and in acts that follow it. That judgment seems infected with all the false assumptions of life in Satan's principality: "Lo! it

44

fell on Rintrah and his rage: / Which now flam'd high &
furious in Satan against Palamabron / Till it became a
proverb in Eden. Satan is among the Reprobate" (9:10–12).
Satan seems among the Reprobate only to a clouded eye,
which recognizes only the momentary flaming of his wrath.
The irony of the proverb is manifest: Satan is no Reprobate,
for his wrath is not the purifying flame of prophecy, but a
hypocritically concealed perversion; indeed, Satan is truly
anti-Reprobate, as we shall soon see. Even so, the Assembly
passes judgment not against the murderer, but against the
wrath that moved him. The reaction is disaster:

> Los in his wrath curs'd heaven & earth, he rent up
>   Nations,
> Standing on Albions rocks among high-reard Druid
>   temples
> Which reach the stars of heaven & stretch from pole to
>   pole.
> He displacd continents, the oceans fled before his face
> He alter'd the poles of the world, east, west &
>   north & south
> But he clos'd up Enitharmon from the sight of all
>   these things. . . .
>
> (9:13–18)

The unidentified anger Los spoke of to Satan in his first
speech is now realized; Los the creator is become Los the
destroyer. Like Satan, he has assumed Rintrah's wrath, but
wrath is as natural in Los as it is perverted in Satan, and the
Reprobate father of the Three Classes can transform his
wrath into fires of creation. For now, however, he is eager
only to destroy. He cuts himself off from all chance of re-
generation: closing up Enitharmon from the grim deeds he
must witness, he completes the process of emanation begun
when he gave birth to her in the first part of the Bard's
Song. His act parallels two that have not yet been described
but that illuminate its significance and will in turn be illum-

inated by it: in several plates we shall learn that Satan simi-
larly closed off his emanation, and at the beginning of Book
II we shall hear of the creation of a place of repose and
comfort for the females by Jesus himself. Los's act suggests
Satan's in its deception and its severance, and Jesus' in its
mercy: a dual suggestion much to the point now, when Los
is in such an ambiguous state, his potential for creative
good undermined by violence.

Meanwhile, Palamabron's plan in calling the Assembly
is being executed: the exonerated dissembler is indeed
caught defending a lie. He accuses Palamabron of malice
and blusters his own omnipotence, and in his fury recapitu-
lates the petrifaction of Urizen:

> Thus Satan rag'd amidst the Assembly! and his bosom
> grew
> Opake against the Divine Vision: the paved terraces of
> His bosom inward shone with fires, but the stones
> becoming opake!
> Hid him from sight, in extreme blackness and darkness,
> And there a World of deeper Ulro was open'd, in the
> midst
> Of the Assembly. In Satans bosom a vast unfathomable
> Abyss.[7]
>
> (9:30–35)

[7] The relationship of these lines to Revelation 12:9 and 20:3 is
significant:

> And the dragon was cast out, that old serpent
> called the Devil, and Satan, which deceiveth the
> whole world: he was cast out into the earth, and his
> angels were cast out with him.

> [An angel] cast him into the bottomless pit,
> and shut him up, and set a seal upon him, that he
> should deceive the nations no more, till the
> thousand years should be fulfilled: and after that
> he must be loosed a little season.

The principal difference between the accounts of Blake's Bard and
St. John is interesting: whereas the biblical Satan is cast out and
sealed up by the forces of God, the Blakean figure is responsible for

Satan has revealed himself the Elect murderer in his bluster and in his darkening. The revelation is met with "a loud solemn universal groan / . . . from the east & from the west & from the south / And from the north"—lines that suggestively recall the fury of Los as he "alter'd the poles of the world, east, west & north & south," and foreshadow the thunders Satan himself is about to utter "from his hidden wheels: accusing loud / The Divine Mercy." The sense in these verbal and imagistic echoes is of universal devastation; on all levels of existence there is turmoil and despair. Significantly, that turmoil is caused both by the Elect Satan and by his Reprobate father Los: no Class of Men can act entirely independently.

Rintrah, revealing the true merciful identity of the Reprobate, seeks to protect Palamabron with walls and moats and columns of fire; when Satan seeks to destroy this protection, he is himself destroyed:

And Satan not having the Science of Wrath, but only
    of Pity:
Rent them asunder, and wrath was left to wrath, &
    pity to pity.
He sunk down a dreadful Death, unlike the slumbers
    of Beulah. . . .

(9:46–48)

The echoes here of previous passages are pronounced and significant. Los has warned Satan that he cannot "drive the Harrow in pitys paths"; he knows no way but dissembling pity, and the awesome harrow cannot be driven by its principles. Pity and wrath are at war here, and Satan is now given over to wrath. Sundered wholly from his natural

his own banishment and imprisonment. But the similarity between the two prophecies is even more important: by echoing John, Blake establishes the apocalyptic milieu of his poem. His Satan sealed within himself during this thousand-year day of mourning is the biblical dragon sealed off for the millennium, but soon to be released to ravage the world.

quality, he is separated from eternal life. His sinking "down a dreadful Death" recalls his cryptic faint, alluded to twice in part two of the Bard's Song: as he fainted beneath the flaming artillery of Palamabron, the arrows of Elynittria, so he sinks now from human consciousness before the fires of Palamabron's shield.

Satan's fury has brought justice upon him. Drawn down into the Female Space providentially created for him by Enitharmon, confined in the limited form of the tangible body, he has ironically fulfilled his destiny, to "go to his own Place Prince of the Starry Wheels":

> Then Los & Enitharmon knew that Satan is Urizen
> Drawn down by Orc & the Shadowy Female into
>   Generation. . . .
>
> (10:1–2)

It is the defeated Urizen, the fallen, constricted, opaque Urizen, with whom the ambitious Satan is identified. His fall makes part three of the Bard's Song directly parallel to part one, the account of Urizen's fall. It turns the poem back on itself in a horrible cycle—or rather, a spiral, because the fall of Satan occurs a generation after the fall of Urizen and leads, not back into the eternity from which Urizen began, but further into the dark reaches of our generative life. Significantly, as we saw the masculine creative principle at work consolidating Urizen and limiting his fall, we see the feminine creative principle at work limiting the fall of the next generation:

> The nature of a Female Space is this: it shrinks
>   the Organs
> Of Life till they become Finite & Itself seems Infinite
> And Satan vibrated in the immensity of the Space!
>   Limited
> To those without but Infinite to those within. . . .
>
> (10:6–9)

Los consolidated Urizen and Enitharmon consolidated Satan, but "Satan is Urizen": the masculine and feminine creative principles are therefore mutual; however different their subjects and operations may seem, the difference is only illusion. A Female Space is ultimately the same rigid, finite form the body of Urizen is; Satan is Urizen.

Satan's space entraps his father as well, "closing Los from Eternity in Albions Cliffs / A mighty Fiend against the Divine Humanity mustring to War" (10:10–11). Los himself, the prototypic Reprobate, suffers the judgment that fell on Rintrah. Raging against the fallen judgment of the Assembly he becomes, like his own son Orc, a suppressed spirit of revolt. He rails against the god and king of the place, against the female jealousy that maintains his oppression. His fury recalls his terrified response to the body of Urizen he created; his castigation of the emanations is but an extension of his separation from Enitharmon.

Finally, after another, close-up look at Satan declaring himself god, someone unnamed asks the reason for the injustice Los reviles. And we learn, in a justification of the ways of eternals to men, that the judgment was no mistake:

If the Guilty should be condemn'd, he must be an
    Eternal Death
And one must die for another throughout all Eternity.
Satan is fall'n from his station & never can be redeem'd
But must be new Created continually moment by
    moment
And therefore the Class of Satan shall be calld
    the Elect, & those
Of Rintrah. the Reprobate, & those of Palamabron
    the Redeem'd
For he is redeem'd from Satans Law, the wrath
    falling on Rintrah,
And therefore Palamabron dared not to call a
    solemn Assembly

Till Satan had assum'd Rintrahs wrath in the day
    of mourning
In a feminine delusion of false pride self-deciev'd.

                        (11:17–26)

We have at last a full definition of the Three Classes of
Men, as well as a demonstration of the mercy of eternity:
Satan, Elect, was vulnerable to eternal death, and so the
verdict of the Assembly fell not upon him but upon the
Reprobate Rintrah, who could survive the edict, and in
whose wrath Los suffers the sentence.

It was feminine delusion, according to the eternal, that
caused Satan's transgression. In the last section of the
Bard's Song the source of that delusion steps forward to ac-
cept the guilt Satan himself denied. In a pattern established
earlier in his Song, a pattern Blake will follow in the general
format of *Milton*, the Bard turns from his definition of the
Three Classes of Men to an account of the female role in
their existence. Leutha, beholding "Satans condemnation"
(no one was fooled by the curious judgment, it seems; even
Satan, granted mercy, condemned himself), descends from
Beulah to the Assembly beneath the Couch of Death to re-
late her part in Satan's deadly act.

Leutha's tale incorporates and explains many elements
of the Bard's Song not yet fully clarified. She announces
boldly, "I am the Author of this Sin! by my suggestion / My
parent power Satan has committed this transgression." The
courage and forthrightness of this confession recalls Los's
"Mine is the fault! I should have remember'd that pity di-
vides the soul" (8:19), and prefigures confessions later in
the poem by Ololon, Milton, and Blake.

Leutha's speech reveals other significant parallels. As
Enitharmon was born of Los, so Leutha was born of Satan,
yet another connection between faltering Reprobate and his
Elect son. And as Satan fell before Elynittria's arrows, so
did Leutha, who yearned for Palamabron: "But beautiful
Elynittria with her silver arrows repelld me. / For her light

50

is terrible to me. I fade before her immortal beauty" (11:38–12:1). The contention of Palamabron and Satan becomes in Leutha's account a contention of their emanations for the love of Palamabron, an amplification necessary to Blake's poetic system, according to which every action has mutual "male" and "female" components. Satan's infatuation with Palamabron's role was, Leutha confesses, her own invention. Repelled by Elynittria, Leutha projected her love for Palamabron upon Satan; she entered into his dreams, "stupified the masculine perceptions / And kept only the feminine awake. hence rose his soft / Delusory love to Palamabron" (12:4–7).

Satan's lapse, then, is Adam's lapse, or Albion's: he yielded to his feminine, weaker portion, perverting his true nature by embracing false desires. He is no evil monster, but a natural human soul deluded; it is the delusion that is responsible for the havoc which ensues. Had Satan maintained his rightful position, had he, once he deviated from it, accepted the mercy of the Assembly, all would have been well. The eternals were right to condemn what was false in him, the Reprobate ardor he was unsuited for, to condemn the sin and not the sinner, and thus attempt to redeem him. But the Elect can no more be redeemed than they can drive the harrow; the initial delusion must be played out.

That playing out requires sacrifice. The crucial sacrifice will be made in this poem by one who has previously violated the principle of such sacrifice. One may not consign, as John Milton did, wrong-doers to eternal damnation, first because they do not deserve it, and second because the necessary balance of humanity will not permit it. Men err, often criminally, disastrously; but even the errant are necessary to life. There are Three Classes of Men, and so there must be. The Reprobate must continually sacrifice to save the Elect, or humanity cannot survive. The mills are as necessary to life as the plow.

In naming Milton to save Satan, Blake symbolically purifies his master of such errors as having damned his own

Satan. Leutha's speech is filled with ironic revisions of *Paradise Lost*, from her own "sinful" relationship with her "Parent power Satan" and the deadly dragon issuing from it to the defiant destructiveness of their mutual act:

> The Harrow cast thick flames & orb'd us round in
> concave fires
> A Hell of our own making. see, its flames still
> gird me round[.]
> Jehovah thunder'd above! Satan in pride of heart
> Drove the fierce Harrow among the constellations
> of Jehovah
> Drawing a third part in the fires as stubble
> north & south. . . .
>
> (12:22–26)

The revision of *Paradise Lost* amounts to a reconsideration of the nature of the rebellion of a third part of the "constellations of Jehovah": Blake complicates the motive of unforgivable pride with a more natural and redeemable motive, a love thwarted by jealousy. Milton's Satan fell by arrogance, Blake's by weakness and delusion (the flaws, significantly, of Milton's Adam and Eve). Milton's Satan could not be saved; Blake's Satan must be saved for the preservation of humanity.

Leutha's explanation of Satan's deed explains as well his previously cryptic faint. Plate 5 announced that "Satan fainted beneath the artillery" (5:2), and later partly clarified that artillery as "the arrows of Elynittria" (5:43); Leutha further clarifies those arrows: "Elynittria met Satan with all her singing women. / Terrific in their joy & pouring wine of wildest power / They gave Satan their wine: indignant at the burning wrath. / Wild with prophetic fury his fomer life became like a dream" (12:42–45). Like his own dull servants in the mills, Satan is not strong enough for Palamabron's heady wine. The artillery that fells him is the joyous sense of eternity. As he faints he casts Leutha "from his inmost brain," casting out female pity as we saw him do plates earlier, condemning himself by his own murderous wrath. Thus we see that what took place before the Assembly in Palamabron's tent on the day of mourning was but a reflection of what took place in the fields themselves on the day of Satan's labor. The act and its consequences are identical. Now we see also the full justification of Blake's non-sequential descriptions. Not only does the seemingly random order of his references quicken our imaginations and resonate suggestively; not only do his series of perspectives generate a sense of numberless perspectives; but this curious pattern of temporally and spatially divergent events unified only by a network of verbal echoes reveals that all the events are a single event. It is one thing to be told that all levels of reality are ultimately one reality perceived differently; it is quite another, considerably more convincing experience to be led to all the levels of reality and to see on all the same populace, the same act.

The technique of the Bard's Song with its interruptions and reversions and accruing definitions is initially confusing. It may even seem comic, as the Bard winds back and forth among the elements of his story like some absent-minded metaphysician too enraptured by his own ideas to relate them coherently. Yet ultimately we recognize that their presentation is not only coherent, but coherent in the only way that would not violate their complexity. The Bard rejects conventional narrative logic because his vision transcends logic. He records events that cannot be comprehended in the limited perspective of fallen reason, and therefore he adopts the involutions, the exotic imagery, and the abrupt tonal shifts with which Ezekiel and the author of Daniel and John of Patmos also chose to challenge that fallen perspective. His vision, like theirs, is one of present error and future truth; his style, like theirs, is sometimes shrill and often hortatory; his narration, like theirs, is a complex union of multidimensional truths. Because his vision of the unity of reality is even more radical than theirs,

he employs the devices of style and narration that he
shares with them even more radically than they do.[8]

Leutha's repentance identifies her act with the original
crime:

> All is my fault! We are the Spectre of Luvah the
> murderer
> Of Albion: O Vala! O Luvah! O Albion! O lovely
> Jerusalem
> The Sin was begun in Eternity, and will not rest to
> Eternity
> Till two Eternitys meet together, Ah! lost! lost! lost!
> for ever!
>
> (13:8-11)

All the events of the Bard's Song are but reflections of the
initial event, the fall of Albion. The second generation of
Zoas fell as the first did; we their issue in time are subject
to the same murderous impulses, and the same creative
ones.

The response of the eternals to Leutha's remorse is the
ratification of Enitharmon's mercy to her son. They give
time to the space she created. The six thousand years of
human history are allotted to Satan's universe, and a guard-
ian is appointed to each period. The Bard's catalogue of the
six guardians enables us to organize the events of his Song
in a symbolic chronology. Insofar as the days of Los's realm
are a thousand years long (7:13), each corresponds to an
age of fallen history. According to Leutha's tale, Satan's day
of labor was under the regency of Jehovah, last of the
guardians set in time: "Jehovah thundered above," Leutha's
refrain says, as Satan "Drove the fierce Harrow among the
constellations of Jehovah." Satan's tentative connection with
Jehovah was suggested in his first reaction to the Assembly's
judgment, when he wrote his laws "upon the clouds of Je-

[8] James Rieger further defines the prophetic obscurity of the
Bard's Song (*op. cit.,* pp. 273-280).

54

hovah" (9:22); now the correspondence is complete. The day of mourning proclaimed by Los is analogous to the seventh thousand years, the millennial reign of the Lamb of God. Satan's day is Jehovah's, and when it is ended Jehovah reacts with Satan's pride:

> loud he call'd, stretching his hand
>   to Eternity
> For then the Body of Death was perfected in hypocritic
>   holiness,
> Around the Lamb, a Female Tabernacle woven in
>   Cathedrons Looms
> He died as a Reprobate. he was Punish'd as a
>   Transgressor!
> Glory! Glory! Glory! to the Holy Lamb of God. . . .
>   (13:24–28)

The end of the day of Jehovah is the completion of created time. It is also, in Los's realm, the end of Satan's devastation. And in the mythic cosmos with which the Bard began his Song, it is the completion of the binding of Urizen, the end of the sixth age and state of dismal woe. On the seventh day Jehovah will rant and Satan will accuse and Los will dance his hideous dance—and at the same time the Lamb of God will appear to redeem them all, for the seventh day is not only the culmination of the previous six, it is the gateway back into eternity. Six thousand years were proclaimed for the universe of Satan; the seventh thousand belongs to Christ. As Rintrah bore the judgment against Satan, Jesus will bear the condemnation of all the sons of Albion. In the sacrifice of Reprobate prophets is the salvation of humanity.

The difficulty is that, although the seventh day ends simultaneously on all levels of reality, the rest of their time schemes do not coincide. Urizen's six days of falling were over long before the sixth and seventh days of Eden recorded in the Bard's Song, and the entire six thousand years of generative history were only decreed on the mournful seventh day in Palamabron's tent. But however long a day lasts on any particular level of reality, twenty-four hours, a thousand years, or an "age" immeasurable to us, the last day will end at the same instant on all levels. Whatever the duration of time decreed for any reality, all time will cease at the same moment. Then "The Elect shall meet the Redeem'd" (13:30), and there will be peace. But until then there will be many meetings of the Elect and Redeemed and little peace:

> But Elynittria met Leutha in the place where she
> was hidden.
> And threw aside her arrows, and laid down her
> sounding Bow;
> She sooth'd her with soft words & brought her to
> Palamabrons bed
> In moments new created for delusion, interwoven
> round about,
> In dreams she bore the shadowy Spectre of Sleep,
> & namd him Death.
> In dreams she bore Rahab the mother of Tirzah
> & her sisters
> In Lambeths vales; in Cambridge & in Oxford, places
> of Thought
> Intricate labyrinths of Times and Spaces unknown,
> that Leutha lived
> In Palamabrons Tent, and Oothoon was her charming
> guard.
>
> (13:36-44)

Even in repose in Palamabron's bed, Leutha has borne and will continue to bear the spectre of peace, creating in her dreams the woeful cycles of mortal history, the reincarnations of Satan. The Bard's prophecy of reconciliation is thus marred by the prospect of the continuation of eternal wars

on the mortal plain; but it is a prospect, like the dream of
Enitharmon in *Europe*, of no considerable duration in the
realm of Los. The six days of conflict will pass there, as they
did in the chaos that preceded them. All nightmares shall
end at the end of the seventh day, and the children of fallen
Albion will once more enter eternity.

Thus the Bard ends his song. Each of its four parts exam-
ines one aspect of a single, manifold event: the fall of man
in all his generations. It is a difficult poem, but a self-con-
tained one. Although it is only one phase of Blake's vision,
it is itself a whole work of art. It is complete on all levels of
its Sublime Allegory, the personal, the historical, and the
philosophical and moral abstract. It is perfectly valid to
read the Song as an account of Blake's feud with Hayley, as
long as we recognize that that account is only its barest,
most skeletal aspect. All the details of the feud, as they ap-
pear in this poem, are details also and more significantly of
a profound philosophical conviction: there are certain dis-
tinctions among men that are natural and inviolable, and
perversions of them can only lead to disaster. A prophet
painting miniature portraits and a dilettante aspiring to
prophecy are equally guilty of such perversion, for neither
is adhering to his nature. Each will suffer, and each must
learn to master his weakest instincts and to respect both his
and his opponent's concerns. Life demands both the harrow
and the mill.

Whether one reads the events of the Bard's Song as bio-
graphical, or as an allegory of the imaginative process or of
political history, its basic coherence depends on its use of
an elaborate system of units of duration. Time is, as Blake
will say explicitly later in *Milton*, the providential duration
established for the lapse of humanity from eternity; it is
measured differently on different levels of reality, but it will
end on all of them at the same, apocalyptic instant. So the
organization of the poem implies in its shifting focuses
among various levels of reality, focuses that ultimately unite

in a clear and striking vision of the end of all fallen reality. The Bard governs our sense of time throughout his poem, making it nonsequential to indicate the complex interrelationships of various "time zones," yet carrying through this seeming disorder a simple and revealing narration common to all levels. There is also a straightforward rhetorical progression in his poem which, together with the simple narrative line, corrects any sense of disunity his irregular perspectives encourage. The Song begins in cosmic vastness, its tone spare and ringing; it moves through frantic action on all levels of creation, reflected in constantly shifting tones and diction, through austere judgment and its tragic consequences, to a passage of lucid and very personal confession. The narration of the Song, organized chronologically, may be seen as a great spiral from cosmic disaster beyond full human comprehension to the all too readily comprehended disasters of our own level of reality, the Mundane Shell. The rhetorical movement from cosmic to personal is also the movement of the action through all the levels of providential time. As the poem ends, that time has almost run its course. The seventh day, the millennial day of mourning, is about to end on all levels of reality. The rhetorical progression of the poem brings us, ultimately, into direct and personal confrontation with the meaning of that end.

At the end of the Bard's Song both Satan and Los have given over to wrath and been cut off from eternity. Satan has cast out pity and Los has but hidden his, so there is a vital distinction in their states. Satan has fallen into eternal death, from which he can never be redeemed but must continually be re-created; Los is merely trapped, still immortal, in the generated universe, railing against his condition and seeking a way out. The cosmic conflicts have been translated to the mortal plane. Because "The Divine Hand found the Two Limits" of descent (13:20), those conflicts must finally be played out there.

W. J. T. Mitchell argues:

The Bard's Song, which functions as the Genesis of the narrative in *Milton*, seems almost ready at several points to become its Revelation. Leutha's description of Satan's work with the harrow (12:25–26) makes him sound like the dragon of Revelation rather than the usurping brother; the quarrel of Satan and Palamabron begins to sound more like Armageddon (8:26–40) than Cain and Abel; the Assembly's judgment begins to look like a Last Judgment when it calls up "Two Witnesses" as did John of Patmos. These echoes remain ironic and unactualized in the Bard's Song; but they create a sense that "the time," in some sense, is always potentially at hand in Blake's world and is not dependent on a scheme of progressive development or cause and effect.[9]

I believe that the echoes are actualized in the Bard's Song, or at least that they are brought to the point of actualization, the instant before time ceases, which the rest of *Milton* will explore. The Bard's Song is in fact both the Genesis and Revelation of Blake's myth, chronicling, on a cosmic level in which a thousand years pass as a single day, the entire history of fallen reality. The Bard's process, however, like Blake's in *The Four Zoas*, has been not merely to move conventionally along from beginning to end, but rather to demonstrate throughout his prophecy the end in the beginning and a beginning in the end. Throughout Blake's myth, Cain and Abel do not produce the warring factions of Armageddon, they are those warring factions; any assembly is for Blake capable of a Last Judgment.

The Bard's Song is to the rest of *Milton* what each of its parts is to the Bard's Song. It is a single aspect of the action of the poem, its mythic prototype, and yet it contains in analogue all the elements of that action. It will be reflected and amplified throughout the rest of the poem. Further-

[9] "Blake's Radical Comedy: Dramatic Structure as Meaning in *Milton*," *Sublime Allegory*, pp. 281–301; p. 287.

more, not only are its component myths and images to be repeated in the body of *Milton*, but its very rhetorical pattern will be followed there. As it moves from cosmic foreboding to personal confession, so will the poem as a whole.

B. Act

The body of Book I is composed of two sections, an account of the action to which the Bard's Song provides a prologue (13:45–24:47), and a vision of the providential workings of time and space liberated by that action (24:48 to the end). The action occurs simultaneously on various levels of existence. It has three distinguishable stages, a series, it would seem, of subactions, but Blake indicates repeatedly, by verbal echoes and by explicit references to the instant each event occurs, that the stages themselves are simultaneous. The three stages are defined by consolidations of major figures in the poem. In the first, the Bard enters Milton; in the second, Milton enters Blake; in the third, Los enters the union of Bard/Milton/Blake. Each consolidation at once inspires new vision and liberates the will to realize that vision.

The Bard's Song, with its implicit condemnation of weak pity and grasping love, has shaken its hearers even as the explicit judgment it describes shook the Assembly. The assembly of the Bard's generation is no wiser than the Assembly of Rintrah's; each questions the pronouncements of its sages, each is in need of purification. Challenged, the Bard claims divine authority even as the eternal in his Song "confirm'd [the judgment against Rintrah] with a thunderous oath" (11:27). His Song has had, he affirms, the very source Blake sought for his own song in its invocation:

> The Bard replied. I am Inspired! I know it is Truth!
>   for I Sing
> According to the inspiration of the Poetic Genius

Who is the eternal all-protecting Divine Humanity
To whom be Glory & Power & Dominion Evermore Amen
. . . .

(13:51–14:3)

The judgment in Palamabron's tent was met with Los's altering the poles of the world and the Assembly's uttering "a loud solemn universal groan . . . from the east & from the west & from the south / And from the north" (9:37–39); the Bard's judgment, too, causes the heavens to resound and the earth to shake:

Then there was great murmuring in the Heavens of
    Albion
Concerning Generation & the Vegetative power &
    concerning
The Lamb the Saviour: Albion trembled to Italy
    Greece & Egypt
To Tartary & Hindostan & China & to Great America
Shaking the roots & fast foundations of the Earth
    in doubtfulness
The loud voic'd Bard terrify'd took refuge in
    Miltons bosom. . . .

(14:4–9)

On all levels of existence, then, there is fear and trembling —a trembling that exactly parallels its mythic precedent yet to be resolved. In that perilous atmosphere Milton alone, fortified by the Bard's presence within him, has the courage to act. The fleeing of the Bard into his bosom is a literalization of the idea that the Bard's Song inspired Milton; it is also a symbol of the failure of eternity to resolve the disputes of Eden, disputes that will only be resolved in time through the agency of Milton. The Bard's flight is thus both the symptom of disaster and its ultimate reversal—as the flames of Rintrah or the battles of Apocalypse are both destructive and renovative. The Reprobate Bard within him, Milton is himself now "Reprobate & form'd to destruction from the mothers womb" (7:37–38):

> Then Milton rose up from the heavens of Albion
> ardorous!
> The whole Assembly wept prophetic, seeing in Miltons
> face
> And in his lineaments divine the shades of Death & Ulro
> He took off the robe of the promise, & ungirded himself
> from the oath of God. . . .
>
> (14:10–13)

Death is already apparent in him as he, like Los before him closed "from Eternity in Albions Cliffs" (10:10), rejects allegiance to the mundane god. The alliances that are to comprise the protagonist of *Milton* are thus suggested at the beginning of its action: Los, Rintrah, the Bard, Milton, and Blake himself have had, and have now, at the poem's moment, the same function on all their levels of reality. Each, inspired from without, sacrifices himself angrily to battle falsehood and preserve truth; each draws the disapproval of his peers and witnesses the devastation of life outside eternity. We have seen this sequence applied to all Reprobate figures but Blake (although it has been imputed to him by subtle similarities between himself and the Bard); his parallel course will be a principal subject of the body of *Milton*. He is the only one of the Reprobate who is solely a figure of our temporal life, the only one who does not descend into the Mundane Shell but, by an act of vision, ascends from it. Thus he will be, by the accident of his birth moment and by his deliberately cultivated receptivity to vision, the key to the redemption of all levels of reality. He is at the nadir; if he can ascend from it, humanity can ascend. It will take all the other Reprobate figures to help him make that ascent: he is their representative, their functional form, in this, the crucial level of reality.

3. Plate 16 (Milton shedding the garment of Puritanism)

As Rintrah bore the judgment of Satan and Los suffered his punishment, now Milton will sacrifice himself for the Elect sinner:

> And Milton said, I go to Eternal Death! The Nations still
> Follow after the detestable Gods of Priam; in pomp
> Of warlike selfhood, contradicting and blaspheming.
> When will the Resurrection come; to deliver the sleeping
> body
> From corruptibilty: O when Lord Jesus wilt thou come?
> Tarry no longer; for my soul lies at the gates of death.
> I will arise and look forth for the morning of the grave.
> I will go down to the sepulcher to see if morning breaks!
> I will go down to self annihilation and eternal death,
> Lest the Last Judgment come & find me unannihilate
> And I be siez'd & giv'n into the hands of my own
> Selfhood.
> The Lamb of God is seen thro' mists & shadows, hov'ring
> Over the sepulchers in clouds of Jehovah & winds of
> Elohim
> A disk of blood, distant; & heav'ns & earth's roll dark
> between
> What do I here before the Judgment? without my
> Emanation?
> With the daughters of memory, & not with the daughters
> of inspiration [?]
> I in my Selfhood am that Satan: I am that Evil One!
> He is my Spectre! in my obedience to loose him from
> my Hells
> To claim the Hells, my Furnaces, I go to Eternal Death.
>
> (14:14–32)

This key speech sets the instant of the poem, the interim between death and resurrection, the moratorium ordered by Los in the Bard's Song. It is at once a declaration of personal intention and a plea for aid from without, its two contradictory impulses perfectly reflected in its shifting rhythms. Beginning and ending with the resolute "I go to Eternal Death," it is a kind of capsule of Blake's convictions of redemption. The progress of the speech is the progress of *Milton*. Its initial affirmation and brief summary of the conditions that make that affirmation imperative are spoken firmly, self-confidently; the beat of the lines is strong and, though not metrically regular, almost martial in its ringing control. The central portion of the speech is a traditional appeal for divine help, and its meeker rhythm is biblical in its lyrical regularity: "O when Lord Jesus wilt thou come? . . . I will arise and look forth for the morning of the grave. / I will go down to the sepulcher to see if morning breaks!" This is not, of course, merely a passive plea for outside control; it has, rather, the positive quality of John Milton's "They also serve who only stand and wait." Going down to the sepulcher is embracing Eternal Death; it is no evasion of responsibility, but a positive act of consciousness demanding enormous courage.

As salvation is a merger of external and internal responsibility, so is the evil that defies it. The last movement of Milton's speech is a confession: "I in my Selfhood am that Satan." The rhythm is once again the stirring, self-confident beat of the opening lines, but the tone has shifted from their asperity to a new and humbler determination. The evil of the opening lines has been recognized as an internal evil; the necessity to exorcise it is therefore even more profound. The second "I go to Eternal Death" has in its context a quieter and yet even more forceful tone than the first. It is as if in the beginning a decision is being made, but at the end it has been made. Decision, in this poem, is action; in the course of this one brief speech, Milton's sacrificial act is both conceived and executed. That course is the course of the entire poem, which begins in bardic anger, moves through a complicated dramatization of mutual responsibility for salvation, and ends in a series of intimate confessions that recapitulate the initial charges.

The next three lines emphasize the identity of decision

and act: "And Milton said. I go to Eternal Death! Eternity
shudder'd / For he took the outside course, among the
graves of the dead / A mournful shade. Eternity shudderd
at the image of eternal death. . . ." It is perhaps too subtle
to rely on Blake's punctuation for such an important point,
yet the punctuation of this quotation of Milton's speech sug-
gests that it is the opening "I go to Eternal Death!" that
causes such consternation in eternity: the concluding state-
ment is followed by a quiet period, not an exclamation
point. Thus Milton's taking the outside course would be si-
multaneous with the rest of his speech. A more reliable indi-
cation of this simultaneity is that as Milton descends,
eternity shudders "at the image of eternal death"—just as,
when he began to speak, eternity wept "seeing in Miltons
face / And in his lineaments divine the shades of Death &
Ulro." These are indeed subtle indications of the simul-
taneity of decision and action, but they are, I believe, sub-
stantial, and they will be supported by more explicit subse-
quent descriptions.

Milton's speech suggests two of Blake's principal argu-
ments with his prophetic master. Frye cites the first:

> But one is struck by the fact that Milton never sees
> beyond this sinister "female will" [of Eve and Dalilah].
> His vision of women takes in only the hostility and fear
> which it is quite right to assume toward the temptress
> who represents moral virtue, . . . but which is by no
> means the only way in which women can be visualized.
> There is no emanation in Milton; no Beatrice or
> Miranda; no vision of the spiritual nature of love.[10]

However much one may disagree with this passage as a
reading of John Milton, it is probably an accurate account
of Blake's reading of Milton. The character Milton's exis-
tence in heaven without his emanation is an implicit criti-
cism of the poet Milton's attitude toward women. It is,

[10] *Fearful Symmetry*, p. 352.

moreover, both a moral and a literary criticism: neither in his life nor in his writings did he, Blake implies, realize "the spiritual nature of love." It is not merely his attitude toward women Blake condemns here, of course; "Emanation" is, after all, not a Blakean translation of "wife," but a representation of all of a person's ideals and productions. Milton's ideals and productions are deficient not only in his alleged insensitivity to women, but in a perhaps more serious insensitivity to his own errors. Thus Blake has Milton return to mortality to loose Satan from "my Hells . . . my Furnaces." He is to redeem Satan, his spectre, from destruction even as Rintrah was forced to do in the Bard's Song, but the action has an added dimension here: Milton calls them his hells, his furnaces, not only because any of us condemns his enemy or that portion of himself he deems his enemy, but because John Milton in his greatest work consigned his Satan to hells of his own design. With God in command and Satan in torment and humanity scheduled for redemption after a mere female dream of history, the universe of *Paradise Lost* would be to Blake static and unprogressive, unforgiving and uninspired. He would have the Bard of that universe restore inspiration to it by recognizing, as Blake implies in the epic invocation of this poem, that it is the universe of each person's imagination, that all of its factions are vital and all must be preserved. So Milton descends to salvage the Elect portion of his own being.

The decision to descend is the first stage in the action of Book I, and even as Milton makes the decision Death and Ulro are visible in him. The second stage is the realization of that image. Milton descends, "taking the outside course, among the graves of the dead / A mournful shade." At the very start of the descent, "on the verge of Beulah," he enters into his Shadow, "a mournful form double; hermaphroditic." S. Foster Damon, Milton O. Percival, Frye, and Bloom have defined Blake's use of the word "hermaphroditic."[11] For

[11] S. Foster Damon, *William Blake: His Philosophy and Symbols* (New York: Houghton Mifflin, 1924), p. 412; Percival, *Circle of*

now, we need only the sense of paradox the word invokes: outside Eden, where males and females are truly one and indistinguishable, and Beulah, where they are distinct but married, the masculine and feminine portions of humanity are in a sterile state of ambiguity opposite both eternal relationships. The senses of ambiguity and of opposition to eternal modes of existence are crucial to Blake's conception of life in time. What Percival calls the "checkmate and consequent sterility" of temporal sexuality is a kind of demonic parody of the union Milton seeks with Ololon. Milton must reenter the ambiguities of mortal existence in order to perfect his own marriage with his emanation. What is unsatisfactory in eternity must be corrected in time, subdued "from Particulars to Generals."

The hermaphroditic shadow is the very body of man, the universe of his fallen perception. It reaches, the poet emphasizes, from the edge of eternity through Ulro to Generation, "Albions land: / Which is this earth of vegetation on which now I write" (14:40–41). All existence outside eternity is a mere shadow of eternity, horrible in its opacity and yet still providential: it is the tissue that binds the mortal remnants of Albion to eternity. Without it the members of Albion would be annihilate.

Milton's descent divides his existence among the various levels of reality. In order to perceive the whole Milton now, we must combine multiple perspectives on him:

> As when a man dreams, he reflects not that his body
>   sleeps,
> Else he would wake; so seem'd he entering his
>   Shadow: but
> With him the Spirits of the Seven Angels of the Presence
> Entering; they gave him still perceptions of his
>   Sleeping Body;

Destiny, p. 280; *Fearful Symmetry*, p. 125; and *Apocalypse*, pp. 282–283.

Which now arose and walk'd with them in Eden, as
    an Eighth
Image Divine tho' darken'd; and tho walking as one
    walks
In sleep; and the Seven comforted and supported him.

Like as a Polypus that vegetates beneath the deep!
They saw his Shadow vegetated underneath the Couch
Of death: for when he enterd into his Shadow: Himself:
His real and immortal Self: was as appeard to those
Who dwell in immortality, as One sleeping on a couch
Of gold; and those in immortality gave forth their
    Emanations
Like Females of sweet beauty, to guard him round & to
    feed
His lips with food of Eden in his cold and dim repose!
But to himself he seemd a wanderer lost in dreary night.

Onwards his Shadow kept its course among the Spectres;
    call'd
Satan, but swift as lightning passing them, startled the
    shades
Of Hell beheld him in a trail of light as of a comet
That travels into Chaos: so Milton went guarded within.
                      (15:1–20)

Milton exists now, because of his decision, in three forms.
Because he entered into death, his eternal portion seems to
the other eternals a corpse on a golden couch. The life
which fled that corpse "vegetates beneath the deep," in-
carnate in this Generation. Because his entry into Genera-
tion is an act of mercy, he maintains even in this earthly life
a providential sense of his eternal nature, a perception of
his true humanity walking with the Seven Angels of the
Presence. He has, then, a double awareness of himself,
while the remaining immortals have a third vision of him
and the mortal beings here on "this earth of vegetation"

have yet a fourth. Only the Seven Angels themselves, presumably, comprehend all these visions.

The Seven Angels are crucial not only to the spatial perspectives of the poem, but also to the temporal "perspectives." They are the Seven Eyes of God of *The Four Zoas*, the watchers of the seven thousand years of fallen existence, the six named by the Bard plus the seventh, millennial guardian, Jesus. That they all watch and support Milton indicates that their reigns are complete, that fallen history is about to be consummated in Milton's great venture. The day of mourning is about to end.

The problem of perspective is not just a cosmic jigsaw puzzle, an intellectual game. It is a central issue to every human being:

> The nature of infinity is this: That every thing has its
> Own Vortex; and when once a traveller thro' Eternity
> Has passd that Vortex, he percieves it roll backward
> behind
> His path, into a globe itself infolding; like a sun:
> Or like a moon, or like a universe of starry majesty,
> While he keeps onwards in his wondrous journey on the
> earth
> Or like a human form, a friend with whom he livd
> benevolent.
> As the eye of man views both the east & west
> encompassing
> Its vortex; and the north & south, with all their starry
> host;
> Also the rising sun & setting moon he views surrounding
> His corn-fields and his valleys of five hundred acres
> square.
> Thus is the earth one infinite plane, and not as apparent
> To the weak traveller confin'd beneath the moony shade.
> Thus is the heaven a vortex passd already, and the earth
> A vortex not yet pass'd by the traveller thro' Eternity.
>
> (15:21–35)

Each observer stands at the point at which two vortices meet. Wherever he looks, he sees a vortex passed, or one yet to be passed through; thus is his standing point an infinite plane, a featureless, endless platform for vision. How much he sees depends on how well he looks. If he looks well, if he sees with fourfold Edenic vision, he embraces what he "sees" as part of himself and there is no distance between perceiver and perceived. If he sees with a fallen eye, he establishes, by the very act of perceiving, his separateness from what he sees: he opens a vortex between perceiver and perceived.

Frye, Hazard Adams, Bloom, and Thomas R. Frosch all define the vortex, as it must be defined, in terms of perception.[12] Frye's useful example of a book as the apex of vision drawn from two reading eyes diagrams the concept neatly: "The book therefore has a vortex of existence opening into its mental reality within our minds. When Milton descends from eternity to time, he finds that he has to pass through the apex of his cone of eternal vision, which is like trying to see the book from the book's point of view. . . ." Frosch acknowledges the value of diagrams in first formulating a definition of the vortex, but pursues the definition beyond the diagram; examining the concept in terms of its constant movement, he suggests that the movement itself is a crucial factor in any definition: the relationship between observer and observed is never static.

The most serious problem with diagrams of the vortex is not just that they cannot comprehend the motion, the three-dimensionality of the device, but that they tend to isolate the vortex as a separate entity, to make it seem independent

---

[12] *Fearful Symmetry*, p. 350; Hazard Adams, *Blake and Yeats: The Contrary Vision* (Ithaca, N.Y.: Cornell University Press, 1955), pp. 104–110; *Apocalypse*, pp. 358–359; Thomas R. Frosch, *The Awakening of Albion: The Renovation of the Body in the Poetry of William Blake* (Ithaca, N.Y., and London: Cornell University Press, 1974), pp. 69–76. For the relation of Blake's conception of the vortex to Descartes', see Donald Ault, *Visionary Physics* (Chicago: University of Chicago Press, 1974), and Martin K. Nurmi, "Negative Sources in Blake," Rosenfeld, pp. 303–318, esp. pp. 307–312.

of both the perceiver and the perceived: perceiver A sees object C through vortex B. Actually, as the Book I passage states, A, B, and C are a continuum; the vortex is not only the mode of A's perception, but the perception itself: the globe, universe, or friend perceived *is* the vortex as it recedes from the observer, who is himself the apex of the figure. The vortex is thus a parody of the Edenic relationship of what in time we must call perceiver and perceived: what is unified in Eden is divided outside of it, and the vortex is at once the emblem and the means of that division. Outside Eden there is no objective reality except the vortex, which, because it is a function of perception, is not itself objective. It only appears objective to the fallen eye.

This may sound perversely abstract, but it is really only a formulation of a basic principle of *Milton* which we can see expressed concretely in the action of the poem. Milton, when he made his decision to descend, saw Jesus as "a disk of blood, distant" (14:27)—"a globe itself infolding; like a sun." On this side of the vortex he will meet Jesus in the clouds of Ololon, and will thus see him "like a human form, a friend with whom he lived benevolent." When Milton and Ololon are united, Milton will be one with Jesus, one with the object of his perception, and the vortex that seemed to divide them will disappear. Milton will be Jesus, and eternal.

The vortex is a condition of fallen humanity. It is formed, as we can see in *The Four Zoas*, of the tension between eternity and eternal death:

Terrific ragd the Eternal Wheels of intellect
    terrific ragd
The living creatures of the wheels in the Wars of
    Eternal life
But perverse rolld the wheels of Urizen & Luvah
    back reversd
Downward & outwards consuming in the wars of
    Eternal Death. . . .

                            (I,20:12–15)

The apex of these conflicting directions is the point at which eternity meets chaos; from it a vortex extends in either direction, a whirlpool created by the opposition of the forces. Standing at that apex one is in a providential calm, the space created by the eternals for Satan's salvation. Wherever he projects his vision he sees the vortex, whether as the starry universe or as his own "corn-fields and his valleys of five hundred acres square": all is vortex. The earth itself, the center of our fallen vision, is merely our vortex point; as such it is part of that "one infinite plane" that by its whirling motion seems a solid form, a cone. So consumed are we fallen beings with the delusions of our existence, however, that we do not recognize the infinity on which we stand.

When Milton left eternity he lost the Edenic vision which sees everything on its own infinite plane. That is why he appears even to himself in several guises, corpse, darkened angel, vegetated man, satanic comet. That is why, also, Albion appears to him to be on alien planes:

First Milton saw Albion upon the Rock of Ages,
Deadly pale outstretchd and snowy cold, storm coverd;
A Giant form of perfect beauty outstretchd on the rock
In solemn death: the Sea of Time & Space thunderd
    aloud
Against the rock, which was inwrapped with the weeds
    of death
Hovering over the cold bosom, in its vortex Milton bent
    down
To the bosom of death, what was underneath soon seemd
    above.
A cloudy heaven mingled with stormy seas in loudest
    ruin;
But as a wintry globe descends precipitant thro'
    Beulah bursting,
With thunders loud, and terrible: so Miltons shadow fell,
Precipitant loud thundring into the Sea of Time & Space.
                        (15:36–46)

What seemed a stormy covering beneath him becomes, as Milton descends through the vortex in the bosom of fallen man, "a cloudy heaven mingled with stormy seas": "what was underneath soon seemd above." The passage though the vortex incarnates Milton, whose shadow, or earthly portion, can enter into the mortal being Blake. Thus yet another dimension of the vortex is established: it is the conical womb through which beings pass from eternity into time. That the womb is in the bosom of Albion reflects Los's giving birth in the Bard's Song: "a red / Round Globe sunk down from his Bosom into the Deep in pangs . . ." (3:29–30). We see now that Los's childbirth was not the anomaly it seemed early in the poem, but simply a fulfillment of this prototypic function of Albion, his parent power.

Milton's descent incarnates him in Blake:

> Then first I saw him in the Zenith as a falling star,
> Descending perpendicular, swift as the swallow or swift;
> And on my left foot falling on the tarsus, enterd there;
> But from my left foot a black cloud redounding spread
>   over Europe.
>
> (15:47–50)

Blake's perception of Milton is described in words that recall the immediately preceding description of Milton's perceiving Albion: "Then first I saw him" echoes "First Milton saw Albion," allying the two figures in their act of seeing even though, looking in different directions, they see different things. That he sees Milton "as a falling star" identifies Blake with the "shades of Hell" who "beheld him in a trail of light as of a comet" earlier on the plate, although the shades with their inimical perception see him only as a frightening phenomenon "That travels into Chaos," while Blake with his more human eye sees him travel to his foot like a small bird: how well one looks determines what one sees. Milton is a fiery comet or a graceful English bird depending on one's perspective.

74

4. Plate 32 ("William")

Milton's entry into Blake's foot suggests an analogy with
the division of Los in the Bard's Song: from Los's back "A
blue fluid exuded in Sinews hardening in the Abyss" (3:35),
just as now from the point of Milton's entry into Blake "a
black cloud redounding spread over Europe." The key dif-
ference is that in the earlier event the imagery is all of sep-
aration, whereas here the principal action is of union. Los
gave birth to the separate form of his emanation and his
spectre divided from him; Milton is born into Blake and his
spectre, too, the shadow into which he entered to be born,
separates from him.

Entering into Blake produces a revelation for the immor-
tal prophet:

> Then Milton knew that the Three Heavens of Beulah
>   were beheld
> By him on earth in his bright pilgrimage of sixty years
> In those three females whom his Wives, & those three
>   whom his Daughters
> Had represented and containd, that they might be
>   resum'd
> By giving up of Selfhood: & they distant view'd his
>   journey
> In their eternal spheres, now Human, tho' their
>   Bodies remain clos'd
> In the dark Ulro till the Judgment: also Milton
>   knew: they and
> Himself was Human, tho' now wandering thro Death's
>   Vale
> In conflict with those Female forms, which in blood
>   & jealousy
> Surrounded him, dividing & uniting without end or
>   number.
>
> He saw the Cruelties of Ulro, and he wrote them down
> In iron tablets: and his Wives & Daughters names were
>   these

Rahab and Tirzah, & Milcah & Malah & Noah & Hoglah.
They sat rang'd round him as the rocks of Horeb
   round the land
Of Canaan: and they wrote in thunder smoke and fire
His dictate; and his body was the Rock Sinai; that body,
Which was on earth born to corruption: & the six
   Females
Are Hor & Peor & Bashan & Abarim & Lebanon
   & Hermon
Seven rocky masses terrible in the Desarts of Midian.

(15:51–17:17)

As during his life, according to Blake, Milton struggled
with his female forms (both human and spiritual, his wives
and his gentler passions) and did not enter through them
as he might have into visions of eternity, so he struggles
now. In Ulro these forms are named after Blakean and bib-
lical women of bad will; in eternity, we shall see, they are
named Ololon. Significantly, their struggle with Milton is
a form of union. They are "now Human, tho' their Bodies
remain clos'd / In the dark Ulro," because their sexual
threefold nature has been complemented by Milton's de-
scent to them: together, they equal a single human entity;
"they and / Himself was Human." A darkened fourfold be-
ing, this union holds potential not only for human perfec-
tion, but also for cosmic perfection: Milton and his female
forms together are "Seven rocky masses terrible in the
Desarts of Midian"; they are the earthly reflection of the
Seven Angels of the Presence, ranged here in satanic
opacity, to be sure, but nevertheless ranged together, wait-
ing for apocalypse. Human perfection will be cosmic
perfection.

Before Milton may realize the fruits of this new vision he
must overcome the opposition of the fallen Zoas, who fear
his prophesied approach. He appears within the Mundane
Shell, the universe created that Albion not be annihilated.
That Shell is a kind of demonic parody of "our Vegetated

77

Earth," the worst of generated existence as Golgonooza is the best.[13] In its "twenty-seven folds of opakeness" (17:26), it is coextensive with Milton's shadow, which reaches from the verge of Beulah through all fallen reality. Horrid as it is, it is not interminable; it "finishes where the lark mounts" (17:27). Even "twenty-seven folds of opakeness" may be penetrated by a fragile bird of song. A true poet may rise in spirit from this vegetated earth through its grim ramifications to the inspired air of Beulah. Where he does so the Mundane Shell ceases to exist for him, spatially disappearing. *When* he does so, we shall see in Book II, the Mundane Shell disappears temporally also, for the mounting of the lark, the achievement of true inspiration, is the signal of apocalypse.

The eternals initially shuddered at Milton's descent because he "took the outside course, among the graves of the dead" (14:34). Now we learn that he had no other choice, "For travellers from Eternity. pass outward to Satan's seat, / But travellers to Eternity. pass inward to Golgonooza." As we shall see, the two paths are complementary, each essential to the completion of the other. Milton's journey outward will be realized in Blake's journey inward. Neither figure of this fallen existence, however, can make his journey without assistance from eternity. Thus Los, in the very next line, is called "the Vehicular terror"; for it is Los, the impaired but still eternal principle of imagination, who must convey these prophets along their way.

Milton's descent causes dissension among the fallen Zoas, who, because he appears within his shadow, assume that he is Satan. Los contends with his emanation, and Orc/Luvah with his; Urizen opposes Milton. The male/female contention and the contention with Urizen, who in another form is Milton's spectre Satan, are, as we shall see, dual aspects

[13] Nurmi defines Blake's vision of the Mundane Shell as "traceable partly to his reaction against a writer who used Newtonian principles to account for the creation: Thomas Burnet" (*op. cit.*, pp. 312–317).

of the struggle Milton wages throughout the poem for full humanity, for apocalyptic wholeness.

The emanations see in Milton's coming the enhancement of their own power. Enitharmon rejoices that she will be freed from Los's protective bonds. The Shadowy Female, who is the spirit of the Mundane Shell, plans to lure him into worship of her false holiness: in a parody of art she will weave the garments of tyranny; in a parody of religion she will "take the Image of God" and "put on Holiness as a breastplate" (18:19–21). She will do so, appropriately, out of a parody of love, "To defend me from thy terrors O Orc! my only beloved" (18:25). Her love, like her art and her godhead, is born of fear and idolatry, the fatal distortions of love in the Mundane Shell.

Los and Orc seek to thwart their emanations, Los by putting out barriers to stop Milton from approaching, and Orc by trying to dissuade the Shadowy Female from luring him on:

Orc answerd. Take not the Human Form O loveliest.
    Take not
Terror upon thee! Behold how I am & tremble lest
    thou also
Consume in my Consummation; but thou maist take a
    Form
Female & lovely, that cannot consume in Mans
    consummation
Wherefore dost thou Create & Weave this Satan for a
    Covering [?]
When thou attemptest to put on the Human Form, my
    wrath
Burns to the top of heaven against thee in Jealousy &
    Fear.
Then I rend thee asunder, then I howl over thy clay &
    ashes
When wilt thou put on the Female Form as in times of
    old

With a Garment of Pity & Compassion like the Garment
   of God
His garments are long sufferings for the Children of Men
Jerusalem is his Garment & not thy Covering Cherub O
   lovely
Shadow of my delight who wanderest seeking for the
   prey.

                              (18:26–38)

This passage is a kind of quarry for images that will later
become significant. Orc offers the Shadowy Female "a
Form / Female & lovely, that cannot consume in Mans con-
summation": a sanctuary like the Beulah created by Jesus
for the emanations weary of Eden's strife (plate 30). In-
stead, the willful consort struggles by falsehood to become
in herself a human fourfold. Hers is an ironic struggle, for
it destroys its own objective: if she would only assume her
rightful female form she would automatically reach four-
fold perfection, because the feminine "Garment of Pity &
Compassion" is truly "like the Garment of God"—an associ-
ation that will be brought into clearer focus when Ololon
herself assumes that garment later in the poem. The gar-
ment imagery culminates in this passage in a line that re-
veals both the way to perfection and the forces that
obstruct it: "Jerusalem is his Garment & not thy Covering
Cherub." The realization of the composite female in her
rightful state completes the Divine Humanity. By contrast,
the Covering Cherub is a kind of fraud, his very name re-
duced to a pun: whereas the true Garment of God glorifies
and enhances him, the Cherub merely covers up his linea-
ments, obscuring him.[14]

    The struggle of Orc and the Shadowy Female echoes the
struggle of Los and Enitharmon, and amplifies the struggle

[14] For further analysis of Blake's use of garment imagery in *Milton*
see Morton D. Paley, "The Figure of the Garment in *The Four
Zoas, Milton,* and *Jerusalem*," *Sublime Allegory*, pp. 119–139, esp.
pp. 131–135.

of Milton and Ololon. All these struggles will be resolved
only when Jealousy and Fear are put aside; it will be, ironi-
cally, for the lowliest of these couples to make that choice
and redeem them all.[15]

As each level of the Mundane Shell she rules contains
both heaven and hell, so does the Shadowy Female herself,
in whose bosom are both "Jerusalem & Babylon shining glo-
riously" (18:41). The contention her dual nature causes
creates a destruction we have seen before; as Los's wrath
once "alter'd the poles of the world" (9:17), so does the
wrath of Orc and his consort:

> Thus darkend the Shadowy Female tenfold & Orc
> tenfold
> Glowd on his rocky Couch against the darkness:loud
> thunders
> Told of the enormous conflict[.] Earthquake
> beneath: around;
> Rent the Immortal Females, limb from limb &
> joint from joint
> And moved the fast foundations of the Earth to wake
> the Dead. . . .
>
> (18:46–50)

[15] Morton D. Paley thinks the inclusion of Orc in *Milton* prob-
lematical, finding him, as energy principle, not fully compatible with
the dominant imagination principle of the poem (*Energy and the
Imagination: A Study of the Development of Blake's Thought* [Ox-
ford: Clarendon Press, 1970], pp. 249–251). Paley suggests that Blake
planned Orc's place in *Milton* when "he had not yet made his final
disposition of the Orc symbol in *The Four Zoas*. He still hoped
somehow to reconcile Orc's revolutionary energy with the regen-
erative Imagination symbolized by Jesus, Milton, and the inspired
Los" (p. 249). Although I agree that Blake probably did greatly
alter his attitude toward "revolutionary energy" as *Milton* developed
(witness his suppression of the angry call to arms of the prose pref-
ace after the first two copies of the poem were engraved), I do not
believe that there is "no place for Orc in this vision of regeneration":
the anguished, passionate, destructive struggle of Orc seems to me
an inescapable aspect, as I have defined it in the text, of the central
struggles of the poem.

Once again Blake has set the time of his poem: it is the instant before the resurrection, before the waking of the dead —the last moment of the millennium.

The battle of male and emanation yields to the battle of male and spectre. Urizen waylays Milton. In the poem's allegory of imagination Urizen stands for all the deadly snares to which inspiration is subject in time, snares Milton did not escape in his mortal span. He is thus the sum of Milton's earthly errors, and therefore an internal enemy. But he is also an external being, the regent of catastrophe, the bound form of our fallen universe; he thus represents the very condition Milton must enter to redeem those errors. Milton must assume his errors to redeem them; he struggles with Urizen now, embracing him in combat, as he earlier in the poem embraced his shadow to redeem it.

As Urizen pours icy waters upon Milton to freeze his imagination, Milton reaches for red clay, molding it with care

> Between his palms; and filling up the furrows
> of many years
> Beginning at the feet of Urizen, and on the bones
> Creating new flesh on the Demon cold, and building him,
> As with new clay a Human form in the Valley of Beth
> Peor.
>
> (19:10–14)

What is happening here is that Milton is taking over the task of Los; he is completing the binding of Urizen, as the fallen Los could not complete it, by adding flesh to the bones Los fashioned ages before. Paradoxically, this further binding is ultimately a releasing; by completing the process Milton reverses it, for when he is finished Urizen will not be merely a stony parody writhing in the deep, but a reborn "Human form in the Valley of Beth Peor."

As Milton and Urizen engage in the struggle that is the central action of the poem, a struggle that at once begins and ends in Milton's self-recognition, Blake pulls back for the widest panorama he will offer of his fallen universe. We see now the effects of Los's wrath and Orc's fiery conflict— only now we are told explicitly for the first time in the poem of the prototypic conflict, the original perversion:

Four Universes round the Mundane Egg remain Chaotic
One to the North, named Urthona: One to the South,
    named Urizen:
One to the East, named Luvah: One to the West,
    named Tharmas
They are the Four Zoa's that stood around the
    Throne Divine!
But when Luvah assum'd the World of Urizen to the
    South:
And Albion was slain upon his mountains, & in his tent;
All fell towards the Center in dire ruin, sinking down.
And in the South remains a burning fire; in the East a
    void.
In the West, a world of raging waters; in the North
    a solid,
Unfathomable! without end. But in the midst of these,
Is built eternally the Universe of Los and Enitharmon:
Towards which Milton went, but Urizen oppos'd his path.

                                    (19:15–26)

The Bard said that "Albion was slain upon his Mountains / And in his Tent, thro envy of Living Form, even of the Divine Vision" (3:1–2); Leutha told us that the sin was Luvah's (13:8–9). Now we learn what that envy was, and how it operated; and we see its awful devastation.

The result of Luvah's action was a drastic reordering of the universe, the prototype of reorderings in succeeding generations when Los "Alter'd the poles of the world" (9:17), when the Bard finished his song (14:4–8), when Orc and his Shadowy Female struggled (18:46–50). In this prototypic reordering the Zoas have fallen from Eden, leaving as their ruins the formless elements of fallen existence, fire, waters, a solid, and a void. The scene is disastrous, and yet it does contain hope. At the center to which all the Zoas fell "Is built eternally the Universe of Los and Enitharmon," the Mundane Egg with which the passage began, and with which it now ends. That providential universe poised between eternity and chaos is the principal milieu of the poem, the ultimate battleground and crucial marriage bed. Perhaps that is why Blake's description of the fallen universe begins and ends with it.

The fall of the Zoas resulted from a contention among them, and produces the contentions we have been examining for two and a half plates. We have seen first the contention of Milton and his generated emanation Rahab/Tirzah, then the battles of Los and Orc with their emanations, and finally the wrestling of Milton and Urizen. Now we return to the original contention: Rahab and Tirzah, in league with Urizen and the Shadowy Female, send out their children to lure Milton to ruin:

> The Twofold form Hermaphroditic: and the
>   Double-sexed;
> The Female-male & the Male-female, self-dividing stood
> Before him in their beauty, & in cruelties of holiness!
>
> (19:32–34)

These sirens are "twofold" or "Double-sexed" because they are children of Generation and incapable of the threefold marriage of Beulah or of Eden's fourfold mental strife. They recall the hermaphroditic shadow Milton entered (14:37), and both Satan and the Shadowy Female with their "cruelties of holiness" (9:21–29 and 18:19–25). They are thus identified with the substance and the two regents of the Mundane Shell. Consequently, the lure they offer is to live this mortal life without inspiration, to realize eternal death.

Like the Shadowy Female, the hermaphrodites offer a delusion of godhead instead of the holiness of true humanity. Like her, they pretend to creativity. Tirzah, they claim, has the creative power of Los: "She ties the knot of nervous fibres into a white brain! / She ties the knot of bloody veins, into a red hot heart!" (19:55–56), even of Jesus: "She ties the knot of milky seed into two lovely Heavens / Two yet but one: each in the other sweet reflected! these / Are our Three Heavens beneath the shades of Beulah, land of rest!" (19:60–20:2). But whereas Los formed brain and heart to prevent extinction and Jesus created Beulah for a rest and a salvation, Tirzah forms only to rule. The body is for her only a vehicle of command, and her version of Beulah is a Bower of Bliss.

Thus Milton, embracing the shadow that is this mortal life, must resist its lures and transcend its delusions in order to redeem it. That is his struggle with the female will, his struggle with Urizen. Each facet of Milton's struggle contains the whole struggle; each is a battle of the fourfold with the twofold soul. Milton began the struggle when he entered into his shadow; it will not end until the last plate of the poem.

Milton does not appear to respond to the sirens, except insofar as his wrestling with Urizen is response. Triumph over Urizen is the only triumph over the hermaphrodites of fallen reality. Presenting that implicit answer to the lure, Blake once again cleanses our perspective:

So spoke they as in one voice! Silent Milton stood before
The darkend Urizen; as the sculptor silent stands before
His forming image; he walks round it patient labouring.
Thus Milton stood forming bright Urizen, while his
    Mortal part
Sat frozen in the rock of Horeb: and his Redeemed
    portion,
Thus form'd the Clay of Urizen; but within that portion

85

His real Human walkd above in power and majesty
Tho darkend; and the Seven Angels of the Presence
    attended him.

(20:7–14)

Milton forms "bright Urizen," who only two lines before
was "darkend." Here we have demonstrated in compression
perhaps too subtle the providential nature of Milton's
descent. Milton in facing his adversary seeks to restore him
to his original glory, the radiance of the Prince of Light.

Milton's strife elicits one of the strangest, most disquiet-
ing tonal shifts in the poem. While the great English
prophet struggles, his awed successor suddenly doubts his
own powers. It is as if Blake himself has felt the waters of
Urizen's deadly baptism:

O how can I with my gross tongue that cleaveth to the
    dust,
Tell of the Four-fold Man, in starry numbers fitly orderd
Or how can I with my cold hand of clay!

(20:15–17)

Blake feels here more closely allied with the Elect Urizen
formed of clay than with the inspired Milton. That identifi-
cation will change as Blake feels the life-giving force of Mil-
ton with him; their union will defeat Urizenic restriction:

For that portion namd the Elect: the Spectrous body
    of Milton:
Redounding from my left foot into Los's Mundane space,
Brooded over his body in Horeb against the Resurrection
Preparing it for the Great Consummation; red the
    Cherub on Sinai
Glow'd; but in terrors folded round his clouds of blood.

(20:20–24)

When Milton entered into Blake, the shadow through
which he descended separated from him. The "black cloud"

86

which "redounding spread over Europe" at their union
(15:50) is now explicitly identified with Milton's spectre.
It hovers around him in a posture like that of Tirzah in the
sirens' speech, "Within [whose] bosom Albion lies em-
balmd" (19:57), aligning both the spectral forms Satan and
Tirzah, and the potentially human forms Milton and Albion.
And once again, Blake orients our temporal with our spatial
perspective: the Cherub glows on Sinai, like Orc on his
mountain, preparing for the Great Consummation.

Only the inspired portion of Milton enters Blake, and be-
cause it does, the later poet can indeed "Tell of the Four-
fold Man." Albion turns on his couch and Blake speaks to
him, first tentatively, as one would speak to a revered elder,
and finally with the confidence of apocalyptic vision
(20:25–40). The effect of Milton's descent is to strengthen
Blake's own voice, as well as to rouse Albion.

From Blake's response to Milton the poem shifts sudden-
ly to that of the eternals:

Thus Milton fell thro Albions heart, travelling outside
     of Humanity
Beyond the Stars in Chaos in Caverns of the Mundane
     Shell.
But many of the Eternals rose up from eternal tables
Drunk with the Spirit, burning round the Couch of death
     they stood
Looking down into Beulah: wrathful, fill'd with rage!
They rend the heavens round the Watchers in a fiery
     circle:
And round the Shadowy Eighth: the Eight close up the
     Couch
Into a tabernacle, and flee with cries down to the Deeps:
Where Los opens his three wide gates, surrounded by
     raging fires!
They soon find their own place & join the Watchers of
     the Ulro.

                                        (20:41–50)

The driving of the seven watchers and their eighth, shadowy companion into Ulro is the completion of Milton's descent. That descent was complete when Milton entered his shadow on plate 14, because that shadow is Ulro. But in order to define this instantaneous process of descent Blake has delineated its beginning and its conclusion in two parallel passages. We earlier saw Milton divided, part of him walking through Eden with his seven comforters, part of him asleep in Beulah, part of him journeying through Ulro (15:1–20). We now see his Edenic and Beulaic portions hounded into Ulro, his descent completed. The progress of these two passages suggests the progress of Milton's own speech upon hearing the Bard's Song (14:14–32), which began in abhorence of satanic selfhood and concluded in embracing that selfhood.

In each of the two descent passages Milton is accompanied by the Seven Angels, first in his walking through Eden and finally in his being sealed off, like Los before him, in Ulro. The sealing off of Milton and the seven angels suggests the assignment of the six watchers, with the implicit denotation of Jesus as the millennial seventh, to satanic space at the end of the day of mourning in the Bard's Song: what the Bard reported and what he inspired are identical acts—an identity that is probably the profoundest definition of prophecy in this prophetic poem. The definition is extended by the presence of Milton in the second instance: the Bard spoke of the establishment of time and his speaking inspires the end of time, for Milton, the eighth angel, is apocalypse.

The progress suggested between the passages defining the start and finish of Milton's course is reinforced by two other parallel passages. Shortly after the first and shortly before the second Blake describes Albion as Milton passes through him (15:3–46 and 20:25–42). In the first description Albion is passive, cold, unconscious as Milton falls through his "bosom" (a neutral word, surely, applied to a male form); in the second he has begun to stir and Blake speaks gently to him as Milton falls "thro Albions heart," through the active, beating, life-giving center of that cold neutral bosom. Milton passes through Albion only once, and therefore the two descriptions are simultaneous—as the descriptions of the beginning and ending of Milton's passage are simultaneous, although they record different aspects of that timeless event.

Between the two passages defining the beginning and ending of Milton's descent, and the two concentric passages describing Albion's role in it, we witness the contentions it arouses among Los's brothers and with their emanations. The descent complete, those contentions begin to resolve. Los, observing Milton's approach in horror, remembers suddenly "an old Prophecy in Eden recorded" (20:57), and makes a parallel descent. The unexpected reversal of Los's attitude exactly parallels the unexpected reversal we saw earlier of Milton's habits in eternity: each, inspired by the wisdom of Eden, has been moved to the "unexampled deed" (2:21) of self-sacrifice in the name of truth.[16]

---

[16] Mitchell finds "an unmistakable element of the ridiculous in the convenient timing of Los's memory here," because Los "finds release from the black waters of melancholy through a hilariously improbable flash of memory" (*Sublime Allegory*, p. 297 and 297n). Although I cannot dispute Mitchell's response to the tone of the passage, I think there is enough precedent elsewhere in Romantic poetry, as well as in Blake's other poems, for sudden reverses of spiritual bleakness, for us to assume that Blake means at least the content of the passage to be taken very seriously. Mary Lynn Johnson cites many of these precedents in " 'Separating What Has Been Mixed': A Suggestion for a Perspective on *Milton*," *Blake Studies*, 6, 1 (1973), pp. 11–17, p. 14. Furthermore, the parallel of Los's instantaneous conversion upon remembering "an old prophecy in Eden recorded" and Milton's instantaneous conversion upon hearing the Bard's prophecy seems also to point to the seriousness of such sudden reversals. See as well my discussion in Chapter Four below, pp. 199–201, of the necessarily spontaneous regeneration of vision. It is true, as Mitchell writes, that Los's reversal "liberates and releases tension rather than maintaining it in some ironic, ambiguous equilibrium" (p. 297n), but I do not think that the reader's resultant exhilaration is meant to be comic, or that there is anything ridiculous in the act that causes it.

Characteristically, Blake reports now not the result of
Los's descent, as we might expect, but the result of Milton's,
for the two are identical:

> But Milton entering my Foot; I saw in the nether
> Regions of the Imagination; also all men on Earth,
> And all in Heaven, saw in the nether regions of the
>   Imagination
> In Ulro beneath Beulah, the vast breach of Miltons
>   descent.
> But I knew not that it was Milton, for man cannot know
> What passes in his members till periods of Space & Time
> Reveal the secrets of Eternity: for more extensive
> Than any other earthly things, are Mans earthly
>   lineaments.
>
> And all this Vegetable World appeard on my left Foot,
> As a bright sandal formd immortal of precious stones &
>   gold:
> I stooped down & bound it on to walk forward thro'
>   Eternity.
>
> (21:4–14)

All that has happened since plate 15, then, in which Milton
"on my left foot falling on the tarsus, enterd there" and
knew for the first time "that the Three Heavens of Beulah
were beheld / By him on earth in his bright pilgrimage of
sixty years," has been a complicated, five-plate explication
of that act. Milton's vision of the under-worlds, his struggle
with his emanation, his struggle with Urizen, his temptation
by the hermaphrodites, the reactions of the Zoas, the turn-
ing of Albion, the descent of Los—all these have been but
facets of the single action of Milton's entering Blake's foot.
What began matter-of-factly on plate 15 and seemed con-
cluded there has been not succeeded but amplified by the
five plates that followed. Now Blake returns to the basic act,

not with his original anatomical precision, but with the fullness of expanded vision. This is the same rhetorical pattern we have noted before, a kind of cryptic, unadorned statement followed by seemingly unrelated events and concluded eventually by a fuller restatement which comprehends all that has passed between. The reason for this circuitous rhetoric is the pure decorum by which Blake's poetry always reflects his ideas: "for man cannot know / What passes in his members till periods of Space & Time / Reveal the secrets of Eternity."

In the second account of the union it is Blake's expanded vision, not Milton's, that is emphasized. Each of those visions is an image of eternal death and of the emanation on a parallel level of reality. But whereas Milton sees "the Cruelties of Ulro" and the satanic female forms, Blake from his different perspective sees a fair world of gems and gold, and the Edenic beauty Ololon. These two visions are necessary complements. As we have seen, each stage in Milton's descent produces a change both in Milton and in the universe ostensibly external to him. Passing into Blake at once grants Milton vision of his own and his emanation's humanity, and permits Blake and all men in earth and heaven a vision of "the nether regions of the Imagination." Milton's vision intensifies his quest for Ololon; Blake's reveals the way to find her:

> And all this Vegetable World appeard on my left Foot,
> As a bright sandal formd immortal of precious stones &
>   gold:
> I stooped down & bound it on to walk forward thro'
>   Eternity.
>
> (21:12–14)

And he will find her, not only in her Ulro-form of the perverse Rahab/Tirzah, but in the full beauty of her eternal portion:

There is in Eden a sweet River, of milk & liquid pearl.
Namd Ololon; on whose mild banks dwelt those who
    Milton drove
Down into Ulro: and they wept in long resounding song
For seven days of eternity, and the rivers living banks
The mountains wail'd! & every plant that grew, in
    solemn sighs lamented.

                            (21:15-19)

Once again, Blake sets the moment, now with a new and
touching sense of the mercy of time. Ololon has wept seven
days, although she has been silent at night rather than in-
convenience anyone (she is, after all, a Daughter of Beulah
and thus responsible for the sweet sleep of others). Each
morning, between the harnessing of the sun and the "clar-
ions of day" "the Family / Of Eden heard the lamentation,
and Providence began" (21:23-24). That is, at each turn of
a thousand-year day a new watcher is set over time to
guard it. On the seventh day, as Los listens, Ololon calls
together the Divine Humanity and repents of driving Mil-
ton into Ulro, preparing to descend herself to save him.
Here the full complication of the poem's simultaneity be-
comes apparent: Milton descends from the environs of
Eden to Ololon in Ulro, and Ololon descends from the en-
virons of Eden to Milton in Ulro—but each descends upon
seeing the other already in the deeps. Their descents, on
this seventh day, are simultaneous heralds of the end of
Los's day of mourning.

    It will be my practice throughout this study, in order to
maintain consistency of reference and to indicate the paral-
lelism of Milton and Ololon, to refer to Ololon as a single
female being. Blake himself uses both plural and neuter
singular pronouns as well as the feminine singular to refer
to "her." In doing so he indicates the stage of her repen-
tance: she is plural, we shall see in Book II, until her incar-
nation brings her to Milton as his bride (36:13-20). As a
plural being she is sixfold—rigid, numbered, delineated—

in her fallen aspect (2:18–20; 17:1–17), and a multitude—a river in flood, a pillar of cloud—in her redemptive aspect (21:15–19; 35:34–41). Her appearance in Blake's garden in Book II will be the humanizing of her multitudes, the vortical transformation of her "universe of starry majesty" into "a human form, a friend."[17]

Ololon's prayer of the seventh day brings startling action. The Divine Humanity begins to gather, changing from "a globe itself infolding; like a sun" to "a human form, a friend" (15:24, 27) as Ololon's vortical vision—and ours—alters:

> But all the Family Divine collected as Four Suns
> In the Four Points of heaven East, West & North & South,
> Enlarging and enlarging till their Disks approachd each other;
> And when they touch'd closed together Southward in One Sun
> Over Ololon: and as One Man, who weeps over his brother,
> In a dark tomb, so all the Family Divine. wept over Ololon.
>
> (21:37–42)

The groan of Ololon and the Divine Family echoes the groans of the eternals and the lamentations of the Zoas at Milton's descent; they are the groans of all reality before apocalypse.

Ololon's response is a decision to descend to Milton, as he has decided to descend to her. Like his decision, hers opens a whole new vision of reality:

---

[17] So Jesus himself will be consolidated in Blake's garden at the end of the poem: "with one accord the Starry Eight became / One Man Jesus the Savior. wonderful!" (42:10–11).

Ololon's name suggests both "All alone" and, as Peter F. Fisher points out in *The Valley of Vision* (p. 248), the Greek word for women's lamentation to the gods (ὀλολυγή). The name suggests also, appropriately, that Greek word ὠλώλειν, "to have lost" or "to have perished."

Is Virtue a Punisher? O no! how is this wondrous thing:
This World beneath, unseen before: this refuge from the
    wars
Of Great Eternity! unnatural refuge! unknown by us
    till now!
Or are these the pangs of repentance? let us enter
    into them. . . .
                           (21:47–50)

As Milton entered into his shadow, Ololon enters the "world
beneath." The acts are identical; both are acts of repen-
tance, both lead to eternal death, both herald apocalypse:
"Then the Divine Family said. Six Thousand Years are
now / Accomplish'd in this World of Sorrow":

So spake the Family Divine as One Man even Jesus
Uniting in One with Ololon & the appearance of One
    Man.
Jesus the Saviour appeard coming in the Clouds of
    Ololon!
                        (21:51–52, 58–60)

Ironically, Milton appears as Satan in his descent, Ololon
as Jesus in hers. The heroic prophet seems an Elect tyrant,
the meek sufferer seems the Reprobate savior. This surpris-
ing division exists not because Ololon is purer than Milton,
but because her act completes his and thus perfects their
union. Milton, after all, however satanic he seems, is himself
the eighth Eye of God, a form of Jesus even as Ololon is a
form of Jesus; the union of the eight with Ololon is the ful-
fillment of the eight, the act by which they, not just she, be-
come Jesus. For Blake to say here that Jesus appears with
Ololon is to imply that Ololon and Milton are united in their
descent. Their union is the realization of the Divine Hu-
manity, an act that requires the renovation of their Elect
portion. Thus Milton, who has embraced the fallen world
in his descent and appears in it as its god, brings Satan into
the union to be recreated eternal.

Blake completes his weaving of the strands of descent by turning from Ololon's decision back to Los's, which introduced it. Again, the refracted pattern of action serves to indicate the identity of its elements: by moving back and forth among the separate descents of all the travelers from eternity, Blake suggests that, interchangeable, they are in fact one. Los, joining with Blake, reinforces that suggestion:

> While Los heard indistinct in fear, what time I bound
>   my sandals
> On; to walk forward thro' Eternity, Los descended to me:
> And Los behind me stood; a terrible flaming sun: just
>   close
> Behind my back; I turned round in terror, and behold.
> Los stood in that fierce glowing fire; & he also
>   stoop'd down
> And bound my sandals on in Udan-Adan; trembling I
>   stood
> Exceedingly with fear & terror, standing in the Vale
> Of Lambeth: but he kissed me, and wishd me health.
> And I became One Man with him arising in my strength:
> Twas too late now to recede. Los had enterd into my
>   soul:
> His terrors now possess'd me whole! I arose in fury &
>   strength.
>
>   (22:4–14)

Los's descent gives him, like Ololon, the appearance of Jesus: the flaming sun, the gathering into One Man proclaim the redemptive force of his merger with Blake, as they do the perfecting love of Ololon's descent. The perspective shift is the same vortical one we have noted before in the courses of Milton's and Ololon's descents: Los seems first a "terrible flaming sun," the disc of the vortex passed, and ultimately "a human form, a friend," who "kissed me, and wishd me health." This transformation is in all cases a

95

humanizing of vision, and thus the preparation for apoca-
lypse. That Blake accepts the terrible principle of imagina-
tion as his friend, that Ololon receives the mighty savior
"as One Man, who weeps over his brother," that Milton
himself will enter into the "One Man Jesus the Saviour"
(42:11), all indicate a new, apocalyptic perception of the
vortex which is "one infinite plane" with our fallen earth.
What was remote and terrifying has become immediate and
loving; the perceiver has accepted it as part of himself, as
Milton accepted his satanic shadow, in order to reintegrate
the shattered form of fallen man.

Los's descent is simultaneous with Milton's. As Milton
entered Blake's foot the sandal of Generation appeared
there, and he "stooped down & bound it on to walk forward
thro' Eternity" (21:14). Now we learn that as he bound the
sandal, Los "also stoop'd down / And bound my sandals on
in Udan-Adan," participating thus in the union of Blake and
Milton. Blake's tying on the sandal is his acceptance of the
generative world as his means of entering into eternity.
Los's binding it on promises an end to that mortal world,
for it signals the end to the moratorium he proclaimed in
the Bard's Song by taking "off his left sandal placing it on
his head" (8:11). The seventh day is about to end; the
eighth dawn is apocalypse. Moreover, it is both Blake's san-
dals they bind on: the poet's stride is now unbroken. In-
spiration is no longer lame, but strong and firm; Los-Blake-
Milton strides toward Golgonooza.

The entry of Los into Blake acts as the entry of Milton
had: it strengthens his visionary courage. He says he "arose
in fury & strength," and from this point on in Book I his
voice will bear witness to it. He will utter no hesitation, no
equivocation, no submission.

As if to illustrate the new identity of Los and Blake, the
poet once again introduces a dramatic speech without an-
nouncing its speaker. From Blake's new resolution we move
immediately into Los's declaration:

I am that Shadowy Prophet who Six Thousand Years ago
Fell from my station in the Eternal bosom. Six
    Thousand Years
Are finishd. I return! both Time & Space obey my will.
                                        (22:15–17)

Los, too, is strengthened by this union. He announces tri-
umphantly the end of history, which is the end of equivoca-
tion and fear. The six thousand years granted to Satan's
world on the moratorium day in the Bard's Song, the day
Los in his wrath was closed in the Mundane Shell, are over.
The periods of fallen reality are moving into alignment as
each nears its end: The fabric of history is completed as the
moratorium, the millennium outside of sanctioned history,
itself draws to a conclusion. For all fallen reality, the next
step is apocalypse.

Los hastens to Golgonooza with his vegetated counter-
parts. The gnomic lines of plate 17 are realized: "For travel-
lers from Eternity. pass outward to Satan's seat, / But trav-
ellers to Eternity. pass inward to Golgonooza." As Milton
journeyed from eternity by the "outside course," Blake, a
mortal soul, may enter eternity only through the city of art,
through poetic inspiration. Both the immortal Milton and
his living successor are dependent on "Los the Vehicular
terror" (17:31), on pure inspiration, for fulfillment of their
journeys.

But the journey is not yet complete. As Milton was tried
by opposition, so Los is now. The earlier objections of the
Zoas to Milton's passage are translated to a new generation.
Los's sons balk. They fear Milton, as Los feared him, as the
liberator of Satan:

    for this is he come! behold it written
Upon his fibrous left Foot black! most dismal to our eyes
The Shadowy Female shudders thro' heaven in torment
    inexpressible!

And all the Daughters of Los prophetic wail: yet
    in deceit,
They weave a new Religion from new Jealousy of
    Theotormon!
Miltons Religion is the cause: there is no end to
    destruction!

                        (22:34-39)

Rintrah and Palamabron with their partial vision see only
the shadow into which Milton entered on descending.
Where Blake saw "a bright sandal formd immortal of
precious stones & gold" (21:13), they see only a "fibrous left
Foot black." To Blake the generative world is illuminated,
but they see only its threatening darkness. Generation,
whatever delights it may hold for us, is opaque to those who
remember Eden.

That the sons of Los see Milton's blackened foot indicates
further that the instant they rise up to bar Milton's entry
into Golgonooza is actually a prelude to the act of consoli-
dation we have been witnessing: when Milton enters
Blake's left foot his shadow "redounds" from them, and
their mutual left foot is free of its blackness. That Rintrah
and Palamabron see it darkened means that they see it be-
fore the union—a paradox, apparently, because that union
is, as we have seen, the initial and the sole act of the body
of the poem: Milton's descent was his incarnation in Blake,
and it liberated both of them from shadowy error. That
paradox is one of the principal means Blake uses of indicat-
ing the simultaneity, the identity, of the acts of the poem.
He must describe a very complex event that has no dura-
tion; to do so, he describes each individual facet of the
event, establishing the congruency of each new facet with
the previous ones by demonstrating, usually through repeti-
tion of key images, that they have the same history and the
same effect. In the lighting flash of Milton's progress to
Blake's foot he is conceived on all levels of reality as satanic;
the eternals shudder at death and Ulro in him (14:11-12

and 33–35), the spectres call him Satan (15:17–18), and so do all of the generation of Los. When Milton reaches Blake, satanic error is dispelled. That Rintrah and Palamabron see only the satanic portion of Milton indicates the instant of their rebellion against him in the system of congruencies Blake has set up.

Their fearful speech suggests another congruency. They cite the deceitful shuddering of the Shadowy Female and the weaving of a religion of jealousy—acts we saw four and a half plates earlier, when Los objected as much as his sons do now to Milton's descent. But here Los's own daughters wail and weave; the females of all generations, like the males, are infected with error. The particular error the daughters represent is one of Blake's chief complaints against the historical John Milton: not only did he fail his emanation and unremittingly consign his Satan to hell, but he also allowed vision to lapse into dogma; he embraced, morally and esthetically, "Laws from Plato & his Greeks" (22:53), instead of from inspiration. His Puritanism bred the Deism of a century later, and although this is the fault more of his angelic followers than of his own will, he is still responsible.

Rintrah and Palamabron have raised up as "two Witnesses" Whitehead and Wesley, their counterparts in time because they themselves were called "Two Witnesses" in the Bard's Song (9:8), but the temporal like the eternal witnesses have gone unheard: "The Witnesses lie dead in the Street of the Great City / No Faith is in all the Earth" (22:59–60). Despairing, Los's sons call for an end to injustice and error:

Awake thou sleeper on the Rock of Eternity Albion
    awake
The trumpet of Judgment hath twice sounded: all
    Nations are awake
But thou art still heavy and dull: Awake Albion awake!
Lo Orc rises on the Atlantic. Lo his blood and fire

Glow on Americas shore: Albion turns upon his Couch
He listens to the sounds of War, astonishd and
    confounded. . . .

                                                    (23:3-8)

Once again the poem's simultaneity is clarified: the sons of
Los call on Albion to wake and then watch as he turns and
falls back into sleep—the same turn Blake himself noted
three plates earlier, attributing it not to the exhortations of
Rintrah and Palamabron, but to the "electric flame of Mil-
tons awful precipitate descent" (20–26). Thus Milton's de-
scent and the exhortations provoked by his arrival in
Blake's person at Golgonooza are simultaneous. The cries
of Rintrah and Palamabron and "the sounds of War" Albion
hears are by this simultaneity identified with Los's wrath
as he alters the poles of the world, with the groans of the
eternals as Milton descends, with the anguish of Orc as he
battles his Shadowy Female, and with the lamentations of
Jesus and Ololon at her descent. All of these sounds are
cries of despair at the injustices of humanity, and at the sor-
rows of what is to come. Because "The trumpet of Judgment
hath twice sounded," what is to come is Orc's Great Con-
summation: apocalypse.

The end Rintrah and Palamabron propose for injustice
and error is itself an act of injustice and error: they would
chain Milton, as their father once chained Orc, lest he de-
stroy them. Los is not immune to their fear; he knows what
Milton looks like in his descent:

Like the black storm, coming out of Chaos, beyond
    the stars:
It issues thro the dark & intricate caves of the
    Mundane Shell
Passing the planetary visions, & the well adorned
    Firmament
The Sun rolls into Chaos & the stars into the Desarts;
And then the storms become visible, audible & terrible,

Covering the light of day, & rolling down upon the
    mountains,
Deluge all the country round. Such is a vision of Los;
When Rintrah & Palamabron spoke; and such his stormy
    face
Appeard, as does the face of heaven, when coverd
    with thick storms
Pitying and loving tho in frowns of terrible
    perturbation. . . .

                    (23:21–30)

This is Milton's own course, and Los's vision is the vision
Milton saw as he passed the vortex:

    the Sea of Time & Space thunderd aloud
Against the rock, which was inwrapped with the
    weeds of death
Hovering over the cold bosom, in its vortex Milton
    bent down
To the bosom of death, what was underneath soon
    seemd above.
A cloudy heaven mingled with stormy seas in loudest
    ruin;
But as a wintry globe descends precipitant thro'
    Beulah bursting,
With thunders loud, and terrible: so Miltons shadow fell,
Precipitant loud thundring into the Sea of Time & Space.

                    (15:39–46)

What Los has seen is Milton himself, "Like the black storm,
coming out of Chaos"; the vision is reflected in Los's face
"coverd with thick storms"; it is also the vision each sees as
Milton passes the vortex. Milton, Los, and their vision of the
universe are all the same fearful storm at the point of the
vortex: center is circumference, poet is inspiration, man and
universe are in this vast moment identical.

The storm, though, is dark and threatening; Los disperses

it, as we shall see Milton eventually disperse his shadow, by firmness and forgiveness:

> And Los thus spoke. O noble Sons, be patient yet
>   a little[.]
> I have embracd the falling Death, he is become
>   One with me
> O Sons we live not by wrath. by mercy alone we live!
> I recollect an old Prophecy in Eden recorded in gold;
>   and oft
> Sung to the harp: That Milton of the land of Albion
> Should up ascend forward from Felphams Vale & break
>   the Chain
> Of Jealousy from all its roots; be patient therefore
>   O my Sons. . . .
>   (23:32–38)

As Milton embraced his shadow, Los embraced the shadowy Milton, ending the wrath by which he was imprisoned in Satan's temporal space. His plea that his sons follow his example incorporates a history of time that parallels the Bard's history of eternity. The speech is a kind of Bardic interpretation of fallen history, with echoes of speeches by the other Reprobate bards of the poem, all of whom are now united in the body of Blake and the spirit of Los. "I have embracd the falling Death, he is become One with me" suggests Milton's "I in my Selfhood am that Satan: I am that Evil One" (14:30), and Los's basic plea is simply an application of the merciful judgment in the Bard's Song:

> O go not forth in Martyrdoms & Wars
> We were plac'd here by the Universal Brotherhood &
>   Mercy
> With powers fitted to circumscribe this dark Satanic
>   death
> And that the Seven Eyes of God may have space for
>   Redemption.
>   (23:49–52)

There is to be no more contention, however just the cause. "The Elect shall meet the Redeem'd. on Albions rocks they shall meet / Astonish'd at the Transgressor, in him beholding the Saviour" (13:30–31): the Bard's prophecy is imminent. Milton, who comes in the appearance of the Elect Satan his shadow, is indeed the Savior beheld within the Transgressor.

Los knows this much, but he does not know everything: "But how this is as yet we know not, and we cannot know; / Till Albion is risen. . . ." So Blake did not know that it was Milton who entered his foot, "for man cannot know / What passes in his members till periods of Space & Time / Reveal the secrets of Eternity" (21:8–10). The full revelation is yet to come, and it is for that apocalypse that Los prepares his sons. Reminding them that all their history has been a period of woe and repression since the thousand-year day of "Palamabrons Harrow, & of Rintrahs wrath & fury," he beseeches them not to succumb to the temptations of anger and fear, to the siren call of the hermaphrodite Corporeal War. He pleads for imagination, for control of the purely instinctive by the inspired faculties of human life. Rintrah and Palamabron must not yield to their instinctive fear of Milton and destroy him, for inspiration (here a prophecy in Eden) dictates that he must live. By permitting him to live they reverse the downward spiral of hatred and jealousy propagated by their brothers; permitting Milton passage into Golgonooza at once frees him to achieve the union he seeks, and frees them from the threat of vegetating helplessly. And their choice is critical, for they are the last of Los's sons still loyal to imagination, and if they give over as their brothers did to Tirzah's death-in-life, there will be no one left to help Los protect true life. Without the regenerative power of the realms they govern, Albion is doomed in all his members to be merely "A Polypus of soft affections without Thought or Vision" (24:38)–an undifferentiated mass of generated life without redeeming imagination. So Los, reduced to Generation without the vision that makes him human, which gives the universe form and keeps it from collapsing into utter ruin, would be his own spectre, Satan. That is what it means to recognize that "I in my Selfhood am that Satan." That is the recognition Los demands now of his sons, but they are not whole enough to make it. They hear not only his pitying speech, but also the "thun[d]ers rolling" about his "stormy face"; he is "Pitying and loving tho in frowns of terrible perturbation" (23:30), and they are baffled, assuming "that wrath now swayd and now pity absorbd him" (24:46). Such is the paradox of Los's position, an eternal trapped in time, a savior in the form of a transgressor. Rintrah and Palamabron do not see enough to have faith in the coming end of perturbation. But they descend anyway to the environs of the city of art, commanded if not appeased by their father's conviction.

The action of Book I is now complete. The Bard has entered into Milton, who, together with Los, has entered into Blake. Each merger has occasioned fear and contention among those who witness it, and new vision for the merged figures. We may delineate the parts of the Book I narrative according to these mergers, although because of the refracted character of the narrative any delineation of its parts is tenuous. Milton's decision and concomitant descent, symbolized by the Bard's taking refuge in his bosom, occupies lines 13:45–14:42. His incarnation in Blake, bounded narratorially by passages describing the start and finish of his passage and his falling through Albion's heart, occupies lines 15:01–20:50. Los joins the triple union of Bard/Milton/Blake in 20:51–24:47. The units of the action are not nearly so distinct, however, as this calculation implies, because the poet's focus shifts so often among the many aspects of the multiple union (for example, Blake's vision upon Milton's entering his foot does not occur in the passage on their merger, but in the next unit, 21:4–14, during the description of Los's involvement). This shifting focus militates against our understanding the three mergers as sequential, suggests instead that they are simultaneous.

As we have seen, the appearance of the Bard within Milton is his decision to descend; the decision is the descent; the descent is the merger with Blake; Milton's merger with Blake is Los's merger with Blake. Each of these phases of the pivotal action, Milton's descent through the vortex, is a momentous decision occasioned both by fear and by faith in prophetic truth; consequently each is represented in terms of the conflicts that produce it: the Bard's feud with the eternals, the Zoas' strife with their emanations, Milton's battles with spectre and emanation, Los's argument with his sons. All levels of fallen reality are represented in these combats and resolutions; and all are focused, by the relentless spiral of eternity into time, on the lowest level of reality, Blake's "earth of vegetation." It is there and only there, at the point at which two vortices meet, that the fatal spiral can be reversed. It is there that time, its seven ages and seven days and seven thousand years, must be consummated. That consummation depends on imagination, which since the beginning of the first age has maintained humanity by its providential structures. Should those mundane structures be penetrated by a sense of eternal truth, they must be abolished and Albion restored to eternity. The entry of Bard/Milton/Los into Blake is such a penetration; it transports the mortal poet into the city of inspiration, where he attains a vision of eternal providence and thereby reverses the spiral's course.

C. Golgonooza

At each merger of major figures in the action section of Book I, one of those figures has a vision of his own identity and his relation to the rest of the universe. In the remaining lines of the book, 24:48–29:65, those visions are translated into a grand, impersonal vision of the providence of time and space. These lines are a kind of coda to Book I, reinterpreting the themes and experiences of earlier parts of the book in an entirely new tonality.

As there are Three Classes of Men and Three Heavens of Beulah, so there are three localities of the city of Los. Golgonooza, the principal locality, is the city itself, protected beneath and all around by two supportive localities, Bowlahoola and Allamanda, the natural law and social commerce that nurture vision. The two supportive localities are new, in *Milton*, to Blake's myth, and have been variously interpreted. Damon calls Bowlahoola the digestive and Allamanda the nervous system,[18] Frye interprets them as the stomach and the heart,[19] and Erdman as the bowels and alimentary canal[20] of civilization. All these interpretations, based on verbal associations or on explicitly defined function, are anthropomorphic, as the myth dictates. All the creations of Los, from the bound form of Urizen to the geography of the city of salvation, are imitations of the human form of Albion. By recreating that form, the prototypic artist preserves it in order that it may be regenerated. The fallen universe (Urizen's bound form), fallen civilization (Golgonooza and its environs), even the individual fallen soul is patterned after the Eternal Man, who lies asleep on his couch. The awakening of any of these facsimiles to eternity will be Albion's awakening, for each is a type and member of Albion.

Blake's account of Golgonooza is primarily an account of its surrounding realms. Bowlahoola and Allamanda are the threshold of vision, the only access of fallen beings to eternity. Like all other dualities in Blake's myth, Bowlahoola and Allamanda are contraries, set against the negation of the wilderness of Entuthon and the formless lake of Udan-Adan that bound them. Bowlahoola, as its howling name suggests, is a primal state of frenzied, anguished action, the realm of flaming Rintrah's plow. Allamanda, calm, gracious, systematic, is the soil of Palamabron's cultivation. Blake describes them in two nearly equal passages (24:48–27:41 and

---

[18] *William Blake*, p. 420. [19] *Fearful Symmetry*, p. 260.
[20] *Blake: Prophet Against Empire* (1954; rpt. Garden City, N.Y.: Doubleday Anchor, 1969), p. 432.

27:42–29:46) which reflect in construction and language the states' individual characteristics. When we have passed from Bowlahoola through Allamanda we shall see briefly, in the book's final nineteen lines, Golgonooza itself.

The Bowlahoola passage, like Bowlahoola, is tortuous, seething, half horrifying and half sweet. Bowlahoola is itself a place of contraries. It is where the substance of mortal existence is created, and where that substance is annihilated. The poetry in which Blake describes it fluctuates between these two functions, and, to complicate things further, moves about among various perspectives on them.

The Bowlahoola plates begin with a passage in which Blake may have carried decorum to an indecorous extreme. "Bowlahoola is the Stomach in every individual Man" (24:67), and the opening verse paragraph describing it is replete with what sound more like symptoms of dyspepsia than anything else:

> The hard dentant Hammers are lulld by the flutes
> lula lula
> The bellowing Furnaces['] blare by the long sounding
> clarion
> The double drum drowns howls & groans, the shrill
> fife. shrieks & cries. . . .
> (24:63–65)

Blake apparently thought these verbalized stomach growls "terrible but harmonious" (24:66); whether we agree or not, they do illustrate his point.

We have a brief intermission from the rumblings of Bowlahoola in a sudden shift in perspective, a pan back to the largest significance of this disconcerting violence:

> Los is by mortals nam'd Time Enitharmon is nam'd Space
> But they depict him bald & aged who is in eternal youth
> All powerful and his locks flourish like the brows of
> morning
> He is the Spirit of Prophecy the ever apparent Elias

Time is the mercy of Eternity; without Times swiftness
Which is the swiftest of all things: all were eternal
    torment:
All the Gods of the Kingdoms of Earth labour in Los's
    Halls.
Every one is a fallen Son of the Spirit of Prophecy
He is the Fourth Zoa, that stood arou[n]d the Throne
    Divine.
                                                (24:68–76)

From seething belly to saving time may seem an illogical
progression, but it has the kind of inspired logic that dic-
tates all the pattern of *Milton.* In order to see Los "in eter-
nal youth / All powerful," to recognize time as the "mercy
of Eternity," one must have passed into the inspired state
called Golgonooza, and one enters that state only through
the "bellowing furnaces" at its base, where selfhood is de-
stroyed and the soul recast without it. One may emerge
from those furnaces either into the wilderness around
Golgonooza, where Blake was until Milton entered him, or
into Golgonooza, where Blake/Los/Milton enters now; the
only way into Golgonooza is through those furnaces of Gen-
eration. The progression of the poetry from furnace to vi-
sion parallels the progression of the human spirit.

The furnaces are translated by vision into another image
of compression and transformation, the wine-presses of
Los:

The Wine-press on the Rhine groans loud, but all
    its central beams
Act more terrific in the central Cities of the Nations
Where Human Thought is crushd beneath the iron hand
    of Power.
There Los puts all into the Press, the Opressor &
    the Opressed
Together, ripe for the Harvest & Vintage & ready
    for the Loom.
                                                (25:3–7)

The vehicle of the imagery thus shifts from anatomy to geography, from creation to apocalypse, but the tenor has remained the same: the souls of men are being prepared by destruction for new life. The belly gives birth and the presses kill, but each transforms the fallen soul and brings it closer to eternity.

Los ordains that transformation. He orders his laborers to reorganize fallen history, binding all generated souls according to their proper Classes, and thus "Separating what has been Mixed / Since Men began to be Wove into Nations by Rahab & Tirzah" (25:28–29). His orders show him to be indeed the "mercy of Eternity":

> The Elect is one Class: You
> Shall bind them separate: they cannot Believe in
> Eternal Life
> Except by Miracle & a New Birth. The other two Classes;
> The Reprobate who never cease to Believe, and the
> Redeemd,
> Who live in doubts & fears perpetually tormented by the
> Elect
> These you shall bind in a twin-bindle for the
> Consummation—
> But the Elect must be saved [from] fires of Eternal
> Death,
> To be formed into the Churches of Beulah that they
> destroy not the Earth. . . .
>
> (25:32–39)

Los, who originally raged against the salvation of the Elect in the Bard's Song, now professes the same mercy. He has been, by his union with the Bard and Milton in Blake, restored to Edenic vision. Where once he ranted and altered the poles of the world, now he pacifies and commands their reordering.

Los's proclamation of apocalypse, in its grim detailing of fallen reality and its plea for restraint and mercy, echoes his

earlier speech to Rintrah and Palamabron, and it has the
same effect: discontent and grudging obedience. Both Gen-
eration and Golgonooza are infected with peril and mis-
trust. But Blake pulls back from these dark minute particu-
lars as if to remind himself and us that any apocalyptic
rumblings in time are negligible in the clearer air of eter-
nity. As the Bard earlier pulled back from the atrocities of
mortal history to the panoramic vision which sees them
as natural cycle (plate 6), Blake now shifts his focus from
the devastations of the Mundane Shell to its grand coher-
ence. The Edenic vision Los has brought him translates the
shrill harps and flutes of Bowlahoola, the agonies of genera-
tive existence, into the music of the spheres:

> Thou seest the Constellations in the deep & wondrous
>   Night
> They rise in order and continue their immortal courses
> Upon the mountains & in vales with harp & heavenly song
> With flute & clarion; with cups & measures filld with
>   foaming wine.
> Glittring the streams reflect the Vision of beatitude,
> And the calm Ocean joys beneath & smooths his awful
>   waves!
>
> (25:66–71)

Those vast constellations are the sons of Los, but the
humblest beings of natural reality are sons of Los as well.
Blake looks himself now at "the little winged fly" he earlier
urged Albion to examine (20:27), and finds in its dance
even as in the motions of the stars an emblem of Edenic har-
mony. "The gorgeous clothed Flies that dance & sport" and
the prophetic mountain trees that teach us to withstand the
wind are "Visions of Eternity / But we see only as it were
the hem of their garments / When with our vegetable eyes
we view these wond'rous Visions" (26:10–12). Blake's
splendid pastoral vision of the laborers of Bowlahoola
ends in a sigh of loss that he cannot long maintain it. He is

mortal and his eye is vegetable, and his concerns are the concerns of Generation. His pastoral ease gives way to foreboding.

Los himself is vigilant against disaster: "For Los against the east his force continually bends / . . . Lest those Three Heavens of Beulah should the Creation destroy" (26:18–20). He faces the threat of Satan, who "Stood opake immeasurable / Covering the east with solid blackness" (9:39–40). His stance is significant, especially because Blake is so specific about it: souls return to the body at his left, the north, which means that he reverses Urizen's position in the Bard's Song (with his "Right arm to the north, his left arm to the south" [3:25], Urizen must face west).[21] At the same time, the directions of the souls at Los's sides suggest a reversal of Jesus' position in traditional graphic representations of the Last Judgment, including Blake's own. Why should Los reverse both Jesus and Urizen? Is the implication that Urizen is in a position to be saved—*i.e.*, that he is a lifeless Jesus?

Facing east, Los faces the great wine-press, which is built "eastward of Golgonooza, before the Seat / Of Satan" (27:1–2). The press is thus between Los and Satan; Judgment, the last vintage, is at once the barrier and the bridge between Reprobate and Elect. The press is a summary of the dualities of Bowlahoola. It is both "War on Earth" and the "Printing-Press of Los" (27:8–9), both bloody destruction and inspired creation. Around it sport insects, vermin, "idle Weeds": "The Toad & venomous Newt," "the Nettle that stings with soft down"—all the parasitic deceivers of nature revealed in their drunkenness as the poisonous creatures they are. Paradoxically, they are not only poisonous but fair, fair in the "gorgeous raiment" they throw off and in their naked energy. These bugs and weeds are the brothers of "the gorgeous clothed flies" and "the Trees on mountains" who are the sons of Los.

---

[21] Their positions imply that they face each other, which presumably they do, in the persons of Los and Satan.

The press is "the Wine-press of Los" (27:1), but Luvah laid its foundation (27:2), and the orgy conducted around it is the play of the children of Luvah. The scene has a pernicious familiarity:

> The cruel joys of Luvahs Daughters lacerating with
> knives
> And whips their Victims & the deadly sport of Luvahs
> Sons.
> They dance around the dying, & they drink the howl &
> groan
> They catch the shrieks in cups of gold, they hand them
> to one another:
> These are the sports of love, & these the sweet delights
> of amorous play
> Tears of the grape, the death sweat of the cluster
> the last sigh
> Of the mild youth who listens to the lureing
> songs of Luvah. . . .
>
> (27:35–41)

These are the joys the Shadowy Female, emanation of Luvah, described as her dominance of fallen men (18:5–25), these the revels of the Bard's Song:

> Between South Molton Street & Stratford Place:
> Calvarys foot
> Where the Victims were preparing for Sacrifice
> their Cherubim
> Around their loins pourd forth their arrows &
> their bosoms beam
> With all colours of precious stones, & their inmost
> palaces
> Resounded with preparation of animals wild & tame. . . .
>
> (4:21–25)

> While the Females prepare the Victims. the Males at
> Furnaces

And Anvils dance the dance of tears & pain: loud
  lightnings
Lash on their limbs as they turn the whirlwinds loose
  upon
The Furnaces, lamenting around the Anvils. . . .

(5:15-19)

The Bard's descriptions sounded all but arbitrary in their
unexpected excitement. They seemed to have no real context.
Now, twenty-two plates later, we recognize their propriety.
The historical frenzy of the English tyrants, the archetypi-
cal frenzy of the males and females, is the ruthless activity
in Bowlahoola: the destruction of selfhood which is the re-
construction of humanity.

The definition of Bowlahoola begins at the forge, where
"loud sport the dancers at the dance of death, rejoicing in
carnage" (24:62). It ends at the wine-press and the same
orgy. At Los's anvil substance is created; at his press it is
destroyed. Both acts are providential, both are horrible,
depending on the observer's perspective. Throughout his
description of Bowlahoola Blake shifts perspectives con-
stantly to suggest the range of truths about this source of
both mortal flesh and immortal inspiration. The passage's
conglomeration of tones, oratorical, prophetic, orgiastic, pas-
toral, suggests as much about the nature of Bowlahoola as
any explicit definitions do.

Bowlahoola and Allamanda are interinvolved: "And
every Generated Body in its inward form, / Is a garden of
delight & a building of magnificence, / Built by the Sons of
Los in Bowlahoola & Allamanda" (26:31-33). The ma-
terial substance of fallen reality is created in Bowlahoola,
formed in Allamanda. In the first, "the Spectres choose their
affinities" (26:38), their Class of Men; in the second, their
choices are realized in mortal shape. The first process is, as
we have seen, tortured and convoluted. The second, its con-
trary, is gracious and direct. The Allamanda passage,
27:42-29:46, has none of the upheaval, none of the confus-

ing shifts in perspective of the Bowlahoola passage. It is a great calm chant, a hymn to the creative forces of inspiration.

The formation of the spectral substance into the Three Classes, the sowing of the seeds of Bowlahoola, begins with the artist Antamon, who draws a fair outline "such as the Spectre admiring / Puts on the sweet form" (28:17–18). Anxious Theotormon and Sotha flesh out that outline and contend with the weak spectres who, seeking cruelty, must be driven "in fear into their Net / Of kindness & compassion" (28:24–26). The sons of Ozoth define and limit the senses of the now generated spectre, rendering him opaque and yet preserving his internal vision so that he is "like the diamond which tho cloth'd / In rugged covering in the mine, is open all within / And in his hallowd center holds the heavens of bright eternity" (28:36–38).[22] Thus are the Three Classes of Men created individually, the fair Redeemed by Antamon's golden pen, the raging Reprobate in the nets of Sotha and Theotormon, and the opaque Elect in the rigid forms of Ozoth. Each is both a triumph and a failure: the sweet Redeemed form is, perhaps, like Palamabron in the Bard's Song, too mild to hold his place; the terrific Reprobate has both the beauty and the danger of pure energy; the blackened Elect, shut out from eternity, has yet its heavens protected within him because there has been a limit set to opacity.[23] And even as these Three Classes are separate and individual, they are all part of the fabric of man: in creating the Redeemed Antamon draws the outline of the body; Sotha and Theotormon frighten the weak spec-

[22] Interestingly, it is the legions of Theotormon and Sotha ("Their numbers are seven million & seven thousand & seven hundred") and the sons of Ozoth ("And the numbers of his Sons is eight million & eight") who perform the second and third tasks; Antamon, the original artist and creator of the design they follow, works alone. Inspiration always is, it seems, a personal matter. The numbers of Theotormon and Sotha and of the sons of Ozoth are, of course, significant in Blake's myth. Sevens yielding to eights suggests the approach, with the completion of fallen humanity, of apocalypse.

[23] Compare Satan in the Bard's Song, 9:30–35.

tre into the net of flesh woven by the daughters to Anta-
mon's design; Ozoth locks the spectre in, protecting his tiny
spark of eternity against the sea of chaos. Each of us is all
Three Classes in one form; we belong particularly to that
Class which predominates.

The "beautiful house" the sons of Los create for each
shapeless spectre is reflected in two other of their creations,
the "wondrous buildings" of time and the "immortal Tent"
of space. Blake describes these vaster structures in two par-
allel passages which illustrate that Allamanda, like Bowla-
hoola, has its own internal contraries.

Four plates earlier, in what seemed an abstract digression
from his description of Bowlahoola, Blake celebrated Los
as time, "the mercy of Eternity." Now, in his description of
Allamanda, he amplifies that celebration:

> But others of the Sons of Los build Moments &
>   Minutes & Hours
> And Days & Months & Years & Ages & Periods;
>   wondrous buildings
> And every Moment has a Couch of gold for soft repose,
> (A Moment equals a pulsation of the artery)
> And between every two Moments stands a Daughter of
>   Beulah
> To feed the Sleepers on their Couches with maternal
>   care.
> And every Minute has an azure Tent with silken Veils.
> And every Hour has a bright golden Gate carved with
>   skill.
> And every Day & Night, has Walls of brass & Gates of
>   adamant,
> Shining like precious stones & ornamented with
>   appropriate signs:
> And every Month, a silver paved Terrace builded high:
> And every Year, invulnerable Barriers with high Towers.
> And every Age is Moated deep with Bridges of silver
>   and gold:

And every Seven Ages is Incircled with a Flaming Fire.
Now Seven Ages is amounting to Two Hundred Years
Each has its Guard. each Moment Minute Hour Day
    Month & Year.
All are the work of Fairy hands of the Four Elements
The Guard are Angels of Providence on duty evermore
Every Time less than a pulsation of the artery
Is equal in its period & value to Six Thousand Years.
For in this Period the Poets Work is Done: and all
    the Great
Events of Time start forth & are concievd in such
    a Period
Within a Moment: a Pulsation of the Artery.

                   (28:44–29:3)

This passage has a revealing symmetry: it begins and ends
with the same subject, suggesting by this circularity both
the cyclical nature of all reality and the climactic importance
of the subject itself. The subject in this description of the
providence of time is the poetic moment that transcends
time. That moment is the most elusive of the units of time
constructed like "wondrous buildings" by the sons of Los,
for it is at once smaller and greater than the other units. In
the two series of those units, otherwise arranged in order
of magnitude, "Moments" are named first and are thus os-
tensibly the smallest. Yet Blake speaks at the end of the pas-
sage of a six-thousand-year "Period within a Moment," a
period being ostensibly the vastest unit of time, yet con-
tained within what seemed to be the smallest. The period
itself is the six thousand years of fallen history, contained
within the moment which must include the millennium to
be complete.[24] The moment itself is thus both immeasurably

[24] The issue is complicated by that span of seven ages "Incircled
with a Flaming Fire," a span that both the numerical symbolism and
the engulfing fire suggest might be the moment itself–but Blake
destroys the expectation by making the seven ages equal to only a
small portion of a "period," two hundred years. The reversal of
expectation is startling, especially because in this poem, which has

vast and immeasurably small, recognizable only in that one determinable span of creativity that also bears its name, the "Moment" of individual vision, the instantaneous comprehension of the history of mankind.

In the initial passage celebrating Los as time, Blake mentioned that "Enitharmon is nam'd Space," but spoke no more of her. Now he corrects the slight, celebrating providential space as he has just praised merciful time. He always has, throughout the poem, maintained the partnership of time and space, never except in that single brief passage examining one without the other, always cleansing mutually

---

many significant numbers, two hundred has no explicit significance. I suggest that it is the span between Milton's birth and the creation of this poem, and thus represents a "generation" of prophetic poetry, the length of time in which one poet beats Urizen into form and dies, leaving his successor the same seven-age task. If that is the definition of the seven ages, the implication is that a single poet's inspiration is but a small part of the inspired moment, a kind of miniature moment, that poetry is a progressive vision that gathers truth and power with its ages as the moment gathers to a close. This is rather like Keats's march of intellect, and like Blake's own description, in Book II, of the relay of inspiration from poet to poet, from lark to lark, until apocalypse. The difference between Keats and Blake on this point is, however, instructive. For both, all later poets build on the works of their predecessors, but for Keats this process yields continual improvement in the works of genius, whereas for Blake there can be no qualitative improvement and historical pressure alone determines the greater success of one poet's genuine vision over another's. For Keats, Wordsworth is profounder than Milton because he writes in a more advanced age (letter to John Hamilton Reynolds, May 3, 1818). For Blake, no poet can be profounder than Milton ("To suppose that Art can go beyond the finest specimens of Art that are now in the world, is not knowing what Art is; it is being blind to the gifts of the spirit," *A Descriptive Catalogue*, p. 535), but another may have more immediate effect if he writes at a more critical time in the downward spiral of history toward apocalypse.

Edward J. Rose suggests that the paradox of the moment as smallest and greatest is the paradox of any perception of time: "Time is described [in this passage] in terms of duration or Chronos, but the smallest, most mi-*nute* segment of time . . . is equal to the whole of time 'in its period & value' because it is time as Kairos" ("Los, Pilgrim of Eternity," *Sublime Allegory*, pp. 83–99, p. 85).

our temporal and spatial perspectives. He has spoken at greater length of time in Book I, to be sure, a proportion we shall have cause to examine in the next chapter, but he has never spoken of it without some reference to its counterpart. Now in the coda of Book I he adjusts that proportion; from a twenty-three-line hymn to ordained time he moves immediately to a twenty-three-line hymn to created space, for the two are equally the gifts of Los's providential art:

The Sky is an immortal Tent built by the Sons of Los
And every Space that a Man views around his
    dwelling-place:
Standing on his own roof, or in his garden on a mount
Of twenty five cubits in height, such space is his
    Universe;
And on its verge the Sun rises & sets. the Clouds bow
To meet the flat Earth & the Sea in such an ordered
    Space:
The Starry heavens reach no further but here bend & set
On all sides & the two Poles turn on their valves of gold:
And if he move his dwelling-place, his heavens also move.
Wher'eer he goes & all his neighbourhood bewail his loss:
Such are the Spaces called Earth & such its dimension:
As to that false appearance which appears to the
    reasoner,
As of a Globe rolling thro Voidness, it is a delusion
    of Ulro
The Microscope knows not of this nor the Telescope.
    they alter
The ratio of the Spectators Organs but leave Objects
    untouchd
For every Space larger than a red Globule of Mans
    blood.
Is visionary: and is created by the Hammer of Los
And every Space smaller than a Globule of Mans blood.
    opens

Into Eternity of which this vegetable Earth is but a
    shadow:
The red Globule is the unwearied Sun by Los created
To measure Time and Space to mortal Men. every
    morning.
Bowlahoola & Allamanda are placed on each side
Of that Pulsation & that Globule, terrible their power.

                                    (29:4–26)

This splendid passage is an apotheosis of much that has
gone before. Its spare eloquence is as much a product of
what preceded the passage, as of the passage itself; the lines
are powerful not just in their purity of vision, but in the re-
flections they bear of previous visions. They are the ulti-
mate manifestation of the vortex. *Milton* is to a great extent
a study of human perspective, of the way we as fallen men
perceive our universe, and the way with expanded vision
we might perceive it. Blake has indicated the disparity of
those ways of seeing in touchstone passages throughout
Book I; here on the book's last plate he resolves that dis-
parity, comprehending in his now inspired imagination
both mundane and eternal vision, presenting them not, as
they have always appeared to be, as conflicting and mu-
tually exclusive modes of seeing, but as one continuous vi-
sion, limited sometimes by our fallen comprehension but by
no means condemned to that limitation. For everything we
see is part of the one great vortex of vision which extends,
like Milton's shadow, from eternity "to the depths of dirast
Hell." Even the sky which seems our spatial boundary is
vulnerable to penetrating vision. It is but a tent imagined
by Los for our protection, and it expands to eternity or con-
tracts to the space immediately above our heads according
to the way we are capable of seeing it. A man standing on
the vortex point of earthly vision, "on his own roof, or in his
garden on a mount / Of twenty-five cubits in height," per-
ceives it as "a vortex not yet pass'd." Even its form is vorti-

cal, as Frye points out: "The tent is pyramidal in shape, the pyramid being its demonic parody, its stony frozen form (cf. the pyramidal shape of the shepherds' tents in one of Blake's *Nativity Ode* illustrations)."[25]

Earlier Blake said,

> every thing has its
> Own Vortex; and when once a traveller thro' Eternity
> Has passd that Vortex, he percieves it roll backward
> behind
> His path, into a globe itself infolding; like a sun:
> Or like a moon, or like a universe of starry majesty,
> While he keeps onwards in his wondrous journey on the
> earth
> Or like a human form, a friend with whom he livd
> benevolent.
>
> (15:21–27)

We have watched each of the principals of the poem pass through these stages of vision, seeing his universe first as globe and finally as friend. Now Blake explicitly condemns the earlier vision: "As to that false appearance which appears to the reasoner, / As of a Globe rolling thro Voidness, it is a delusion of Ulro." All space except its integral unit, the spatial equivalent of a moment of time, the providential limit of contraction, is imagined. Those who recognize the act of imagining transcend the limitations it seems to impose: knowing that what seems fixed and externally ordained is but a product of one's own fixed senses liberates those senses and permits them to transcend what they perceive.

The progress implicit in this culminating passage is vast. Not only has Blake in his purified vision personally rejected all the spatial delusions of Ulro; in doing so, he has found himself at the point of a vortex (on a roof or on a mount of twenty-five cubits: thus even spatially on the point of a

[25] "Notes," p. 136 fn.

pyramid extending downward to the earth), looking out-
ward into another vortex. He reverses Milton's own posi-
tion, for to Milton, as to all travelers through eternity, "the
heaven [is] a vortex passd already, and the earth / A vortex
not yet pass'd" (15:34–35). For Blake the earth is a vortex
passed, and heaven one yet to be passed. Because Blake at
this moment is the embodiment of Milton, Milton, too, has
achieved this reversal of perspective. He has come a full
cycle from mortality through regeneration.

Arriving at Golgonooza, both Milton and Blake have
completed journeys through the vortex. Traveling from op-
posite directions, they have reached finally the same per-
spective. Milton's outside path and Blake's inward one have
culminated in a purified vision of the universe which neith-
er figure could have achieved without the other. The
achievement of that vision is the initiation of apocalypse.

Splendid visions of beneficent sons of Los are not all of
Allamanda. Its cultivated land verges on the wilderness of
Entuthon, and Allamanda is not immune to horror:

But Rintrah & Palamabron govern over Day & Night
In Allamanda & Entuthon Benython where souls wail:
Where Orc incessant howls burning in fires of
    Eternal Youth,
Within the vegetated mortal Nerves; for every
    Man born is joined
Within into One mighty Polypus, and this Polypus is Orc.
But in the Optic vegetative Nerves Sleep was
    transformed
To Death in old time by Satan the father of Sin & Death
And Satan is the Spectre of Orc & Orc is the generate
    Luvah. . . .
                                            (29:27–34)

The sons of Ozoth limited and preserved the perceptivity
of vegetated souls, and their act was providential. Yet it was
horrible as well, confirming the loss of eternity. The subject

of their ambiguous beneficence is the sum of fallen reality, known collectively as Orc. Spectrous Satan and eternal Luvah are mutual identities of Orc, who is at once the polypus, the unorganized material out of which generated life is formed, and the fiery spirit of rebellion which may free men from that generated life. The polypus is Orc/Satan, the freedom Orc/Luvah; Orc is the embattled potential of all men. Los organizes the polypus[26] and releases the spirit:[27] such is the operation of imagination on the natural man.

We are back in the dark vision of the Bard's Song, an ominous return after the beauty of the vision of Los's creation. Once again we are told of the constriction of what should be eternal forms, of the senses' debasement in physical restraint. Once again we are reminded of the dual nature of Los's providence, its pain as well as its glory. We are back in the ambiguous prophecies of the Bard's conclusion, in which Leutha called Satan "The Spectre of Luvah the murderer / Of Albion" (13:8–9). That sin, she said, "was begun in Eternity, and will not rest to Eternity / Till two Eternitys meet together" (13:10–11). It is to that relief that Los directs his labor:

> On Albions Rock Los stands creating the glorious
>   Sun each morning
> And when unwearied in the evening he creates the Moon
> Death to delude, who all in terror at their splendor
>   leaves
> His prey while Los appoints, & Rintrah & Palamabron
>   guide
> The Souls clear from the Rock of Death, that Death
>   himself may wake
> In his appointed season when the ends of heaven meet.
>   (29:41–46)

---

[26] Compare lines 24:36–39.

[27] Los ascends to Blake to permit Milton, in fulfillment of the prophecy in Eden, to free Orc (20:59–61 and 22:32–33).

We have passed through Bowlahoola and Allamanda, and their contraries are clear to us. Now we may enter Golgonooza, where we shall find not only the contraries of Los's creation, but also its negation:

> Then Los conducts the Spirits to be Vegetated, into
> Great Golgonooza, free from the four iron pillars
>   of Satans Throne
> (Temperance, Prudence, Justice, Fortitude, the four
>   pillars of tyranny)
> That Satans Watch-Fiends touch them not before they
> Vegetate.

> But Enitharmon & her Daughters take the pleasant
>   charge.
> To give them to their lovely heavens till the
>   Great Judgment Day
> Such is their lovely charge. But Rahab & Tirzah pervert
> Their mild influences, therefore the Seven Eyes of
>   God walk round
> The Three Heavens of Ulro, where Tirzah & her Sisters
> Weave the black Woof of Death. . . .

> Such is the World of Los the labour of six thousand years.
> Thus Nature is a Vision of the Science of the Elohim.[28]
>   End of the First Book

The contention of Rahab and Enitharmon is the struggle of the whole of Book I, the struggle of Milton against Urizen, of Los against the polypus, of creation against chaos. The

---

[28] Percival accounts for the identification of nature with the Elohim, the third of the seven watchers, when he says, "Elohim comes with the flood and shapes the world which rises out of it" (*Circle of Destiny*, p. 246). The science of the Elohim, then, is a science of reconstruction after catastrophe, which is Los's action throughout the six thousand years of fallen history. Los's creation is a vision of the science of the Elohim whenever it occurs; it is identified by function, not by sequence, with the third watcher.

battle began in the Bard's Song and has not ended. Yet much has happened between the Bard's Song and this concluding chant which echoes it, and the third section of the book is in many ways a redaction of the first two. Although the action and even many of the images of the book's conclusion are those of its beginning, they have a new dimension and a new finality. What happened in the environs of Eden has happened here in Generation, but the transposition is not simply part of an endless cycle. The difference between the events is the difference between the Preludia of *America* and *Europe*: in one the Shadowy Female is ravished, in the other she has been ravished many times and her misery is about to end. In the Bard's Song time and space were created; in the Golgonooza passage they have been recreated continuously, and are, like the cycles of the Shadowy Female, about to end. Because a limit has been set by Jesus to the fall of Albion and his members, the prototypic actions of the Bard's Song cannot be played out again and again on endlessly receding levels of reality; they can be played out only to the limit established by Jesus, and that limit is the generative world of the body of Book I. Concluded there, they are concluded for all reality. By the five and a half-plate chant with which Book I ends, they have been concluded.

Entering into Golgonooza is the visionary consummation of the three-part action of Book I. The Bard's joining with Milton caused Milton's first full vision of fallen reality; Milton's union with Blake caused Blake's; Los's union with Bard/Milton in Blake affirmed those visions by bringing the consolidated Reprobate protagonist into Golgonooza. We have seen that the three unions of the Book I action were the same union, all prompted by and elucidating the same vision, a vision of the providential nature of the limits set to Albion's fall and of the function of the Reprobate in that providence. Part three of Book I is a five and a half-plate elaboration of that crucial vision. The act itself culminates in Golgonooza. So, too, does the vision.

124

Entering the city of art entails recognizing that what is torment to the purely vegetable sense is harmony to the Edenic, that the violent contractions of Bowlahoola are on a broader level of reality the rhythmic order of "the Constellations in the deep & wondrous Night" (24:66). Our generative life is part of the infinite plane that reaches to eternity; its forms and acts are but eternal forms and acts on a minute scale. Apocalypse has been here all along; it takes only a visionary eye to see it: "whenever any Individual Rejects Error & Embraces Truth a Last Judgment passes upon that Individual."[29] It is all a matter of perspective, of retracing the vortex into eternity. For a vegetated soul to do that he must "pass inward to Golgonooza": he must achieve the imaginative recognition that the minute particulars of his life, the globule of blood in the artery's pulse, are but the most contracted forms of eternal truth. To achieve that vision, to recognize eternity in time, is to begin the abolition of time.

We have noted three parts in this first book of *Milton*, the prologue to an act, the act itself, and the vision associated with that act. Each part is distinct in content and technique, but none is independent of the rest. The Bard's vision at eternal tables, the consolidation of Bard/Milton/Blake/Los, and Blake's vision in time form a natural progression in which each element realizes and is realized by the others, in which vision is affirmed as action.

Each part of the book has a characteristic technique, which we might name the bardic, the disjunctive narrative, and the visionary. The first is familiar to us from the earliest of Blake's longer poems. Its mixture of mythic and apocalyptic elements, ringing, urgent, and foreboding, appears somewhere, at least embryonically, in every work of Blake's prophetic poetry. The disjunctive narrative, with its intricate weavings of various phases of action, theme, and tone, began in the biblical parodies and flowered in *The Four Zoas*. Its complicated system of internal suggestions

[29] "A Vision of the Last Judgment," p. 551.

and reflections is a hallmark of Blake's art. That rarefied third technique, epitomized in the time-space passages but at work throughout the final section of Book I, is new. Its origin may lie in Oothoon's elegy of *Visions of the Daughters of Albion* or in parts of Night the Ninth, but it is not fully realized in either. It is like the bardic style in its mythic dimension, but its pace is steadier and less urgent. It is, rather, a distillation of the bardic manner, a reduction of its material to the most familiar particulars which yet somehow retain the intoxicating majesty of prophecy. There is a kind of ecstasy here, intrepid and unalloyed, which recalls in impact though not in style the great sunburst of Milton's Book of Light or the gracious climax that is Eliot's last *Quartet.*

But Blake's poem does not end with this triumph of style and vision. The conflicts of Book I have not been resolved; its protagonists are in Golgonooza, but Golgonooza is only the temporal representation of eternity. If time is to be abolished, Golgonooza must be abolished: the vision of Eden must be replaced by its reality.

III. Loom

In the progress of Book I from bardic urgency to visionary eloquence we have charted a journey from the environs of Eden through Ulro to Golgonooza. Book II charts a parallel journey, but one of a very different character: beginning in Beulah, it passes through Ulro not to a theoretical state of pure vision, but to a particular garden in a particular region of England. Even the conception of Ulro is different in the second book: Milton passes through a whirlpool and through seas of time and space—images of cosmic abstraction; Ololon passes through the polypus, the sum of undifferentiated matter—an image of tangible concreteness. In its structure and in its imagery Book II is a personal human realization of the grand myth of Book I.

Passages in the progression of Book I gain color and impetus from previous passages that express analogous or identical material. Book II approaches the same material yet again, but from such a radically different perspective that what we have already learned as a moving philosophy of history and of poetic responsibility becomes a profound vision of personal fulfillment. Book I is concerned with the "masculine" assertiveness of the poet, his responsibility to his vision and his compeers; Book II is concerned with the "feminine" portion which is his inspiration and support, the mercy he learns to exercise in Book I. The second book is an expansion of the single plate of Book I in which Ololon appears: on plate 21 she, having lamented for seven mornings her driving Milton into Ulro, repents and descends to him; Book II is an extended analysis of that act which, like all acts described in *Milton*, is identical with its consequences. Book I is about the Three Classes of Men, Book II is about the Three Heavens of Beulah. Book I is a poem of struggle, Book II of resolution. Book I, in subject and style, is the incessant beating of the hammer of Los; Book II, in subject and style, is the graceful throbbing of the looms of Enitharmon.

The structure of Book II exactly parallels that of the much longer Book I. Each has three major parts, a prologue of events leading to an act of union, a refracted account of that union, and an epilogue expanding upon a vision associated with that union. In Book I, the union is primarily the consolidation of the masculine forces of creativity; in Book II, it is the concomitant merger of the feminine forces with the masculine. That merger is implicit in Book I, for the ultimate consolidation of Reprobate figures would have been impossible without it: only the feminine quality of repentance could have permitted both Milton and Los to accept the obligations they do accept. Book II makes that merger, which is the pivotal factor of every decision in the poem, explicit. As the crucial center sections of the two books thus complement each other, so do their first and third sections.

A. Beulah

The Bard's Song has four distinct parts, a myth of creation, an account of a pivotal action, a judgment on that action, and an act of contrition for it. The first section of Book II is also a prologue in four parts, each directly comparable to its counterpart in the Bard's Song. The first, 30:1–31:7, is a myth of creation; the second, 31:8–63, details the result of the action in the Bard's Song; the third, plate 32, is a judgment necessitated by that action; the fourth, plate 33, is a complicated act of contrition promoted by that judgment.

The first part of the Book II prologue begins with what is probably the most astonishing tonal shift anywhere in Blake's poetry. The warnings and contentions of Book I,

with their ominous culminating passage on "the veil of
human miseries," have yielded suddenly to a gentle
satisfaction:

> There is a place where Contrarieties are equally True
> This place is called Beulah, It is a pleasant lovely
> Shadow
> Where no dispute can come. Because of those who Sleep.
> . . . .
> Beulah is evermore Created around Eternity; appearing
> To the Inhabitants of Eden, around them on all sides.
> But Beulah to its Inhabitants appears within each district
> As the beloved infant in his mothers bosom round
> incircled
> With arms of love & pity & sweet compassion. But to
> The Sons of Eden the moony habitations of Beulah,
> Are from Great Eternity a mild & pleasant Rest.
>
> (30:1–3, 8–14)

From Golgonooza to Beulah, from time to the emanation of
eternity, from a prophesied end to a remembered begin-
ning: Blake's vision expands to comprehend a reality be-
yond that of vegetated life. He has reached, by passing in-
ward to Golgonooza, not only vision, but the well-spring of
vision. He can see now and describe the "Realms of terror
& mild moony lustre" whose regents he invoked at the start
of his poem as the "Muses who inspire the Poets Song."
Thus Beulah becomes for him and for us, as well as for the
eternals for whom it was created, a place of rest.

Although this description breaks drastically with the tone
of what preceded it, it retains not only dramatic but also
thematic continuity. That great world of Los with which
Book I ends is a direct copy of this eternal world pictured
now for the first time. The pattern for Golgonooza sur-
rounded by Allamanda is Eden surrounded by Beulah,
"Poetic Inspiration" (identified with Eden in 30:19) sur-
rounded by its social source of nourishment and protection;

both eternal and temporal complexes rest on Ulro. As Los modeled Urizen's fallen body after the anatomy of Albion's, so he modeled his temporal world after the geography of the eternal. By maintaining eternal forms in time, Los has kept open a potential communication between the realms. He has provided fallen reality with a pattern of eternity, a lifeless form that need only be invested with eternal vision to be revived.

How we see Beulah is a function of where we stand. From Generation it may seem "Realms of terror," for it is the source of inspiration, which is a fearful gift. From Eden it is the surrounding region, simply part of the landscape. But from inside its bounds it seems a compassionate maternal bosom, encompassing and sustaining. So every aspect of reality changes with our perspective on it, seeming, like the vortex that governs perspective, geometry or benevolent friend according to the way we choose to see it. Blake's vision now places him in Beulah, and his poetry will reflect the "love & pity & sweet compassion" of this idyllic realm.

As the first part of the Bard's Song chronicled the creation of Urizen's form and of Golgonooza, the first part of the prologue of Book II relates the creation of Beulah. The emanations, frightened by the mental strife of Eden, beg of Jesus "a Temporal Habitation" (30:29) where they may rest from it.[1]

> So spake the lovely Emanations; & there appeard a
>   pleasant
> Mild Shadow above: beneath: & on all sides round,
> Into this pleasant Shadow all the weak & weary

---

[1] Their fears echoes Orc's fear for his emanation in Book I: "But if we who are built but for a time . . . / Behold these wonders of Eternity we shall consume" (30:26–27) parallels Orc's concern that the Shadowy Female "Consume in my Consummation" (18:28). The remedy for each fear is the same: Orc's emanation may "take a Form / Female & lovely, that cannot consume in Mans consummation" (18:28–29) just as the emanations may enter into their "female" state of repose.

Like Women & Children were taken away as on wings
Of dovelike softness, & shadowy habitations prepared
    for them
But every Man returnd & went still going forward thro'
The Bosom of the Father in Eternity on Eternity
Neither did any lack or fall into Error without
A Shadow to repose in all the Days of happy
    Eternity. . . .

                              (30:32–31:7)

The creation of Beulah is thus, like the creation of Golgo-
nooza, an act of salvation, Los's of the fallen masculine
forms and Jesus' of the failing feminine forms. The emana-
tions have pled, "Give us a habitation & a place" (30:24),
begging of Jesus the very act Los performs in building
Golgonooza, in "Giving to airy nothing a name and a habita-
tion" (28:3). The parallel offers a potential renovation of
one of the grimmest images in the poem, the opaque shad-
ow that is the consolidation of error: Los's city of art is the
redemptive epitome of the shadowy Mundane Shell even
as Beulah, which Blake four times in the quoted passage
alone calls "shadow" or "shadowy," is a benevolent refuge
for faltering beings. Los, and through him the Bard, Milton,
and Blake, is identified in his act of creation with the ulti-
mate Reprobate Redeemer, Jesus.

As Milton descended into his shadow, Ololon descends
into "this pleasant Shadow Beulah," and the second part of
the prologue begins. Part one defined the relationship of
Beulah and Eden; part two defines that of Beulah and
Generation:

And the Shadows of Beulah terminate in rocky Albion.

And all Nations wept in affliction Family by Family
Germany wept towards France & Italy: England wept &
    trembled
Towards America: India rose up from his golden bed:

As one awakend in the night: they saw the Lord coming
In the Clouds of Ololon with Power & Great Glory!

And all the Living Creatures of the Four Elements, wail'd
With bitter wailing . . .
Orc howls on the Atlantic: Enitharmon trembles: All
 Beulah weeps. . . .

(31:11–27)

Beulah weeps as Ololon weeps, and all Generation laments
with them, for it is the time of weeping, the moment of the
loosing of Orc. As the Bard prophesied, the Elect meet the
Redeemed, Germany weeping toward the Latin lands, En-
gland toward America. The conflict that has tormented all
levels of reality, setting Los against Urizen, Milton against
Satan, has engulfed the lowest level of reality and become
the final conflict, the battles of apocalypse.

All Beulah weeps, but to us in Generation the lamentation
is a lyric promise of new birth; for those embroiled in cor-
poreal miseries, even the anguish of a higher state must
seem a respite and a joy. Instead of explicitly defining this
vital difference in perspective, as he did throughout Book
I, Blake simply illustrates it here with a corresponding shift
in style. The description of vegetated war yields abruptly
to a celebration of natural peace (31:28–63). The progres-
sion forms an ironic counterpart to the second part of the
Bard's Song: in Book I this segment is one of deliberate and
disastrous action, of Satan's usurping the harrow and the
ensuing havoc; in the parallel section of Book II, all conten-
tion gives way to a sublimely delicate pastoral hymn. Eden
is a place of strife, Beulah of gentle repose. Yet even in its
respose Beulah prophesies the doom of time. That sublime
hymn is not a denial of the conflicts of nations and families,
but a consummation of them. This is the only way gentle
Beulah can describe apocalypse, but it does describe
apocalypse.

In Book I Blake defined time and space in matching twenty-three-line stanzas. In Book II he describes the heralds of the end of time and space in matching eighteen-line stanzas. The interinvolvement of the time and space stanzas is repeated in the second pair, which reflect and complement each other and, not incidentally, amplify their Book I counterparts as well.

Time and space are cosmic artificialities. The harbingers of their destruction are two humble natural beings, the lark and the wild thyme, heralds of morning and of spring.

In Book I we learned that the Mundane Shell "finishes where the lark mounts" (17:27); now the significance of that cryptic image begins to come clear:

> Thou hearest the Nightingale begin the Song of Spring;
> The Lark sitting upon his earthly bed: just as the morn
> Appears; listens silent; then springing from the
>   waving Corn-field! loud
> He leads the Choir of Day! trill, trill, trill, trill,
> Mounting upon the wings of light into the Great
>   Expanse:
> Reecchoing against the lovely blue & shining heavenly
>   Shell:
> His little throat labours with inspiration; every feather
> On throat & breast & wings vibrates with the effluence
>   Divine
> All Nature listens silent to him & the awful Sun
> Stands still upon the Mountain looking on this little Bird
> With eyes of soft humility, & wonder love & awe.
> Then loud from their green covert all the Birds begin
>   their Song
> The Thrush, the Linnet & the Goldfinch, Robin & the
>   Wren
> Awake the Sun from his sweet reverie upon the
>   Mountain:
> The Nightingale again assays his song, & thro the day,

And thro the night warbles luxuriant; every Bird of Song
Attending his loud harmony with admiration & love.
This is a Vision of the lamentation of Beulah over Ololon!

(31:28-45)

It is not only where the lark mounts that the Mundane Shell
ends, but when he mounts: the instant of these lines is the
apocalyptic instant of the entire poem, the instant in which
the sun, stilled for the length of the moratorium day, is
awakened by the chorus of inspiration, the instant when
spring and fall are united (the nightingale begins the Song
of Spring, but the lark in response arises from autumn's
"waving Corn-field"), when the birds of night and day sing
together. This is the instant when Ololon's lamentation was
heard in Eden and "Providence began" (21:24), but now,
instead of drowning her song, the clarions of day echo it
throughout Generation.

The structure of the passage is, like the structure of the
time passage, cyclical; it opens and closes with the song of
the nightingale. Again, the structure is a perfect analogue
of the meaning: the nightingale, having inspired the lark,
falls silent, only to join finally the chorus all birds of song
must join. So John Milton, to whom this passage is surely a
tribute, wrote and died, only to be resurrected later in the
song of Blake, the lark whose humbler voice he inspired.[2]
The unity of the songbirds is the unity of the prophetic
poets in Book I, of the Bard and Milton and Blake and Los.
Their singing together fulfills the prayer of Moses that is
the motto of *Milton*: "Would to God that all the Lords peo-
ple were prophets." The instant in which all men are
prophets, in which all voices sing together, is the instant of
apocalypse.

The circular rhetoric of the lark and time passages is a
device Blake uses throughout the poem to emphasize key

---

[2] Later in Book II the lark itself will be identified with Milton;
by then the nightingale will have disappeared from the poem's
imagery, and the lark will stand for every bird of song.

passages and to unify the often contradictory impulses that comprise the passages. Milton's first speech, beginning and ending "I go to Eternal Death," begins in hatred of satanic selfhood and ends by embracing that selfhood (14:14–32); Rintrah and Palamabron castigate Los for his pity at the beginning and end of their fearful speech (22:29–23:30), counseling wrath to avenge the destruction of the merciful; Blake himself will address Ololon in a brief speech beginning and ending with a plea for comfort for his emanation, but meanwhile concerned with his own affliction (36:27–31). The device of circularity is not new in *Milton*; Blake used it throughout his career, from "The Tyger" through the Argument to *The Marriage of Heaven and Hell* to the more diffuse version of it in the reflecting actions of Nights One and Nine in *The Four Zoas*. But it has a special force in this poem about the mutuality of contraries, reinforcing insistently the identity of the polarities it circumscribes.

In the instant of the lark's song the second of Los's early-rising messengers awakes. To the song of all the birds the wild thyme leads a dance of all the flowers, a dance that may recall the terrifying dance of Los himself in the *Book of Urizen* and *The Four Zoas*, or of Urizen after his binding in the Bard's Song; though here, described in the language of the Song of Songs with echoes of *Lycidas*, the motion is "all in order sweet & lovely":

> Thou percievest the Flowers put forth their precious
>   Odours!
> And none can tell how from so small a center comes
>   such sweets
> Forgetting that within that Center Eternity expands
> Its ever during doors, that Og & Anak fiercely guard[.]
> First eer the morning breaks joy opens in the flowery
>   bosoms
> Joy even to tears, which the Sun rising dries; first
>   the Wild Thyme
> And Meadow-sweet downy & soft waving among the
>   reeds.

Light springing on the air lead the sweet Dance: they
    wake
The Honeysuckle sleeping on the Oak: the flaunting
    beauty
Revels along upon the wind; the White-thorn lovely May
Opens her many lovely eyes: listening the Rose still
    sleeps
None dare to wake her. soon she bursts her crimson
    curtaind bed
And comes forth in the majesty of beauty; every Flower:
The Pink, the Jessamine, the Wall-flower, the Carnation
The Jonquil, the mild Lilly opes her heavens! every Tree,
And Flower & Herb soon fill the air with an
    innumerable Dance
Yet all in order sweet & lovely, Men are sick with Love!
Such is a Vision of the lamentation of Beulah over
    Ololon. . . .

                                        (31:46–63)

After both of these idyllic passages Blake has had to remind
us that they are "a Vision of the lamentation of Beulah over
Ololon," for they are so gracious and so fair that they erase
all sense of the horror they entail. The end of time they sig-
nal may sound in the soft tones of gentle Beulah an instant
of harmony and love, but it is an instant to be achieved in
Generation only by agony and devastation. These two pas-
sages reflect not only the time and space passages of Book
I, with their exalted sense of the constructs of Los's world,
but also two far less reassuring passages in the Allamanda
section: on plate 27 Blake described the creatures around
the wine-press of war on earth, the venomous insects and
the stinging weeds; what are they but the dread obverse of
lark and thyme? The wasp and hornet, nettle and thistle are
the mundane forms of those creatures that, imaginatively
realized, are called lark and wild thyme, messengers of Los.
Neither wasp nor lark is the whole emblem of the apocalyp-
tic instant, for that instant comprises both anguish and re-

lease, both poison and song. The wasp is what we see in
Generation, the lark what Beulah celebrates; the man who
perceives their identity renovates in his imagination both
Generation and Beulah.

The space stanza refined earlier definitions of the vortex
by relating them to individual mortal experience. It reaf-
firmed also the ability of every individual mortal being to
discover eternity within himself, for "every Space smaller
than a Globule of Mans blood. opens / Into Eternity"
(29:21–22). The wild thyme stanza refines those concep-
tions further: "opening a center," which is what one does
when he passes within himself from the temporal to the
eternal vortex,[3] yields the joys of eternity not only to the
explorer himself but to those around him. The "precious
Odours" released from the eternal centers of the flowers can
inspire us all to seek that center. The seeking, of course, is
not easy; the center is guarded: "Bowlahoola & Allamanda
are placed on each side / Of that Pulsation & that Globule,"
according to the space stanza; Og and Anak guard the cen-
ter of the wild thyme.

Both time and the lark seem more active, more progres-
sive than the stationary space and wild thyme. This parallel
is given more force by a key alignment in the Book II pas-
sages: the lark by his singing is identified with the sense of
hearing, whereas the flowers are identified with all the
other senses. They are fragrant and visually gorgeous; they
are "downy & soft" and they open to the sun and dance
voluptuously.[4] Together, lark and thyme symbolize all the

---

[3] Frye's definition of the process suggests a vortical change of
awareness: "As soon as a man acquires anything that can be called
wisdom, [his] hostile and suspicious fear relaxes and he begins to
be aware of an inner balance. This changes him from a center to a
circumference of perception. His imagination begins to surround
his experience like an amoeba: he becomes capable of sympathy
because he has given other people shelter in his mind, and no longer
thinks of them as opaque; and, as he can thereby see through them,
he is equally capable of disinterested enmity. This process of mental
growth Blake calls 'opening a centre' " (*Fearful Symmetry*, p. 349).

[4] The tongue is usually identified with the sense of touch by

fallen senses. The most potent sense, the one through which inspiration acts to renovate the others, receives a symbol and a stanza to itself; as the other senses respond to it they are given a corresponding symbol and stanza. This is precisely the relationship between time and space: they are mutual factors of fallen reality, yet only one is independently mobile and can thereby act to renovate them both.

We have seen the interrelatedness of time and space, and the interrelatedness of their emblems, lark and thyme. The identification of a mobile bird with the active male regents of time and of a stationary flower with the passive female regents of space[5] seems standard enough. But the particular flower Blake chose for this otherwise unpuzzling iconography creates a significant confusion within that iconography: "Wild Thyme" irresistibly suggests a punning identification not with space, but with its contrary. This aural identification is, of course, hardly inappropriate: even the names of the emblems he designates indicate what was for Blake the necessary mutuality of contrary principles.

Time and space are the totality of fallen experience; lark and thyme represent our ability to perceive them. The former are abstract, the latter concrete, the former cosmic, the latter personal. Each pair is appropriate to its book, for as Book I dealt with a myth of creation-fall-redemption, Book II will describe the relevance of that grand myth to every fallen person.

In the second part of the Bard's Song Satan usurped the harrow and divided fallen man. The corresponding seg-

---

Blake, but taste is presumably represented separately in the passage in the herb in the third line from the end.

[5] Although most critics have assumed the opposite identification (see, for example, Erdman, *Prophet*, p. 401, or Irene Taylor, *op. cit.*, p. 253), the precise parallelism of the time with the lark passages and the space with the thyme passages contradicts them. Moreover, Peter Alan Taylor notes that in 35:54–60 Blake associates the thyme with Ololon in that both sit by the "Fountain in the Rock of Odours" ("Providence and the Moment in Blake's *Milton*," *Blake Studies*, 4, 1 [Fall 1971], p. 56).

ment of Book II interprets Satan's action in terms of our fallen reality ("Nations wept in affliction Family by Family"),[6] and offers an antidote to it: by renovation of the senses, fallen people can be united and restored to eternity. The third section of Book II's prologue, plate 32, also interprets and redresses its counterpart. The parallelism of the two third sections is unmistakable: each takes place around a couch of the dead (Albion's, Milton's), each is concerned with Satan's division of the nations. In Book I we see the fall and division itself; we see Satan's new opacity and the creation of female space. In Book II we learn, in a passage of that impassioned technicality that is now a familiar rhetorical device, of the meaning of that division to our fallen universe, and of its imminent resolution.

Plate 32 is a conversation of Milton's eternal portion with the Seven Angels. It opens with Milton's discontent:

> I have turned my back upon these Heavens builded on
>   cruelty
> My Spectre still wandering thro' them follows my
>   Emanation
> He hunts her footsteps thro' the snow & the wintry
>   hail & rain[7]
> The idiot Reasoner laughs at the Man of Imagination
> And from laughter proceeds to murder by undervaluing
>   calumny. . . .

(32:3-7)

This is a curious speech, an unsettling one because it disrupts our perspective in order to redefine it. The heavens from which Milton turns away are the heavens we have seen him enter, the "heavens of Albion" of the invocation,

---

[6] Los identified the falseness of Satan's division into "Nations or Families" in his orders to his laborers (25:26ff.).

[7] An echo, perhaps, of the third part of the Bard's Song, in which Enitharmon appeared weeping in Generation, "An aged Woman raving along the Streets" (10:4).

"the heavens beneath Beulah" which constitute Ulro-Generation.[8] How, if he has voluntarily entered those heavens, has he turned his back on them? This is the paradox of the vortex: Milton does exist simultaneously on several levels of reality. That his various portions are not in agreement underscores the basic conflict of the poem, the contention of Milton and his spectre. This particular version of that conflict offers a necessary counterbalance to our usual conception of the natures of the combatants. Milton's tone here borders on elite disdain; he could hardly care less what happens to that nasty spectre. The spectre, on the other hand, is performing, with whatever perverted motives, the necessary constructive function of Milton himself, seeking out Ololon. There is, we must understand, positive value in the spectrous portion of a divided being, and destructive error in the immortal part. The Elect not only needs but deserves preservation. Milton's Edenic portion has recoiled from the action it set in motion itself; it disowns its own shadow. Until it embraces that shadow and renovates it, Milton will remain a divided self. That we have already seen Milton embrace his spectre Urizen in Book I indicates the position of this speech in the action "sequence" of the poem: it is a close-up analysis of the instant of Milton's descent, a study from a different angle of Milton's division into Edenic, Beulaic, and Ulroic portions (15:1–20). In Book I we saw that division as the first phase of a process without duration, a process concluded by the driving of Milton's eternal vestiges into Ulro by the outraged eternals (20:41–50). Now in Book II we return to the first phase again; we see Milton on his couch with his comforting angels, as we saw him earlier, but this time we recognize in his spectrous part the internal causes of his division. Here, as in the Book I death-couch passage, the end

[8] They are called heavens, we can assume from the geography with which the book opens, because they are what one sees looking outward from Eden.

of the division is imminent: the angels will soon tell Milton that he is "a State about to be Created / Called Eternal Annihilation" (32:26–27): his immortal portion is about to descend into his satanic shadow.

The Seven Angels dispel Milton's hesitation. Using their own dual nature as an object lesson, they warn him that his spectre yet contains a portion of his living individuality, and may not be abandoned:

> We are not Individuals but States: Combinations
>   of Individuals
> We were Angels of the Divine Presence: & were Druids
>   in Annandale
> Compelld to combine into Form by Satan. . . .
>
> . . . .
>
> Distinguish therefore States from Individuals in
>   those States.
> States Change: but Individual Identities never
>   change nor cease:
> You cannot go to Eternal Death in that which can
>   never Die.
>
>   (32:10–12, 22–24)

States are the means by which the eternals salvaged the fallen Elect. The space created by Enitharmon, in the form given to it by Los and the duration authorized for it by the eternals, is divided into "Twenty-seven Churches" (32:25), the units of the Mundane Shell. Each of those units shelters a collection of fallen individuals, who pass successively from unit to unit, "state" to "state," until they may pass beyond states altogether, until they reattain Eden. To return thus to imaginative reality the identity must be whole, its parts fully integrated; vortical multidimensionality does not exist in eternity. Milton's spectre pursuing Ololon through the deeps is compound both of error and of Milton's human individuality. Milton cannot abandon him without abandoning a part of himself, and thus his hope for return to Eden.

The difference between immortal Milton and his spectre is the difference between Angels of the Presence and druids in Annandale, between freedom and tyranny. Joined "in Freedom & holy Brotherhood" the spirits are human; "Compelld to combine into Form by Satan" they are "Shapeless Rocks" (32:12–17). So Milton in free union with spectre and emanation is human ("they and / Himself was Human," 17:5–6), while in bondage to his oath he is the rock Sinai (17:14). "Los's Mathematic power" redeems (29:38); Satan's condemns (32:16–21). The process by which tyranny is converted to freedom, spectre to living identity, is the annihilation of what makes it tyrannous in the first place. But that "Selfhood" cannot be vanquished from without; it must truly be converted, informed so fully by its own humanity that it ceases to exist as selfhood. It cannot perish any more than Jesus will permit Satan to perish, but it can be changed, and therefore cease to exist as it was known.

In part three of the Bard's Song Eden passed judgment on Satan; in the corresponding part of Book II, the Seven Angels tell Milton to "Judge then of thy Own Self" (32:30). They have taught him to preserve his identity, annihilating only the created states that contain and restrict it. To judge of his self is to liberate his spectre and re-create it human, to fulfill the judgment of Eden that Satan "must be new Created continually moment by moment" (11:20). This we have seen him do in building Urizen anew with red clay.

Part four of the Bard's Song describes the female response to part three; the corresponding section in the second book presents a feminine counterpart to the doctrine of states and individuals. As the fallen male form is divided, so is his female portion; Milton has his spectre, Ololon her shadow Rahab. The spectre is no more terrifying than the female shadow, and his recreation is no more crucial than hers. Plate 33, the last part of the Book II prologue, describes the renovation of the shadowy female Elect, who must "be continually Redeem'd / By death & misery of those [she loves] & by Annihilation" (33:12–13).

Beulah chants Jesus' castigation of Babylon, shadow of his emanation Jerusalem, whose vegetated jealousy has "Cut off my loves in fury till I have no love left for thee" (33:7). This is the prototypic male-female conflict, the cycle of jealousy and fear reflected in the relationships of Orc and the Shadowy Female and Milton and Ololon. But Jesus foresees an end to the cycle. Milton's descent will cause Ololon/Rahab to repent of her jealousy, and that in turn will bring Babylon to return Jerusalem to Jesus. The parallel of Ololon and Jerusalem in his speech and the contingency of Babylon's redemption on Rahab's remind us once again of the identity of eternal and temporal beings, and of the dependence of the once eternal on the temporal for resurrection.

The final segment of the prologue is the same in each book of *Milton*: the errant female will, Leutha or Ololon, recognizes her guilt and repents. Leutha's repentance in Book I brings the Bard's prophecy of reconciliation: the Elect shall meet the Redeemed in love and forgiveness. Ololon's repentance, prophesied by Jesus and implicit in the chanting of that prophecy not only by Beulah but by Ololon herself (we have heard, it seems, the divine voice in "the Songs of Beulah in the Lamentations of Ololon" [33:24]), promises reconciliation, too, and by the same terms the Bard established: Ololon shall bring "maidens" to her lord as Elynittria brought Leutha to Palamabron. As Milton descended to find Ololon after Leutha's lament in the Bard's history, so Ololon descends to find Milton after the divine promise in her own lamentation. Each of these crucial laments thus prepares the way for the reunion of Milton and Ololon in Generation.

All four parts of the Book II prologue interpret their parallel parts in the Bard's Song, and offer antidotes to its gloom. If the fallen universe had to be created in anguish and bitterness, still there is hope for it because its model is fair Beulah, a providential place of ease and revitalization. If Satan perverted the true order of existence and brought still more anguish and bitterness, which we see now in the strife of nations in our fallen world, yet we may, by purifying our senses and thereby understanding these dread conditions, end them. If the judgment against Rintrah caused Satan in his pride and Los in his wrath to be closed up in Canaan, a judgment against what is annihilable in the self can end the imprisonment and return all its victims to eternity. If Leutha's repentance was vain because Satan would not respond, Ololon's repentance will fulfill the Bard's prophecy, for Milton has already turned to seek her.

Thus the first four plates of Book II are clearly related structurally and thematically to the Bard's Song. Their relation to the rest of Book II is the relation of the Bard's Song to the body of Book I. They form, like the Bard's Song, a prologue to the action of their book, though at first they may seem simply a part of that action. Part one, the story of the creation of Beulah, is clearly antecedent, but the laments of part two seem merely an amplification of the action itself. They accompany the descent of Ololon, and that descent is the action. But they take Ololon only as far as Beulah, and Beulah is, after all, as natural and familiar a setting for her as Eden; it is Ololon's descent "to death in Ulro among the Transgressors" (21:46) that is the book's significant action, action decided upon and in fact taken in Book I. A lament as she passes Beulah is, after plate 21, past history. Part three is antecedent by much the same logic: the Angels' injunction anticipates Milton's self-judgment, but by the time we read that injunction he has already judged of himself and descended. The tone of the fourth part is what makes it antecedent: the disapproval in the divine voice suggests that at the time of the speech Ololon had not yet repented, although Jesus prophesies that she will; but we heard her repent twelve plates before. The four parts of the prologue of Book II predate the action of the book and underscore its motives and its urgency just as the Bard's Song operates in Book I.

B. Act

The action of Book I comprises lines 13:45–24:47, Milton's descent to his entry into Golgonooza with Los-Blake. It is made, as we have seen, in three phases: his decision and descent through Albion's bosom, incarnation in Blake, merger with Los. The parallel sacrifice of Ololon also has three phases, her own decision and descent, her incarnation, her union with Milton. Although the units of the Book I action are difficult, if not impossible, to delineate by plate and line, the Book II units are clearly defined by Ololon's location in each: the first, lines 34–35:17, takes her through Beulah to "the Gates of the Dead"; the second, 35:18–36:32, sees her pass through the polypus to Blake; the third, 37–42:23, describes her union in Blake's Felpham garden with Milton.

The Bard's Song was met by the eternals with anger and skepticism. Serene Beulah accepts the opening songs of Book II more generously: "And all the Songs of Beulah sounded comfortable notes / To comfort Ololon's lamentation" (34:1–2). Ololon, like Milton, ignores the response to her decision:

But Ololon sought the Or-Ulro & its fiery Gates
And the Couches of the Martyrs: & many Daughters of
    Beulah
Accompany them down to the Ulro with soft melodious
    tears
A long journey & dark thro Chaos in the track of
    Miltons course
To where the Contraries of Beulah War beneath
    Negations Banner. . . .
                              (34:19–23)

Ololon seeks the descended Milton, as he had sought the descended Ololon. She passes through "The Four States of

Humanity in its Repose," a feminine universe extending from Beulah through Or-Ulro (34:8–18). The three states subsidiary to Beulah, Alla, Al-Ulro, and Or-Ulro, are unprecedented in Blake's poetry and appear in *Milton* only briefly, to indicate the parallelism but also the separate perspectives of Ololon's descent and Milton's. Or-Ulro is ostensibly the Ulro of the poetic universe with which we are already familiar, viewed through feminine eyes.

As Milton began his descent he beheld the twenty-seven-fold shadow that was his spectre, vegetating "Like as a Polypus" beneath Beulah (15:8). As Ololon begins her descent she beholds the same horror:

> Then view'd from Miltons Track they see the Ulro: a
>   vast Polypus
> Of living fibres down into the Sea of Time & Space
>   growing
> A self-devouring monstrous Human Death Twenty-seven
>   fold[.]
> Within it sit Five Females & the nameless Shadowy
>   Mother
> Spinning it from their bowels with songs of amorous
>   delight
> And melting cadences that lure the Sleepers of Beulah
>   down
> The River Storge (which is Arnon) into the Dead Sea:
> Around this Polypus Los continual builds the Mundane
>   Shell. . . .
>
> (34:24–31)

The twenty-seven-fold polypus is the Mundane Shell itself, the material of fallen reality. It is also the shadow into which Milton entered on the verge of Beulah, and thus when Ololon enters into it she will be joining, in their darkened portions, with Milton.

The six females who spin the polypus are not only the vegetated form of sixfold Ololon; they are as well a demonic

146

parody of Enitharmon and her daughters, who spin out the fabric of life in Cathedron. The difference between Enitharmon's creative spinning and Rahab's destructive spinning is largely one of context: Enitharmon spins her web of death in the city of art, where it will be invested with living truth; Rahab spins hers in chaos, where it will remain unformed and unproductive. Each spins a different substance: Enitharmon's threads are the spectres of eternal death, but Rahab lures sleepers from Beulah into her looms; Enitharmon weaves the dead into potential life, Rahab, the living into death. The parallel says much about the constructive but precarious function of art, a function that imitates eternity but may as easily be imitated by hell. It says much, too, about the nature of Ololon, who is, through their mutual selfhood, identified with Enitharmon, as Milton is identified with Los.

The River Storge is the female version of the river of Milton's contention with Urizen, the Arnon. Damon calls the latter "the river of generation"[9] and the former "the river of parental affection";[10] the female version is thus more intimate, even domestic, but no less pernicious, because "parental affection" in Blake's fallen universe is a distillation of jealousy and fear, the destructive motive force of generated death. Male or female, Arnon or Storge, fallen reality is a landscape of chaos relieved only by the providential world of Los. Blake emphasizes the unity of that horror, regardless of perspective, by repeating with only minor modifications for Ololon at Storge the vision of the ruined "Four Universes" that Milton confronted on the Arnon. The eight lines in which he describes the polypus are followed immediately by eight lines defining the cosmic origin of that perversion, the fall of the four Zoas into ruin (34:33–39). The two stanzas thus define the cause (collapse of the Zoas) and the result (false creation of the emanations) of the fall.

Ololon questions the perversions she must witness outside eternity:

9 *William Blake*, p. 414.   10 *William Blake*, p. 425.

They said. How are the Wars of man which in Great
     Eternity
Appear around, in the External Spheres of Visionary Life
Here renderd Deadly within the Life & Interior
     Vision. . . .

.   .   .   .

And War & Hunting: the Two Fountains of the River of
     Life
Are become Fountains of bitter Death & of corroding
     Hell
Till Brotherhood is changd into a Curse & a Flattery
By Differences between Ideas, that Ideas themselves,
     (which are
The Divine Members) may be slain in offerings for sin
O dreadful Loom of Death! O piteous Female forms
     compelld
To weave the Woof of Death. . . .

                              (34:50–52, 35:2–8)

Ololon asks the same questions she asked of the Divine Humanity in Book I: "Is Virtue a Punisher? O no! how is this wondrous thing: / This World beneath, unseen before . . ." (21:47–48). Is what was fair and good in Eden deadly and terrible here? Is Ololon Rahab? With all her expanded apprehension of fallen reality, she cannot yet accept it as part of the infinite plane that reaches to eternity. She has not yet become part of it:

So spake Ololon in reminiscence astonishd, but they
Could not behold Golgonooza without passing the
     Polypus
A wondrous journey not passable by Immortal feet, &
     none
But the Divine Saviour can pass it without annihilation.
For Golgonooza cannot be seen till having passd the
     Polypus

It is viewed on all sides round by a Four-fold Vision
Or till you become Mortal & Vegetable in Sexuality
Then you behold its mighty Spires & Domes of ivory &
    gold. . . .
                    (35:18–25)

Ololon sees only the horrors of the fallen universe, not its glory Golgonooza, for that she may not see until she assumes the flesh of its reality. As the angel told Milton, "You cannot go to Eternal Death in that which can never Die" (32:24); Ololon may not pass the gates of the dead except in a state that can be annihilated. The passage is itself the annihilation, for only the Divine Saviour, the divine portion of all travelers from eternity, can survive it. To reach this inspired condition one must pass inward to Golgonooza (achieve "Four-fold Vision") or outward to Satan's seat (become "Mortal & Vegetable"), depending on one's starting point. Mortal Blake passed inward to where he viewed and described Los's world "on all sides round"; immortal Ololon must, like Milton, pass the satanic polypus before she can join Blake there.

The eight lines describing Ololon's predicament are matched by eight lines that summarize its resolution:

And Ololon examined all the Couches of the Dead.
Even of Los & Enitharmon & all the Sons of Albion
And his Four Zoas terrified & on the verge of Death
In midst of these was Miltons Couch, & when they saw
    Eight
Immortal Starry-Ones, guarding the Couch in flaming
    fires
They thunderous utterd all a universal groan falling
    down
Prostrate before the Starry Eight asking with tears
    forgiveness
Confessing their crime with humiliation and sorrow.
                    (35:26–33)

Twice before Blake has used the device of paired stanzas to indicate the congruency of action and consequences, in the two eight-line verses of plate 34 in which we witness with Ololon first the female weaving of the polypus (34:24–31) and then the collapse of the male principles that caused it (34:32–39), and, more dramatically, in the Book I account of Los's descent, in which an eleven-line description of that act from fear through decision to consummation is followed immediately by the great eleven-line speech in which Los recognizes himself as "that Shadowy Prophet" and proclaims the end of history (22:4–25). In all three cases the matching stanzas define a pivot of vision, a passage through the vortex points; it is as if one might imagine oneself standing between the two stanzas and seeing in either direction the equal cones spiral out into eternity and into time.[11]

Ololon's falling down prostrate is the moral analogue of her descent. It is the act of contrition we saw briefly in Book I, seen now from the perspective of the polypus and not through the clarified fourfold vision of Blake/Milton. The change in perspective seems to be a change in the *dramatis personae*: in Book I Ololon confessed to the Divine Family, who, uniting with her, became Jesus. Here she begs forgiveness of the Starry Eight, of the Seven Angels of the Presence and the eighth, apocalyptic angel who is Milton himself, no longer dark but restored to brilliance by union with Ololon. The Divine Family and the Starry Eight are both manifesta-

---

[11] Thomas W. Herzing discusses the philosophical assumption that explains this identification of action and consequences:

> Blake does not deny causation; he postulates a more comprehensive causal theory, infinite spiritual causes operant in an infinite spiritual world. Blake is arguing that the world is infinite and, if that is true, a finite causal theory will not be satisfactory. There can be no natural cause for spiritual effects, for that would imply a total confusion of orders—as if a man were to create God or a rock were to create life.

("Book I of Blake's *Milton*: Natural Religion as an Optical Fallacy," *Blake Studies*, 6, 1 [1973], pp. 19–34, p. 32.

tions of Blake's god in his separate members; each manifestation has been completed by Milton or Ololon, who are themselves completed only by each other. There is no change in *dramatis personae* in Book II, only a clarification of the consequences of Ololon's contrition, which has united her with Milton and realized the Divine Humanity.

The "universal groan" Ololon utters at her prostration echoes the groans we have heard throughout the poem at the inception of apocalypse. It is also a kind of birth cry signaling her incarnation, for by falling down in humility she has entered the polypus: the Starry Eight rejoice in her act as a "descent thro Beulah to Los & Enitharmon" (35:36), to Golgonooza, which the previous stanza asserted she could not view without becoming mortal.

The second phase of Ololon's act, incarnation in the polypus, has begun. She is now coextensive with that proliferate horror, for she reaches "from Ulro to Eternity" (35:38). She is also coextensive with Milton; they occupy the same area and are therefore united, but they are united in their satanic as well as their Edenic portions and cannot yet recognize each other.

The first phase of Ololon's descent, which took her as far as the gates of the dead, yielded a vision of the horror of Ulro. The second phase, which carries her through those gates and into Golgonooza, liberates a vision of the providence of time and space. As we might expect by now, that vision of time and space in Golgonooza is related in paired stanzas:

There is a Moment in each Day that Satan cannot find
Nor can his Watch Fiends find it, but the Industrious find
This Moment & it multiply. & when it once is found
It renovates every Moment of the Day if rightly
        placed[.]
In this Moment Ololon descended to Los & Enitharmon
Unseen beyond the Mundane Shell Southward in Miltons
        track

Just in this Moment when the mourning odours rise
    abroad
And first from the Wilde Thyme, stands a Fountain in
    a rock
Of crystal flowing into two Streams, one flows thro
    Golgonooza
And thro Beulah to Eden beneath Los's western Wall
The other flows thro the Aerial Void & all the Churches
Meeting again in Golgonooza beyond Satans Seat. . . .

                                 (35:42–53)

This is the creative moment of the artery's pulse, the instant
between the sun's first rising and the clarions of day. In this
moment Ololon's lamentation was heard in eternity, and
"Providence began" (21:24); "In this Moment Ololon de-
scended to Los & Enitharmon." Lamentation and descent,
we see once again, are identical.

The moment is safe from Satan because it is an inspira-
tion he cannot, by definition of his state, recognize. It is
secure from his menace even as the city itself is secure, the
Golgonooza into which Los conducts fallen spirits "That
Satans Watch-Fiends touch them not" (29:50).

That moment, like the moment of the artery's pulse, is at
once minute and vast, as brief as inspiration and as long as
all time. The streams are similarly local and universal. They
arise from a single point, a single fountain, yet together they
define the limits of all reality from eternity through Ulro
and back in to Golgonooza. Their paths suggest the paths
of Blake and Milton "inward to Golgonooza" and "outward
to Satan's seat." And the streams, we learn, are also coun-
terparts of two other familiar figures who follow their
paths: the six-line stanzas on the moment and the streams,
on time and space, are followed by two seven-line stanzas
on lark and thyme (35:56–67).[12] "The Wild Thyme is Los's

[12] In the engraving, line 67 is at the very bottom of plate 35 and
the text of plate 36 begins at the very top, with no intervening
design or punctuation, so it is possible that this second pair is not a

Messenger to Eden," and "The Lark is Los's Messenger thro
the Twenty-seven Churches" (35:54 and 63). As the two
streams meet in Golgonooza, as Milton and Blake meet
there (for they are transported there in the instant of their
merger), so do thyme and lark: the flower covers the Rock
of Odours "Beside the Fount above the Larks nest in Gol-
gonooza" (35:58); each emissary, leaving Los's city with his
message, will return there to herald the end of time.

Like the three pairs of stanzas that define the pivot of a
visionary act, *Milton*'s four pairs of stanzas on time and
space (the principal pair in Book I, 28:44–29:26, and
35:42–53) or lark and thyme (the principal Book II pair,
31:28–63, and 35:54–67) all underscore the parallelism of
the contraries they comprehend. But parallelism in this
poem, structural or thematic, is more than merely an equal-
ity of opposing forces—it is a mutuality of those forces, a
progressive opposition whose synthesis is apocalypse. Ac-
cordingly, the congruency of the passages on time and
space or act and consequences indicates more than their
equality; it suggests their identity, their consolidation as
well. Time and space may reflect the contention of active
male and passive female, the lark and thyme may go in dif-
ferent directions, eternity and time may conflict and an act
may be reversed by its consequences—but time and space,
lark and thyme, eternity and time/space, act and conse-
quences still operate mutually for the salvation of humanity
from satanic opacity. Significantly, five of the seven pairs of
stanzas in *Milton* occur in Book II, where they act as a kind
of echo, an almost subliminal substantiation of the consoli-
dating unity of opposites that is the action of the book.

The twenty-seven churches the lark penetrates are the
states of creation through which individual identities pass,

---

pair, that the second seven-line unit is actually part of a nineteen-
line unit broken only accidentally at seven. Still, 35:61–67 seems
thematically and rhetorically unitary; like the preceding seven-line
passage it begins and ends with a spatial identification that circum-
scribes its mythical content.

the twenty-seven periods of fallen history. They culminate, according to the angels, in the twenty-eighth state, Milton, "Eternal Annihilation" (32:25–28). The lark sends his message through them in a system of relays, one lark per "church," until the circuit is accomplished and the last lark reaches Golgonooza again. The relay of the larks is the passage of inspiration from poet to poet throughout the generations: each generation has produced prophets as well as tyrants. We saw in Book I the end of the relay, as Milton, the lark of the previous generation, passed into Blake and Los joined with them, transporting them to Golgonooza. Now we see it end again in the very different context of Book II: "the Twenty-eighth bright / Lark met the Female Ololon descending into my Garden" (3:9–10). Consolidation of male with male or male with female, Golgonooza or Felpham—Milton's descent, his second coming, is its consummation. He is the twenty-eighth state and the twenty-eighth lark, the signal of apocalypse.

The lark could meet Ololon, "For Ololon step'd into the Polypus within the Mundane Shell" (36:13). As Milton's incarnation brought him to Blake, so does Ololon's: "as the / Flash of lightning but more quick the Virgin in my Garden / Before my Cottage stood" (36:18–20). She seems in her descent a flash of lightning, as Milton seemed a falling star, "swift as lightning" (15:18), in his: the parallel suggests the identity of their passages to Blake.

The garden in which Ololon appears is the tangible portion of Golgonooza; it is where Blake's mortal part was carried when his imagination entered the city of art:

> For when Los joind with me he took me in his firy
> whirlwind
> My Vegetated portion was hurried from Lambeths
> shades
> He set me down in Felphams Vale & prepard a beautiful
> Cottage for me that in three years I might write all
> these Visions. . . .
>
> (36:21–24)

The seat of imagination is not just a miraculous construction of ineffable wonder, but the place where any person receives inspiration. A humble cottage is a vast and splendid city when one knows vision there, just as this earth of vegetation is one infinite plane to the mind which sees that "Satanic Space is a delusion" (36:20), that nature is but one small aspect of eternity. To see only nature, only Felpham, is to miss eternity and overlook Golgonooza. Blake sees both realms, and presents both, in the grand visions of Book I and in the humbler dimensions of Book II through which they operate.

Milton's merger with Blake caused both poets to see the immortal's emanation in the deeps. Ololon's appearance to Blake causes him for the first time to think of his own wife, who, though not wailing in the abyss, is yet "sick with fatigue" within their cottage (36:31–32). He invites Ololon to join her, suggesting a consolidation of the feminine forms which corresponds to the consolidation of masculine forms in Book I. That Ololon does not enter the cottage does not, as we shall see, impair the consolidation, for by the end of the poem Catherine Blake will have appeared beside her husband in the garden. Meanwhile, Ololon has more urgent business. Her incarnation complete, she seeks the third phase, the consummation, of her action.

The third phase of the action of Book II is presented cinematically in a complicated system of close-up focuses on all aspects of the action, aspects we have seen before, but never in such intimate detail. All the elements of the act of purgation are gathered into this great climax in Blake's garden, this marriage of repentance and forgiveness.

Ololon asks immediately for Milton, speaking familiarly to Blake because she appears as a Daughter of Beulah, the muse of his vision:

The Virgin answerd. Knowest thou of Milton who descended
Driven from Eternity; him I seek! terrified at my Act
In Great Eternity which thou knowest! I come him to seek

When on the highest lift of his light pinions he arrives
At that bright Gate. another Lark meets him & back to back
They touch their pinions tip tip: and each descend
To their respective Earths & there all night consult with Angels
Of Providence & with the Eyes of God all night in slumbers
Inspired: & at the dawn of day send out another Lark
Into another Heaven to carry news upon his wings
Thus are the Messengers dispatchd till they reach the Earth again
In the East Gate of Golgonooza, & the Twenty-eighth bright
Lark. met the Female Ololon descending into my Garden
Thus it appears to Mortal eyes & those of the Ulro Heavens
But not thus to Immortals. the Lark is a mighty Angel.

For Ololon step'd into the Polypus within the Mundane Shell
They could not step into Vegetable Worlds without becoming
The enemies of Humanity except in a Female Form
And as One Female. Ololon and all its mighty Hosts
Appeard: a Virgin of twelve years nor time nor space was
To the perception of the Virgin Ololon but as the
Flash of lightning but more quick the Virgin in my Garden
Before my Cottage stood for the Satanic Space is delusion

For when Los joind with me he took me in his firy whirlwind
My Vegetated portion was hurried from Lambeths shades
He set me down in Felphams Vale & prepard a beautiful
Cottage for me that in three years I might write all these
Visions
To display Natures cruel holiness: the deceits of Natural
Religion
Walking in my Cottage Garden, sudden I beheld
The Virgin Ololon & addressd her as a Daughter of Beulah

Virgin of Providence fear not to enter into my Cottage
What is thy message to thy friend: what am I now to do
Is it again to plunge into deeper affliction? behold me
Ready to obey, but pity thou my Shadow of Delight
Enter my Cottage, comfort her, for she is sick with fatigue

5. Plate 40 ("Blake's Cottage at Felpham")

So Ololon utterd in words distinct the anxious thought
Mild was the voice, but more distinct than any earthly
That Miltons Shadow heard & condensing all his Fibres
Into a strength impregnable of majesty & beauty infinite
I saw he was the Covering Cherub & within him Satan
And Raha[b] . . .

Descending down into my Garden, a Human Wonder of
    God
Reaching from heaven to earth a Cloud & Human Form
I beheld Milton with astonishment & in him beheld
The Monstrous Churches of Beulah, the Gods of Ulro
    dark
Twelve monstrous dishumanizd terrors Synagogues of
    Satan.

(37 : 1–9, 13–17)

The act in Eden which terrifies Ololon is her having driven
Milton into Ulro—the very act Rahab and her sirens have
been attempting throughout the poem. Rahab, however,
seeks to trap him there in slavery to her false power, to
vegetate him, and he merely ignores her enticements.
Ololon has awakened him to the falseness of his own posi-
tion in eternity, and his descent to her is liberation. She
does not seduce him, she merely seeks him out. Because she
seeks, she finds: that she asks her question provides its an-
swer. Her voice is the voice of eternity, the voice of inspira-
tion;[13] Milton recognizes it and appears, descending into
Blake's garden in what is his material form, the horrible
shadow that is his spectre.

Milton's descent came before Ololon's, but hers is com-
pleted first. Milton descended to find her, and she is waiting
for him when he arrives—although it was his descent that
precipitated hers. This teasing paradox frames the action

---

[13] It is that voice of more than mortal clarity which can be heard
but not reproduced by generated men, "for the Nerves of the
Tongue are closed" (29:40).

of the poem. It is neither idle nor perverse, but deliberately devised to indicate both the necessarily paradoxical nature of any human conflict and any human marriage, and the elastic properties of the moment of the artery's pulse. We can explain it partially by recalling that it was the Ulro form of his emanation, Rahab/Tirzah, that Milton descended to redeem, and that his act of mercy is rewarded by the presence of the eternal form Ololon at the end of the journey. But Rahab and Ololon are not truly separate entities, but rather distinguishable aspects of the same being. And Ololon in eternity is called "those who Milton drove / Down into Ulro" (21:16–17); whichever aspect of her is responsible for the deed, it is that aspect called Ololon that is called to account for it. The paradox remains, for it is the paradox of vortical perception.

The terrifying appearance of Milton is the very first image the fallen world had of him in Book I: "Onwards his Shadow kept its course among the Spectres; call'd / Satan" (15:17–18). We are witnessing that very descent again, from the new perspective of Blake's Felpham garden. Originally, watching him fall from our Edenic perspective of early Book I, we knew him "guarded within" (15:20) by the Seven Angels of the Presence; now, in the very different light of Generation, we see him guarded within by Satan and Rahab. Even Blake's own perspective is altered here, an alteration that defines the conflicts of generated life. His garden is the embodiment of Golgonooza, but it is that only in the moment of vision; otherwise it is as likely to be the embodiment of Udan-Adan. When Milton descended to him in Book I, Blake stood in Udan-Adan and was by the descent translated into Golgonooza; here in his garden Blake has suffered still the confusions of Udan-Adan, as his anguished questions to Ololon make clear: "What am I now to do / Is it to plunge into deeper affliction?" (36:29–30). He is only now, as Milton and Ololon appear to him, attaining that illumination which transforms confusion into vision. In the mythic dimensions of Book I he stood in the lake of illusion and saw Milton "as a falling star" (15:47); here in his more personal, more urgent confusions he has a more personal, more urgent perception of him. There was no time for him to fear in Book I, but the close-up focus of Book II makes all the terrors of Milton's shadow apparent. For anyone standing in Generation, for Blake or for us who observe him, a vision of eternity is first a vision of the horrors of time.

Ololon's appearance in his garden has conjured for Blake a terrific vision of Milton's shadow, which is the Mundane Shell. When Milton came to him in Book I, Blake saw the vegetable world "as a bright sandal formd immortal of precious stones & gold" (21:13). But that was a Blake who lived in Udan-Adan and could stride forward through eternity—a mythic representation of the Blake we see now standing in a real garden in a real vale. This man cannot bear the world on his foot; he cannot overlook its darknesses and perversions, for he lives among them. The vegetable world is both satanic shadow and jeweled sandal; the shadow must be annihilated before the sandal may be worn into eternity. In order that it may be annihilated, Blake exposes it in nearly a plate of pounding, sonorous poetry, a concentration, according to Bloom, of "most of his negative symbols in a powerful catalogue of dread."[14] He names the twelve synagogues of Satan which are the demonic forms of Los's twelve sons, and the twenty-seven heavens of the Mundane Shell, with all the exotic suggestiveness of John Milton's own catalogues in *Paradise Lost* or the *Nativity Ode*.[15]

The catalogue of spectrous horrors is not a digression from the union of Milton and Ololon, but an explanation of it:

[14] Commentary, p. 840.
[15] For a full account of these gods and churches see Damon, pp. 426–427, and Bloom, Commentary, p. 841.

The Heavens are the Cherub, the Twelve Gods are Satan
And the Forty-eight Starry Regions are Cities of the
  Levites
The Heads of the Great Polypus, Four-fold twelve
  enormity
In mighty & mysterious comingling enemy with enemy
Woven by Urizen into Sexes from his mantle of years[.]

(37:60-38:4)

The sexual division that Milton and Ololon have descended
to reverse is, like Satan's division into nations and families,
a corruption of the genuine identities and communities of
fallen humanity. Sexual division is more pernicious than
Satan's false categories because it antedates them, as
Urizen's generation antedates Satan's, and in fact even
causes them. As Leutha confessed, "emanation," the separa-
tion of female from male, was the source of Satan's own fall
(as, we may infer from other Blake prophecies, it was the
source of Luvah's and of Albion's before him). We prob-
ably ought to remind ourselves at this point that "female"
is not a biological term with Blake, that it does not mean
"woman" but rather a kind of spiritual analogue of woman-
ness; we all have emanations, whatever our gender. The
female portion in each of us is that which can emanate from
us, our emotions and our desires and our products. What
Blake means by sexual division is not that the world is made
up of girls and boys, but that each of us is by the conditions
of our existence separated from what would, in Edenic real-
ity, motivate and delight us from within. Ololon is not Mil-
ton's estranged wife; she is part of his own soul. "Marriage"
is a metaphor. We shall pursue its implications further in
the next chapter.

Urizen authored sexual division, and thus Milton's seek-
ing reunion with his emanation has been all along, as we
have surmised with no explicit proof, a feature of his strug-
gle with Urizen. Both aspects of that struggle, annihilation

of the spectre and reunion with the emanation, are to be resolved in this final section of the action of Book II.

With that knowledge our perspective on Milton shifts:

And Milton collecting all his fibres into impregnable
    strength
Descended down a Paved work of all kinds of precious
    stones
Out from the eastern sky; descending down into my
    Cottage
Garden: clothed in black, severe & silent he descended.

                                               (38:5–8)

These lines echo the description of the descent a plate earlier ("That Miltons Shadow heard & condensing all his Fibres / Into a strength impregnable . . ."), when all we could see of the "Cloud & Human Form" was the cloud. Now we see the human being, and the echo assures us they are the same. Looking closer at the spectre we see the man within, "clothed in black, severe & silent." The black garb is Milton's Puritanism, the black cloud that "redounding spread over Europe" at his union with Blake (15:50), his shadow itself as it might appear around this now incarnate man. It is also the "robe of the promise" he took off as he entered into Albion's bosom (14:13), which clarifies the exact timing of his appearance now in Blake's garden: it is simultaneous with his original decision, but yet it is a kind of slow-motion close-up of that act, which was completed in Book I but will not be complete in Book II until the dark garments of the promise are annihilated.

If Milton is silent, his adversary is certainly not. He thunders desperately at Milton, "not daring to touch one fibre" but yet anxiously trying to frighten him off. He is a "mighty Demon / Gorgeous and beautiful" (38:11–12), but yet he is an empty, even pathetic figure. Blake, who is one with Milton, is also one with his spectre:

I also stood in Satans bosom & beheld its desolations!
A ruind Man: a ruind building of God not made with
    hands;
Its plains of burning sand, its mountains of marble
    terrible:
Its pits & declivities flowing with molten ore & fountains
Of pitch & nitre: its ruind palaces & cities & mighty
    works. . . .

(38:15–19)

The way to annihilate a spectre is to enter it and renovate
it. Blake's "I also stood in Satans bosom" echoes Milton's "I
in my Selfhood am that Satan": each poet has recognized
his satanic portion and has thus begun its recreation. Milton
descended to release his selfhood from hell; Blake makes
that possible now by quieting hatred and fear, by arousing
even a measure of pity for this "ruind Man." Satan is still,
to be sure, pernicious; he succors Babylon and holds Jeru-
salem prisoner. But his glory and his strength have deserted
him and left him who was brilliant and beautiful a black-
ened wreck. Perceived from without Satan threatens; per-
ceived from within his own dark bosom he suffers and
fades. To know that is to end fear-wrought allegiance to the
Mundane Shell. Blake's recognition is echoed by Milton:

Satan! my Spectre! I know my power thee to annihilate
And be a greater in thy place, & be thy Tabernacle
A covering for thee to do thy will, till one greater
    comes
And smites me as I smote thee & becomes my covering.
Such are the Laws of thy false Heavens! but Laws of
    Eternity
Are not such: know thou: I come to Self Annihilation
Such are the Laws of Eternity that each shall mutually
Annihilate himself for others good, as I for thee[.]
Thy purpose & the purpose of thy Priests & of thy
    Churches

Is to impress on men the fear of death; to teach
Trembling & fear, terror, constriction; abject selfishness
Mine is to teach Men to despise death & to go on
In fearless majesty annihilating Self, laughing to scorn
Thy Laws & terrors, shaking down thy Synagogues as
    webs. . . .

                               (38:29–42)

Milton will not fear the "ruind Man," will not in fear seek
battle and destruction, will not perpetuate the cycle of fear
represented so disastrously by Orc and the Shadowy Fe-
male. The temptation to conquer the feared in order to be
feared is the temptation, devised for Milton by the children
of Rahab and Tirzah, to become "King / Of Canaan and
reign in Hazor where the Twelve Tribes meet" (20:5–6).
He is as adamant in rejecting it now as he was in Book I. He
will not be the Covering Cherub obscuring Satan's evil,
"The Spectre of Albion in which the Spectre of Luvah in-
habits" (37:45). He will annihilate not Satan but himself.
In destroying what can be destroyed in his own being, he
will necessarily destroy satanic falsehood. In being unafraid
of that destruction he will expose the folly of the satanic
priests who rule by fear of death; exposing them will expose
the falseness of their god, who thus will cease to be a god.
All of this he will accomplish not in battle but in sacrifice.

    Milton the Reprobate prophet is also Milton the Re-
deemed creator. Wrath was the constructive mode of Book
I; it burned away falsehood. Pity is the constructive mode
of Book II; it re-creates truth. The consolidated Reprobate
male forms of Book I have been tempered by Ololon's sweet
love. Wrath is no longer left to wrath and pity to pity; the
two are joined together in the book of the Daughter of
Beulah, the "place where Contrarieties are equally True"
(30:1). There was, of course, evidence of the mutuality of
Reprobate and Redeemed in Book I. As Eve Teitelbaum
notes, "Palamabron and Rintrah . . . always appear together

with only the disastrous exception told by the Bard."[16] Los himself, who in the Bard's Song condemned pity and ordered Satan to "leave me to my wrath" (4:14), gives over that wrath in the body of Book I and demands an end to jealousy and war. His sons recognize the existence of both Reprobate and Redeemed in him, although they are incapable yet of understanding the mutuality of the principles; they think their father vacillates, "that wrath now swayd and now pity absorbd him" (24:46). That mutuality is only suggested in the book of the hammer. It is fully realized in the book of the loom by Milton's prophetic vision and wise restraint.

Milton has broken the chain of jealousy. Satan responds with the same kind of bluster that was his downfall in the Bard's Song: all will bow before him "Till All Things become One Great Satan, in Holiness / Oppos'd to Mercy, and the Divine Delusion Jesus be no more" (39:1–2). Satan proclaims the triumph of the polypus over creation, of Ulro over Eden. The results of his bluster are as catastrophic to him now as they were in Palamabron's tent: the "Delusion" appears in the garden, and Satan is again caught defending a lie:

> Suddenly around Milton on my Path, the Starry Seven
> Burnd terrible! my Path became a solid fire, as bright
> As the clear Sun & Milton silent came down on my Path.
> And there went forth from the Starry limbs of the Seven:
>   Forms
> Human; with Trumpets innumerable, sounding articulate
> As the Seven spake; and they stood in a mighty
>   Column of Fire
> Surrounding Felphams Vale, reaching to the Mundane
>   Shell, Saying

[16] "Form as Meaning in Blake's *Milton*," *Blake Studies*, II, 1 (1969). p. 45.

Awake Albion awake! reclaim thy Reasoning Spectre.
Subdue
Him to the Divine Mercy, Cast him down into the Lake
Of Los, that ever burneth with fire, ever & ever
Amen!
Let the Four Zoa's awake from Slumbers of Six Thousand
Years. . . .

(39:3-13)

In the inevitable pattern defined in the vortex passage, the Seven Angels appear first as "a solid fire, as bright / As the clear Sun," and then, when the beholder's perspective clears, as Forms Human. They speak as a friend benevolent, bidding Albion arise. Their appearance in a column of fire is the consummation of Milton's appearance as a comet, Ololon's as a flash of lightning; Satan, on the other hand, has come with his own trumpets and fire flashes, but in a dismal cloud (38:13 and 50, 39:23). Their light will disperse that cloud as Los dispersed the storms about his face in Book I (23:31). For their presence sets the instant of the poem, which is the instant of the raising of the Zoas, the instant before apocalypse.

The words of the angels shatter Satan's lie, and he is reduced to hungering vainly for his own flesh. He thrashes in despair, "not daring to touch one fibre" (38:14) of the body he bears within him, because it is Milton's and thus his own. He will not defy death as Milton has done; he fears annihilation. He has become the Satan of *Paradise Lost* at his most pathetic, the vain opposite of God fighting a hopeless battle for supremacy, the "adversary" whose very adversity is God's gracious gift: he is "So permitted / (lest he should fall apart in his Eternal Death) to imitate / The Eternal Great Humanity Divine" (39:25-27).

Satan thus stalemated, Albion tries to heed the angels' call. He rises on his couch, "his face . . . toward / The east, toward Jerusalems Gates" (39:33-34). Like Los, who turned eastward and reversed Urizen's westward dance (26:18), Albion looks toward Jerusalem, in the direction from which Milton approaches with the Angels of the Presence. Los descended to Blake "to walk forward thro' Eternity" (22:5); now Albion strives to rise, "to walk into the Deep" (39:50), his fallen domain. He would enter into Generation, as Milton entered the Mundane Shell, to be rid of it. But it is not time yet for resurrection. Only the "Starry Seven" have called to him to rise, for Milton, the eighth angel, is at this instant still engaged in conflict; the Four Zoas are not themselves reunited, for Urizen/Satan is still rebellious; Albion's emanation Jerusalem is still in bondage.

When Milton entered Generation through his bosom, "Albions sleeping Humanity began to turn upon his Couch" (20:25). Later Rintrah and Palamabron described that turn: "Albion turns upon his Couch / He listens to the sounds of War, astonishd & confounded: / He weeps into the Atlantic deep, yet still in dismal dreams / Unawakend!" (23:7–10). Now, as Milton enters Blake's garden (which is mortal Blake's perspective on that descent through Albion's bosom), we see that same turn in detailed geographical symbolism. Albion turns throughout all England, his fallen body. Instead of weeping westward into the Atlantic, he faces toward Jerusalem. His left foot moves from its center at London, that he may stride forward, but he is not yet strong enough: "He strove to rise to walk into the Deep. but strength failing / Forbad & down with dreadful groans he sunk upon his Couch / In moony Beulah. Los his strong Guard walks round beneath the Moon" (39:50–52). Albion has been identified with Los in his position and in his attempt to stride forward, because he has been touched by inspiration. And although that inspiration has not yet saved him, its personification guards him and waits. Apocalypse is not achieved, but it approaches.

The groans of Albion are the weeping that Rintrah and Palamabron heard, the groans of all reality we have noted so many times throughout the poem, at Los's altering the poles of the world, at the Bard's prophecy, at Milton's descent, at Orc's battle with his consort, at the entry of Los/Blake/Milton into Golgonooza, at Ololon's repentance and descent, at the forges and wine-presses of Golgonooza; they are the thunderings of Satan. These groans are one of the principal motifs by which Blake indicates the simultaneity of the events of *Milton*, but I must stress that the repetition of motifs does not by itself substantiate the stimulaneity. Other authors use motifs to indicate not simultaneity but similarity. What distinguishes Blake's use of motifs like the groans is not their repetition, nor even their universality, but the particular references that accompany key repetitions to the instant of their occurrence. The groans occur throughout reality at the end of the millennium.

The paradigmatic "loud solemn universal groan" is uttered in the Bard's Song (13:37) after judgment is passed against Rintrah but before Leutha repents and confesses—that is, after the call to judgment but before the judgment is realized. The groan is precipitated by Los's altering the poles of the world and Satan's entering into the abyss—by earthquakes and incarnation. It occurs as the Day of Mourning, the millennium of Los's realm, is about to end.

The "great murmuring in the Heavens of Albion" that greets the Bard's Song is reflected in the trembling of Albion, which shakes "the roots & fast foundations of the Earth in doubtfulness" (14:4–8): the earthquakes that mark the end of the day of Los mark the end of Albion's deathly sleep as well. The trembling of Albion is described, as we have seen, three more times throughout the poem, when Milton enters Albion's bosom, when he enters Golgonooza, and when he enters Blake's garden. The tremblings are described in increasingly greater detail: first a quake, then the start of a turn, then a turn, then an attempt to rise. Unless we are to believe that Albion turns—or tries to—four times during the poem, a belief for which there is no thematic or rhetorical evidence and no rational support, we must recognize that those turnings of Albion with their quakes and their groans are not a sequence of similar events but a series of clarifications throughout the poem of a single event, the reviving of Albion on his deathcouch, the resurrection of humanity which precedes Judgment even as the incarnation of Satan preceded his full judgment in the Bard's Song. That Albion's trembling or turn is described as simultaneous with four different events of the poem, the Bard's entering Milton's bosom, Milton's descent, the entry into Golgonooza, and the union in the garden, indicates that those events themselves are simultaneous.

The Bard's Song ends with a prophecy: the six thousand years ordained for fallen history have passed, and the Lamb has been born and crucified; the seventh thousand years has nearly passed. It will end at the Second Coming, the reappearance of the Saviour which will re-form the Elect:

> And the Elect shall say to the Redeemd. We behold it
> is of Divine
> Mercy alone! of Free Gift and Election that we live.
> Our Virtues & Cruel Goodnesses, have deserv'd Eternal
> Death.
> Thus they weep upon the fatal Brook of Albions River.
>
> (13:32–35)

Thus the Bard prophesies directly the climactic action of the body of Book II. The events of his Song will be resolved in the very action that resolves the conflicts of Book I, Redeemed Milton's re-forming Elect Urizen of red clay on the banks of the Arnon.

The millennium does not end in the Bard's Song; Los has removed his left sandal to signal the Day of Mourning, but he will not tie it on again until he joins with Blake in binding on the bright sandal of vegetable reality which appeared on Blake's left foot at his union with Milton. Thus although the millennium of the realm of Los begins before that of the realm of fallen Albion, both periods end simultaneously. The quakes and groans that greet the incarnation

of Satan and precede his full judgment occur before fallen
history is even established; they are prophetic of the quakes
and groans that greet the resurrection of Albion and the in-
ception of his Judgment, even as the Bard's Song itself is
prophetic of the actions of the body of Book I. The groans
of the Assembly occur near the end of the Day of Mourn-
ing, which is Satan's day of judgment; the groans that ac-
company Albion's turn occur near the end of the seventh
thousand-year "day" of reality; they accompany the resur-
rection of fallen humanity as it rises from death to face its
Last Judgment. They begin as the Bard ends his prophecy
and enters into Milton; their last note will be heard when
Rahab divides from Ololon and, shrieking in the female
concomitant of Satan's thundering, leaves her joined with
Milton in divine humanity.

Reality groans on all its levels because its false order is
about to be annihilated. Already that annihilation is begin-
ning to be felt:

> Urizen faints in terror striving among the Brooks of
>   Arnon
> With Miltons Spirit: as the Plowman or Artificer or
>   Shepherd
> While in the labours of his Calling sends his Thoughts
>   abroad
> To labour in the ocean or in the starry heaven. So Milton
> Labourd in Chasms of the Mundane Shell, tho here
>   before
> My Cottage midst the Starry Seven, where the Virgin
>   Ololon
> Stood trembling in the Porch: loud Satan thunder'd on
>   the stormy Sea
> Circling Albions Cliffs in which the Four-fold World
>   resides
> Tho seen in fallacy outside: a fallacy of Satans
>   Churches. . . .
>   (39:53–61)

As Satan fainted before the artillery of Palamabron and Elynittria in the Bard's Song, so Urizen faints on the Arnon before Milton's creative power. The passage begins and ends with the generations of Urizen, with Urizen himself fainting in terror and with his second-generation counterpart howling furiously: each is Milton's adversary, and neither can defeat him, the one because he faints before him and the other because he dares not touch him. In a decorum so subtle Blake himself was probably unaware of it, these references to Milton's adversary frame lines about Milton just as the shadowy Satan surrounds Milton's body.

The passage is yet another clarification of spatial perspective. Milton battles two generations of his adversary in two separate regions of the universe because, having passed through the vortex, he exists in multiple dimensions. Blake originally explained this unsettling principle by a simile of unconsciousness:

> As when a man dreams, he reflects not that his body
>   sleeps,
> Else he would wake; so seem'd he entering his Shadow:
>   but
> With him the Spirits of the Seven Angels of the Presence
> Entering; they gave him still perceptions of his
>   Sleeping Body;
> Which now arose and walk'd with them in Eden. . . .
>   (15:1-5)

His simile is now not of dreaming, but of conscious imagining: "as the Plowman or Artificer or Shepherd / While in the labours of his Calling sends his Thoughts abroad. . . ." In Book II Milton has full command of the multiple vision granted him in Book I. A further contrast between these passages of clarification is also suggestive: in Book I, Milton had a dual awareness of himself in Ulro and Eden; in Book II, the two levels on which he perceives himself are Ulro and Generation. Such is the progress of *Milton*, which has moved from the grand mythic environment of Book I through the milder and more natural milieu of Beulah to the fallen human reality of Blake's garden at Felpham.

Urizen's faint is only a partial resolution of the conflict, a temporary victory, but it releases Milton to face Ololon. Finally he is able, in this close-up examination of the action, to recognize "the Eternal Form / Of that mild Vision" (40:1-2). This is the necessary complement of his recognition upon entering Blake's foot in Book I "that the Three Heavens of Beulah were beheld / By him on earth in his bright pilgrimage of sixty years" (15:51-52). Now he can perceive the Edenic Ololon as well as the mild Daughter of Beulah. In that perception is their union.

Ololon, too, experiences an expansion of an earlier recognition. She repents in Blake's garden, as she repented in Eden and before the couches of the dead, her failure with Milton. Now, however, she knows that failure in all the intimate details of its historical implications:

Are those who contemn Religion & seek to annihilate it
Become in their Femin[in]e portions the causes &
    promoters
Of these Religions, how is this thing? this Newtonian
    Phantasm
This Voltaire & Rousseau: this Hume & Gibbon &
    Bolingbroke
This Natural Religion! this impossible absurdity
Is Ololon the cause of this? O where shall I hide my face
These tears fall for the little-ones: the Children of
    Jerusalem
Lest they be annihilated in thy annihilation.

                                        (40:9-16)

Her question is ever the same: "Is Virtue a Punisher?" "Have I caused this?" But its context has shifted several times since she first asked it in Book I. There it was concerned mostly with Milton himself: "Has the morality I have held been destructive? Have I caused Milton so much anguish?" Then in Book II, when Ololon stood before the polypus, she saw the gross destructiveness of that morality in the natural universe, and asked how the truths of eternity could be so perverted; her answer again was her own guilt, this time in the person of her demonic manifestation Rahab/ Tirzah (34:49–35:17). By the time she confronts Milton directly, however, the subject of her questioning is neither her personal guilt toward him nor her generalized guilt toward the vegetated universe, but rather the specific effects of her guilt on fallen human history. Her concern has shifted from the anguish she has caused immortal Milton in forcing him to Ulro, to the anguish she has caused all mortal beings by promulgating false religion. As she is Milton's emanation and thus represents his work and ideals, her contrite recognition underscores Blake's chief complaint against Milton in this poem: through his work, Milton has encouraged a natural religion he never intended to encourage. The fault lies, as Rintrah and Palamabron cried, with Milton's religion (22:39), and with the poetry that embodied it; for it did declare virtue a punisher, "Heaven as a Punisher & Hell as One under Punishment" (22:52), and in so declaring it provoked the negations of Voltaire and Rousseau.

As Ololon speaks she weeps, in the lamentation that has accompanied her contrition in its every manifestation, in Eden, in Ulro, and here now in Blake's garden. She has wept before at her error and its consequences, and her tears have seemed as much the result of fear as of repentance; but now she affirms that, "These tears fall for the little-ones: the Children of Jerusalem / Lest they be annihilated in thy annihilation." This declaration sets her apart from the Shadowy Female, the sum of Rahab/Tirzah, who feared only that she herself would be consumed in Orc's consummation (18:25, 28). Ololon is no longer part of Rahab's jealous holiness:

No sooner had she spoke but Rahab Babylon appeard
Eastward upon the Paved work across Europe & Asia
Glorious as the midday Sun in Satans bosom glowing
A Female hidden in a Male, Religion hidden in War
Namd Moral Virtue; cruel two-fold Monster shining
    bright
A Dragon red & hidden Harlot which John in Patmos
    saw. . . .

(40: 17–22)

Ololon's words crystallize her demonic portion within
Satan, completing the consolidation of error in the poem.
That consolidation is the necessary step before annihilation,
for only what can be perceived can be altered. Satan is
opacity; illumination must annihilate him. The appearance
of Rahab within Satan graphically identifies him who rules
and is the Mundane Shell of eternal death with the hideous
hermaphroditic shadow into which Milton entered. Ololon's
courageous confession finally has, like Leutha's in the Bard's
Song, defined Satan and the perils of his class. But Leutha,
her confession made, bore Rahab and Tirzah and Death;
Ololon's confession will reverse that dread course, will an-
nihilate the progeny of sin.

As Albion turned toward Jerusalem, Milton turns now to-
ward his emanation:

But turning toward Ololon in terrible majesty Milton
Replied. Obey thou the Words of the Inspired Man
All that can be annihilated must be annihilated
That the Children of Jerusalem may be saved from
    slavery
There is a Negation, & there is a Contrary
The Negation must be destroyd to redeem the
    Contraries
The Negation is the Spectre; the Reasoning Power in
    Man
This is a false Body; an Incrustation over my Immortal

Spirit; a Selfhood, which must be put off & annihilated
    alway
To cleanse the Face of my Spirit by Self-examination.

To bathe in the Waters of Life; to wash off the Not
    Human
I come in Self-annihilation & the grandeur of Inspiration
To cast off Rational Demonstration by Faith in the
    Saviour
To cast off the rotten rags of Memory by Inspiration
To cast off Bacon, Locke & Newton from Albions
    covering
To take off his filthy garments, & clothe him with
    Imagination
To cast aside from Poetry, all that is not Inspiration
That it no longer shall dare to mock with the aspersion
    of Madness
Cast on the Inspired, by the tame high finisher of
    paltry Blots,
Indefinite, or paltry Rhymes; or paltry Harmonies.
Who creeps into State Government like a catterpiller
    to destroy
To cast off the idiot Questioner who is always
    questioning,
But never capable of answering; who sits with a sly grin
Silent plotting when to question, like a thief in a cave;
Who publishes doubt & calls it knowledge; whose
    Science is Despair,
Whose pretence to knowledge is Envy, whose whole
    Science is
To destroy the wisdom of ages to gratify ravenous Envy;
That rages round him like a Wolf day & night without
    rest
He smiles with condescension; he talks of Benevolence &
    Virtue
And those who act with Benevolence & Virtue, they
    murder time on time

These are the destroyers of Jerusalem, these are the
    murderers
Of Jesus, who deny the Faith & mock at Eternal Life!
Who pretend to Poetry that they may destroy
    Imagination;
By imitation of Natures Images drawn from
    Remembrance
These are the Sexual Garments, the Abomination of
    Desolation
Hiding the Human Lineaments as with an Ark & Curtains
Which Jesus rent: & now shall wholly purge away with
    Fire
Till Generation is swallowed up in Regeneration.

                    (40:28–41:28)

Into this last speech of Milton are channeled most of the
major themes and images of the poem: the garments that
either protect truth or conceal it; "ravenous Envy" howling
round the idiot questioner like the Covering Cherub
around Satan, "The Spectre of Albion in which the Spectre
of Luvah inhabits" (37:45), Milton's shadow howling vainly
around Milton's flesh; the murderer virtue, who is Satan in
the Bard's Song or the punisher of Ololon's question; the
fire of Jesus, which is the illuminating flame in which the
Seven Angels appear on Blake's path. They have gathered
throughout the poem, slowly and erratically but yet inevita-
bly moving into the clear focus of Milton's fullest vision—
and our own.

The passionate conviction of Milton's voice has the
urgency of the Bard's "Mark well my words . . . ," but neith-
er the Bard's anger and fearfulness nor his parabolic and
disjointed expression. The line from bardic through vision-
ary and lyric has led to a new kind of bardic eloquence, as-
sured, precise, unequivocal, and profoundly personal. That
new assurance makes this final speech of Milton a kind of
revision of his first speech. In Book I the poet was resolute,
to be sure, but his speech was filled with questions: "O

when Lord Jesus wilt thou come?" "What do I here before
the Judgment? without my Emanation? / With the Daugh-
ters of Memory, & not with the Daughters of Inspiration[?]"
(14:18, 28–29). Now he has learned the answers: Jesus will
come when "Generation is swallowd up in Regeneration,"
which is the annihilation of the selfhood; descent into Gen-
eration is regeneration, is the prelude to Judgment, is the
substitution of Inspiration for Memory; Ololon could have
been here all along, had he only known to seek her here.
The paradox of the poem is that the two speeches are iden-
tical, that the second is merely the manifestation in time of
the first in eternity, that the answers are the asking of the
questions. No time has elapsed between the speeches, for
Milton entered Generation as he spoke the first and arrives
in Generation as he speaks the second. The only difference
between the two is the crucial difference of perspective
which is, after all, the only difference between time and
eternity.

Ololon has just said that she pities the children of Jeru-
salem as in Eden she pitied "This World beneath, . . . un-
natural refuge" (21:48–49). Milton's answer to her now is
couched in the commands with which Jesus answered her
then: "Obey thou the Words of the Inspired Man," he or-
ders, echoing Jesus' "Obey / The Dictate" (21:54–55). His
consolation for her is the consolation the Seven Angels of
the Presence offered him, for the Seven Angels collectively
are Jesus, and Milton speaks now with the inspiration of
Jesus. He has adopted the Angels' doctrine of states and
turned it into an active principle of life this side of the vor-
tex. Not only has he determined to destroy the negation by
self-examination, by that judging of his own self com-
manded by the Angels (32:30), but he has also learned as
they bade him learn "What is Eternal & what Changeable"
(32:31). He had complained to the angels that "The idiot
Reasoner laughs at the Man of Imagination / And from
laughter proceeds to murder by undervaluing calumny"
(32:6–7). Now he firmly vows "To cast aside from Poetry,

all that is not Inspiration / That it no longer shall dare to mock with the aspersion of Madness"; "To cast off the idiot Questioner who is always questioning, / But never capable of answering." Where once he asserted loftily, "I have turned my back on these Heavens builded on cruelty" (32:3), now he has entered willingly into them to fulfill the angels' prophecy, "And thou O Milton art a State about to be Created / Called Eternal Annihilation" (32:25–26).

Exactly what it is Milton has decided to cast off in this passage has given John Middleton Murry some difficulty:

> We are conscious of an abrupt descent in this passage. The universal message declines into a particular denunciation of schools of art which stood in Blake's way. The human excuse for him is obvious. He is retaliating on those who have dismissed him as a madman; he is probably still smarting from the intolerable condescensions of Hayley. But into Hell with Hayley goes Rembrandt also, chief of 'the tame high finishers of paltry Blots Indefinite'.[17]

Murry is the only critic I know who finds this passage a descent, who hears Milton/Blake's voice as shrill,[18] but his complaint is a useful consolidation of error. Blake's attack here is not personal; he cites "Bacon, Locke & Newton," and the unnamed Rembrandt, not as men to be discredited, but as states to be annihilated. They are the minute particulars of the hermaphroditic lure, the preachers of entrapment in time. They are named here because error must be named. Elsewhere Blake calls the error "Natures cruel holiness: the deceits of Natural Religion" (36:25); here he becomes more specific, more concrete, identifying it with its chief proponents that it may be recognized and abolished. There is no vindictiveness in this passage, even where it comes closest to

---

[17] *William Blake* (1933; rpt. New York, Toronto, London: McGraw-Hill, 1964), p. 240.
[18] *William Blake*, p. 239.

autobiography; the tame high finishers of paltry art who de-
risively prevented Blake's acceptance earn only a calm and
confident evaluation, no furious rebuttal. For Blake's con-
cern here is not his own misfortunes and his own suffering,
but the subjugation of true art by false. The anger of the
passage is not that an individual man has been betrayed, but
that art has been betrayed, that inspiration is discredited in
favor of the "imitation of Natures Images drawn from Re-
membrance." Although there is surely personal bitterness in
Blake, who suffered because of this betrayal, Milton's speech
has a far greater concern: false art is not just an affront to a
good artist, but a danger to mankind, for it is only through
true art that one may perceive eternity, and it is only
through perceiving eternity that one may enter it:

> The Last Judgment is an Overwhelming of Bad Art &
> Science. . . . Some People flatter themselves that there
> will be no Last Judgment & that Bad Art will be
> adopted & mixed with Good Art That Error or Experi-
> ment will make a Part of Truth & they Boast that it is
> its Foundation these People flatter themselves I will not
> flatter them Error is Created Truth is Eternal
> Error or Creation will be Burned Up & then & not till
> then Truth or Eternity will appear It is Burnt up the
> Moment Men cease to behold it. . . .[19]

In Book I there are many strong voices; the Bard's Song
and Blake's vision, Milton's declaration and Los's proclama-
tions, maintain a rhetorical volume of considerable inten-
sity. There is, however, no Bard in Book II; Blake when he
speaks for himself speaks, except once when he echoes Mil-
ton, wonderingly and meekly; Los issues no ultimata, and
Satan's are vainglorious rantings; Ololon's voice is soft and
hesitant, although it rises when it must to determination.
Only Milton preserves in Book II the great vigor and pro-

[19] "A Vision of the Last Judgment," p. 555.

phetic power of so much of Book I. His two spare speeches
of consecration dominate the second book. Milton alone of
all the speakers in the poem is consistent in language and tone.
The Bard's voice changes throughout his tale, and becomes
unexpectedly shrill when he is forced to defend himself;
Los pleads as well as declaring; Satan snivels and blus-
ters; Ololon vacillates; Blake's voice changes to accommo-
date his changing vision. Milton only is the same from the
beginning of the poem to its end. His even voice never fal-
ters, never stoops to argue, to defend, to cajole. He con-
vinces by his own conviction. Only once, conversing in the
second book's prologue with his "superiors," does he sound
less than perfectly inspired, and that speech is a kind of
flash-back to the instant before his momentous decision.
From his first words in the poem, from the instant of his de-
cision and descent, Milton, Blake's personification of human
greatness in courageous self-purgation, is pure and sound
and divinely whole.

Milton's speeches anchor the poem with their convic-
tion, their "terrible majesty" (40:28). And almost as power-
ful as the speeches themselves is his silence. He never
misuses his voice. He never speaks when words are unneces-
sary. It is remarkable that in this long poem which bears his
name, a poem largely dramatic, Milton speaks only four
times. In Book I he announces his descent and does not
speak again. The opponents who bar his way elicit no words
from him: his struggle with Urizen is soundless ("Silent
they met, and silent strove among the streams" [19:6]), and
he deigns no reply to the siren hermaphrodites' long plea
("Silent Milton stood" [20:7]); in the second book he enters
Blake's garden "severe & silent" (38:8). That very severity
of discipline makes the speeches he does utter the more im-
pressive. In the spareness as well as the consistent convic-
tion of his speeches Milton epitomizes the finished poet,
who does indeed "cast aside from Poetry, all that is not
Inspiration."

Milton's great declaration occasions the poem's last re-focus of perspective. Ololon asks her questions for the last time:

> Is this our Femin[in]e Portion the Six-fold Miltonic
>   Female. . . .
>   . . . are we Contraries O Milton, Thou & I
> O Immortal! how were we led to War the Wars of Death
> Is this the Void Outside of Existence, which if
>   enter'd into
> Becomes a Womb? & is this the Death Couch of Albion
> Thou goest to Eternal Death & all must go with thee
>
> So saying, the Virgin divided Six-fold & with a shriek
> Dolorous that ran thro all Creation a Double Six-fold
>   Wonder!
> Away from Ololon she divided & fled into the depths
> Of Miltons Shadow as a Dove upon the stormy Sea.
>   (41:30; 41:35–42:6)

She has always asked the same thing: "how is this wondrous thing: / This World beneath, unseen before: this refuge from the wars / Of Great Eternity!" (21:47–49); "Is Ololon the cause of this?" (40:14). In eternity she cried, "Let us descend also, and let us give / Ourselves to death" (21:45–46); now she vows, "Thou goest to Eternal Death, and all must go with thee." Ololon's final speech here in Blake's garden is, like Milton's, a reflection of the first words she spoke, and the relationship between these two speeches is the same as that between Milton's: they are identical, the last speech simply the temporal manifestation of the Edenic situation in the first. The answer to her questions is the asking of them. The only difference is perspective, and now we see fully what a crucial difference that is. For Ololon's decision in Eden was a kind of parenthetical aside, a single plate among twenty-nine other plates that dealt with other things; but here in time, her decision is the crux of the poem's whole action, the trigger of apocalypse. It is only in time that the full extent of Ololon's failure is apparent, for time is ruled and ordered by such failure. Similarly, it is in time that reversal of that failure will have its profoundest effect, for that reversal will abolish time.

This last speech of Ololon ends with her division from Rahab, even as her speech two plates earlier did. The shriek Rahab utters at their division is the last note of Ololon's lamentation; it is the same cry we have heard on all levels of reality throughout the poem, the dread of the imminent end of time. The dramatic difference between the earlier representation of the division and this one is that between the speeches Milton has turned toward Ololon. Now when Rahab divides from her, there is nothing to prevent her union with Milton. Finally we are permitted full vision of the divine marriage, a vision that has been slowly focusing throughout this section of Book II—indeed, throughout the whole poem:

> Then as a Moony Ark Ololon descended to Felphams
>   Vale
> In clouds of blood, in streams of gore, with dreadful
>   thunderings
> Into the Fires of Intellect that rejoic'd in Felphams Vale
> Around the Starry Eight: with one accord the Starry
>   Eight became
> One Man Jesus the Saviour. wonderful! round his limbs
> The Clouds of Ololon folded as a Garment dipped in
>   blood
> Written within & without in woven letters: & the Writing
> Is the Divine Revelation in the Litteral expression:
> A Garment of War, I heard it namd the Woof of Six
>   Thousand Years. . . .
>
>   (42:7–15)

Ololon's appearance fulfills the Bard's prophecy: "The Elect shall meet the Redeem'd. on Albions rocks shall they meet / Astonish'd at the Transgressor, in him beholding the Saviour" (13:30–31). So indeed the redeemer is beheld in the form of the transgressor, for Jesus appears now in this union of Ololon with Milton, whom all Generation has called Satan. The garment he wears recalls the garment of affliction woven for Milton by the Shadowy Female, with "Writings written all over it in Human Words / That every Infant that is born upon the Earth shall read / And get by rote as a hard task of a life of sixty years" (18:12–14). The difference between the garments is the difference between inspiration and dogma, between Angels of the Presence and druids in Annandale.

If earlier it seemed that Ololon entered Blake's garden without Milton, it was only because she had not yet recognized him; if Milton seemed to enter without Ololon, it was because he had not yet perceived her. But now the paradoxes of false perspectives are removed; the eternal forms are revealed in time. Ololon appears to the Starry Eight and renders them Jesus. She who descended to her husband has found him waiting for her; he has entered into the garden and found his bride waiting there. For they are and have been the same being. Ololon's bloody garments and Milton's Seven Angels are both manifestations of the Lamb of God.

Jesus and Los both proclaimed in Book I the end of the six thousand years of fallen history; now, finally, their proclamations are fulfilled. Albion's banishment from eternity is about to end. As Milton entered death through Albion's bosom, we now see Jesus who is Milton purified enter "Albions bosom, the bosom of death":

And I beheld the Twenty-four Cities of Albion
Arise upon their Thrones to Judge the Nations of the
    Earth
And the Immortal Four in whom the Twenty-four appear
    Four-fold
Arose around Albions body: Jesus wept & walked forth

From Felphams Vale clothed in Clouds of blood, to
    enter into
Albions bosom, the bosom of death & the Four sur-
    rounded him
In the Column of Fire in Felphams Vale; then to
    their mouths the Four
Applied their Four Trumpets & them sounded to the
    Four winds. . . .

                          (42:16–23)

The word "four" occurs eight times in these eight lines, with
its phonetic equivalent in "forth" reinforcing the emphasis.
It is as if the insistent repetition of the number of human
completion could erase the imperfect threes of which the
poem is built, the Three Classes of Men and the Three
Heavens of Beulah. And in effect it does, for the Starry
Eight rendered Jesus has also become the Four Zoas who
surround Albion and bid him rise again. His rising will be
the end of the sexual threefold, the end of deception and
illusion, the end of time.

    The action of Book II, and through it of the whole poem,
is now complete. Its three basic units correspond to the
three units of the action section of Book I. Ololon's resolu-
tion, incarnation, and consummation directly parallel Mil-
ton's: both figures descend from eternity, pass through the
vortex (the mode by which the polypus is perceived) to
Blake, and realize by their passage their union and the abo-
lition of time. In Book I the abolition is largely imaginative;
when Los carries Blake/Milton into Golgonooza, into the
moment of inspiration, time ceases to exist for them. In
Book II when Milton and Ololon join together and thereby
annihilate spectrous illusion, time ceases altogether for
everyone.

    The action section of each book has its own peculiar com-
plexity. In the first book Blake's focus plays among the
many different unions that comprise the basic action of the

poem. In Book II his concern is a single union, the most comprehensive one, but his focus shifts constantly among various aspects of that union. It is as if the camera of his imagination selects one of Book I's actions and spends all of Book II circling around it, using increasingly greater lens magnification until we have seen every one of its details in close-up intensity. In the Book I section each union, each phase of the action, occurs simultaneously with all the others, as if they could be superimposed; each has the same duration, which is the duration of the entire act. But in Book II, each time Blake examines the act from a new angle we see it both complete and in various stages of incompletion; that is, each perspective comprehends the act as a whole, but focuses specifically on one brief instant of it, and the sequence of those instants is progressive. Thus we see Ololon pass through the polypus into Blake's garden seeking Milton, whereupon he appears; then we see Milton's resistance of the satanic lure, and Ololon's symbolic division from Rahab; then Milton's redefinition of that resistance in terms of fallen reality, and Ololon's literalization of her division; finally the consummation implied in each of these dramatic scenes is realized in the conversion of the Starry Eight to Jesus. There is clearly a sequence here, but it is a paradoxical sequence in which any individual stage of it contains it all: Ololon's descent into the polypus is her union with Milton, for it makes them coextensive; their resistance of their satanic portions is their union, because those annihilable states were all that prevented that union; the literalization of the resistance only clarifies it as it relates to life on this earth of vegetation; the consummation in the figures of angels and Jesus has been implicit all along, for the angels have been with Milton since he descended, and Jesus has been with Ololon since she descended.

The difference between the two action sections is the variability of time and space in each. In Book I, time is stable and space variable, and we see thereby various spatial levels of reality for the same duration. In Book II, time is the variable; the action takes place almost exclusively in Blake's garden (with Ololon's reminiscence of Edenic perception and her one vision of Milton on the Arnon recalling other levels briefly), but it is examined at different points in its duration. In Book I, we remember, Blake frequently emphasized the moment of the poem, defining briefly when he did so his spatial perspective; in Book II he has alluded frequently to the setting of the action, to its occurrence here on earth in a cottage garden in Felpham. This inverse variability is the natural product of the poem's symbolic structure: Book I is the ringing, visionary book of Milton, of Los, of fixed time; Book II is the more lyrical, more intimate book of Ololon, of Enitharmon, of established space.

If the complication of the action section of Book II has any analogue in Western literature, that analogue must be the dizzying central verses of the book of Revelation. The sevens built on sevens complicated by fours of verses 6 through 16 form a suggestively similar pattern of constantly re-focusing vision. The three principal seven-unit series of the work, the seals, trumpets, and vials that portend doom, seem to be organized seriatim: when the seals are all open the trumpets sound; when the trumpets are all still the vials pour out their wrath. But the sequence is more complicated than that. The three series repeat each other in the events they record and in the images of their recording. At the completion of each, at the seventh seal and the seventh trumpet and the seventh vial, there are voices and thunderings and lightnings and an earthquake (8:5, 11:19, and 16:18); these motifs of disaster are repeated individually throughout the sequence of sevens. The repetition of natural calamity at the conclusion of each series is not in itself a complication of the sequence, but the congruency of those calamities is: the first six vials repeat virtually the same disasters the first six trumpets herald, although the extent of the disaster is greater in the later sequence (in the first, for example, one-third of the seas turn to blood and one-third of the waters are poisoned, and in the second all of the seas turn to blood, and all of the waters), and at the seventh vial it all seems to happen again, though in less detail. But the verses that attend the pouring out of the last vial (16:18–21) record practically the same events that earlier—or what seemed to be earlier—attended the opening of the sixth seal (6:12–17), and they happened with greater finality in the first passage, which saw "the heaven departed as a scroll when it is rolled together." To complicate things further, we are told in 10:6–7 "that there should be time no longer" at the sounding of the last trumpet, but it is not until the pouring out of the last vial that a voice from the temple of heaven announces "It is done" (16:17); the end of time is the beginning of the battles of Armageddon, but that day of wrath was announced before either the last trump or the last vial, at the loosing of the sixth seal (6:17).

I do not mean by introducing these complications to imply that St. John was writing a Blakean poem. What he meant by his congruent sevens is beyond my purpose to surmise, except insofar as such vast and awesome images in such provocative and suprarational order are perfectly appropriate to the vast, awesome, provocative, and suprarational vision they embody (and, perhaps, perfectly necessary to hide the political implications of that vision from imperial Roman understanding). The design of the book of Revelation arises from far different conventions and necessities from those of early nineteenth-century England. I do mean to imply that Blake was writing an apocalyptic poem —even an Apocalyptic poem. I suggest that he adopted the rough and perhaps unintentional congruencies of the central chapters of Revelation, refined them, systematized them, and built the action of *Milton* out of them. We might even see a strong structural relationship between the whole of Revelation and the whole second book of *Milton*—and hence by extension the whole of *Milton*: the biblical work has, like the Blakean work, three parts, a prologue on the history and urgency of the vision, a refracted narrative of events leading to the end of time, and an account of the last harvest and what lies beyond (this last only an implication in *Milton*). In Revelation as in *Milton* the focal action is the consolidation of the forces of good against the forces of evil; in the earlier as in the later work that action is described in a system of contraries (the sealed good vs. the sealed evil, the woman clothed with the sun vs. the whore of Babylon, the measuring of the temple vs. the measuring of the New Jerusalem, the seven angels of god vs. the seven hills of Rome, four beasts of the throne vs. four horsemen, lamb vs. beast). That St. John deliberately built his vision on these complex structural principles I do not propose. That Blake did, imitating or not imitating the single biblical work, the single work, whose images and ideas are most pervasive in his epic poems, I am certain.[20]

[20] In "Opening the Seals" Wittreich, defining the prophetic bond that links Blake to Milton, describes the general structural principles of Blake's late prophecies in terms of David Pareus' seventeenth-century commentary on Revelation. Although Wittreich applies Pareus' observations specifically only to *Jerusalem*, several of those observations seem to me to apply at least as directly to *Milton*. He notes, for example, that "The Book of Revelation, as described by Pareus and many other commentators on the Apocalypse, was composed of a preface (1:1-9), a prophecy composed of seven visions (1:10-22:5), and a conclusion (22:6-21)" (p. 42). Furthermore, "Though each vision in Revelation repeats the same event and represents it in relation to all time, it does so without reiterating the same details or the same totality" (p. 43). "The visions of Revelation, though they seem continuous, are not so, since they push the reader back into contemplation and interpretation of what he has just beheld; but the visions [in Pareus' words] 'do all cohere one with another'. . . . The early visions are more obscure than the later ones so that there is a sense of progression within the repetitions. . . . In Revelation structure, as described by Pareus and more recently by Farrer (Austin Farrer, *A Rebirth of Images: The Making of St. John's Apocalypse* [London: Dacre Press, 1949]), the darker types go before, and the clearer follow after; the darker are revealed by the clearer . . ." (p. 43). Blake may have followed St. John's form in *Milton*, but the ideas of the two men are not identical. Sandler (*op. cit.*) notes that Blake, "having succeeded to the iconoclastic enterprise" of apocalypse, must reveal all error, including that of John of Patmos. She lists Blake's arguments with and reinterpretations of the biblical Apocalypse (pp. 24ff.).

C. Felpham

The prologue of Book II is an interpretation of the pro-
logue of Book I, following exactly its four-part structure.
The action of Book II is an interpretation of the action of
Book I, adopting its technique of a three-part refracted nar-
rative. The epilogue of Book II (42:24-43:1) is an interpre-
tation of the epilogue of Book I, but it imitates neither the
intricate structure nor the technique of its vastly different
counterpart in Book I. The first book ends in a five and a
half-plate hymn to inspiration; it is a resounding chant, an
extended recapitulation of Blake's mythic vision of human
history. Its dimension is vast, its concern abstract. The final
lines of Book II are, on the contrary, subdued and personal.
We have moved from human grapes in the wine-presses of
eternity to a single man outstretched upon a garden path:

> Terror struck in the Vale I stood at that immortal sound
> My bones trembled. I fell outstretched upon the path
> A moment, & my Soul returnd into its mortal state
> To Resurrection & Judgment in the Vegetable Body
> And my sweet Shadow of Delight stood trembling by my
> side. . . .
>
> (42:24-28)

As Albion tried to stand and could not, so did Blake. The
human terror of the creative moment drove his soul from
his body, and he fell senseless, "for man cannot know what
passes in his members till periods of Space & Time / Reveal
the secrets of Eternity" (21:8-10). Then, in the most human
and personal of all Blake's images of apocalypse, his soul re-
turns to his body to await Judgment. As Milton must, as
Ololon must, as Albion who is Jesus must, as all men must
at the trumpet of doom, Blake returns soul to body to await
eternity. Beside him waits his wife, who had been ill in their
cottage when the vision first appeared to him. As Ololon
came into the garden to join Milton, Catherine has come to

join Blake: they are the embodiments in Generation of the union that is the action of *Milton.*

Book I presents us with the cosmic, mythic dimensions of that union; for its purpose, Blake was himself a mythic figure who strode toward eternity with all Generation on his foot; he was the herald of inspiration taking part in the drama of apocalypse. Book II presents us with the individual, human dimensions of the union; for its purpose, Blake is a single human being with a sick wife and a modest garden, a single human being whose vision of his own failures makes possible the return of Jesus to the fallen world, for, "whenever any Individual Rejects Error & Embraces Truth a Last Judgment passes upon that Individual." The mythic Blake chanted a resounding hymn to creativity, an elegant, assured, inspired vision of providence. The mortal Blake faints in his garden, like Satan or Urizen unable to withstand the intoxication, like the prostrate Ololon frightened and humbled.

In one crucial respect the final sections of the two books are the same: as the epilogue of Book I returned in its last lines to the rhetoric and mythic milieu of the Bard's Song, tense, pregnant with apocalypse, so does the epilogue of Book II:[21]

> Immediately the Lark mounted with a loud trill
>   from Felphams Vale
> And the Wild Thyme from Wimbletons green &
>   impurpled Hills
> And Los & Enitharmon rose over the Hills of Surrey
> Their clouds roll over London with a south wind,
>   soft Oothoon
> Pants in the Vales of Lambeth weeping oer her
>   Human Harvest
> Los listens to the Cry of the Poor Man: his Cloud
> Over London in volume terrific, low bended in anger.

[21] Mary Lynn Johnson notes that in this passage the poem even makes a return to "the agricultural labors interrupted at the end of the Song" (*op. cit.,* p. 11).

189

Rintrah & Palamabron view the Human Harvest beneath
Their Wine-presses & Barns stand open; the Ovens
    are prepar'd
The Waggons ready: terrific Lions & Tygers sport & play
All Animals upon the Earth, are prepard in all their
    strength
To go forth to the Great Harvest & Vintage of the
    Nations.

Finis

The end of time must be horrible to those in time. No vision of the promised release is honest without this sense of anguish to come. We have heard throughout the poem the lamentations of all levels of reality at its imminence. Now even mortal Blake perceives the cataclysm. His trembling and his wife's trembling are one with the trembling of the universe.

Yet even in this familiar dark prophecy the Book II epilogue maintains its restraint and integrity. There is no celebration, no orgiastic rite of sacrifice, no furious resistance here, as there has been in previous such passages. The steady calm of the passage is Blake's own expression of the visionary conviction of Milton's speech. It is born neither of ignorance nor of resignation, but of a profound sense that truth is the only good, and that the end of time is the final revelation of truth.

All the familiar apocalyptic images are gathered in this passage, the lark and thyme, the storm, the ovens and presses; yet they are described so simply and quietly that they seem almost literal. We stand in a rural garden, where a lark is no angel nor a flower a mighty demon, where a storm is a natural event however threatening, where even presses and barns and ovens and wagons are part of the landscape. Yet these natural images have been invested with apocalyptic significance by a vision that comprehends not only their familiar manifestations in time, but also their eternal reality—a vision that is both center and circumference of the perspectival vortex. Blake and Catherine united in the garden are not only the incarnation of Milton and Ololon; they are also the inspired imagination united with its product, Los and Enitharmon rising together over England.

Book II charts the union of their emanations with the consolidated masculine forms of Book I. In keeping with the decorum we have noted throughout the poem, it is stylistically as well as thematically the "feminine" counterpart of the first book. The basic mode of Book I is the bardic mode of Eden, with the variant I have called visionary. The basic mode of Book II is the lyricism of Beulah, with its variant, a very intimate kind of prophecy which is a translation into personal, temporal terms of the grand impersonal vision of Golgonooza. Book I progresses from bardic through disjunctive narrative to visionary; Book II follows a parallel course through its emanative modes, lyric, disjunctive narrative, prophetic.

The range of these styles illustrates the basic concern of *Milton*, the perfection of a literary art through which eternity may be realized and time abolished. The profusion of styles suggests an experimentation, a testing of each to see whether it can bear the weight of truth. In a way each can, for as Murry points out, "the total argument of Milton is contained in any of its parts."[22] Yet it is only in one style, the final one, that the apocalyptic vision of the poem is fully expressed; it is only when Blake has adapted the bardic inspiration with which he began to the most personal, most intimate conditions of his life, that that inspiration yields eternity in time. In the progression of styles that is *Milton*, then, we have a kind of formula for perfecting poetic art: one must apply one's inspiration, through that complicated process of gradual understanding that is the heart of each book of this poem, not only to a grand, mythic conception of life, but to its humblest particulars. That is what John Milton had failed to do in his lifetime, for he did not know

[22] *William Blake*, p. 253.

until he entered Blake's foot "that the Three Heavens of Beulah were beheld / By him on earth in his bright pilgrimage of sixty years" (15:51–52). It is what Blake himself had failed to do before he moved to Felpham, for he had thought this vegetable earth a hindrance to vision rather than its beautiful expression. In the course of *Milton* both poets recognize their error; each, "collecting all his fibres into impregnable strength" (38:5) in Blake's Felpham garden, begins the renovation of time by infusing it with eternal vision.

6. Plate 50 (Ololon between two human sheaves)

IV. Contraries and Progression

The hammer and loom perform the same function. Together they create the form and substance of fallen humanity. They are forces not only parallel, not only equal, not only complementary, but absolutely necessary to each other. The hammer created Urizen, the loom Satan—but Satan is Urizen: without the weaving of Satan into flesh the hammering of Urizen into bone is useless. Without both these functions, which together realize eternal humanity in time, Urizen/Satan and with him Albion would fall forever into Ulro.

The interinvolvement of hammer and loom epitomizes the necessary mutuality of all the contraries of which *Milton* is built, of male and female, time and space, eternity and time/space. We have seen this interinvolvement reflected in the rhetorical structure of the poem from its broadest outline to its minutest particulars, from its matching three-part books to its paired stanzas and its circular oratory. We ought now to examine several thematic structures with which the rhetorical structure is itself interinvolved.

The principal thematic development of *Milton* is that of the Three Classes of Men, the frequently hostile yet vitally interrelated categories of fallen humanity. The concept of the Three Classes extends beyond the kind of rudimentary psychological and historical distinctions it implies, distinctions between Reprobate prophet and Elect patron or between revolutionary and tyrant, to inform both the cosmology of the poem and its moral vision of human relationship. We have noted the interinvolvement of the Three Classes in the equal necessity of Satan's mills, Palamabron's harrow, and Rintrah's plow to the realization of the harvest, and in the mutual functions of Redeemed Antamon, Reprobate Sotha and Theotormon, and Elect Ozoth in embodying the formless spectres. We may see it as well in the tenuous interactions of the four states of being and the precarious relationship of the two sexes.

Blake's cosmology is generally conceived to be a developing system which maintains an internal consistency as its tenets proliferate.[1] I question its consistency, which seems to me a misconception responsible for a frustrating inaccuracy in standard definitions of Blake's four states of being. Damon, for example, distinguishes in *A Blake Dictionary* between eternity and Eden, which "partakes of Eternity, but differs from it in that it also partakes of this world."[2] But in *Milton* Blake uses the words "Eden" and "Eternity" interchangeably, and each term refers not to the perfected imaginative state we should expect from Blake's other prophecies, but to a highly ambiguous state which incorporates error and truth, imagination and dogma. Similarly, Beulah differs subtly but significantly in the three last prophetic works: its creation is identified with Albion's fall in *The Four Zoas*, but not in *Milton* and *Jerusalem*, in which its creation antedates the fall and indeed might have prevented the fall if Albion's members had not been so thoroughly corrupt. Even the fallen worlds are mapped differently in *Milton* from in *The Four Zoas* and *Jerusalem*.

A redefinition of Blake's four states of being seems to me essential at this stage of Blake studies, and an accurate redefinition will depend on distinctions among the cosmol-

[1] Morton D. Paley (*Energy and Imagination*) and Mary Lynn Johnson (*op. cit.*) have recently challenged the assumptions of what Johnson calls "the critics' monomyth" (p. 12), Paley in demonstrating the general shift in emphasis throughout Blake's poetry of his basic conceptions of energy and imagination, and Johnson in disputing several specific critical tenets about Blake's cosmos, although she does not indicate any inconsistencies in Blake's accounts of that cosmos.

[2] *A Blake Dictionary: The Ideas and Symbols of William Blake* (1965; rpt. New York: E. P. Dutton, 1971), p. 114.

ogies of the individual prophecies. We might contribute a beginning to that necessary critical redefinition by examining briefly the cosmology of *Milton*, which in its peculiarities of description and alignment reflects the interactions of the Three Classes of Men.

We noted above the ambiguity in the poem's representation of the state of Eden. That highest state of Blake's universe is supposedly the eternal and infinite abode of integrated beings engaged in progressive mental strife, but in *Milton* it is presented as a far less attractive place filled with hostility and error. The Bard sings his jarring song to the eternals, who receive it in anger; the Seven Angels walk through Eden with their darkened eighth, Milton; Ololon weeps repentance all day long, and is heard only at dawn. All three instances of Edenic reality testify to its imperfection. People make mistakes there, are incomplete there, mourn there. Time of some sort or other is even measured in this peculiar eternity (21:18). Damon's distinction between Eden and eternity does not, as we have noted, resolve the incongruity; Blake uses the terms interchangeably in this poem. It may be that we do not see Eden at all in *Milton*, that the realm of Los and the realm of the Bard are fallen states outside Eden, and Eden itself is something or someplace else. But Blake calls these places Eden, and he calls the inhabitants of these places eternals. It may be that our fallen perpsective conditions our sense of Eden, even as it does our sense of Beulah, conceiving its mental strife as horrible when in fact it is wondrous just as we conceived the mournful Song of Beulah as a fair pastoral hymn. But the Bard, who does not share that fallen perspective, is just as appalled by the events he reports and witnesses as we are. It may be that the Eden of the Bard's Song is only a small portion of Eden, that portion associated with the fallen Albion: it is the "Sons of Albion" among whom the Bard sings (2:23), and Albion's children Milton and Ololon who are shattered and mournful. Are there other "Albions" wandering around elsewhere in Eden, whole and unfallen? There

seem to be others in *The Four Zoas*; the figures called
eternals there are saddened, even horrified, by Albion's fall,
but they do not seem to partake of its error. But in *Milton*
no such unscathed brethren are presented, and unless the
"Sons of Albion" are only a faction at the eternal tables,
none are intimated.[3]

There is no Edenic existence unmarred by failure and
loss in *Milton*. Whatever Blake's earlier formulations of the
relation of Albion to Eden have been (and those formula-
tions are themselves ambiguous), as far as we can see in this
poem Albion is the form of all human reality. The eternals
left behind at his fall may be defined as the broken members
of the Divine Family which collectively is Jesus, or Albion's
wholeness. Albion's lapse thus epitomizes in *Milton* the dis-
unity of the Family, as Luvah's lapse epitomizes throughout
Blake's poetry the disunity of the Zoas. The members of the
Divine Family, like the Three Classes of Men, are mu-
tually necessary whatever their error to the survival of eter-
nal humanity; they are interinvolved. The eternal portions
of Albion's disunity dwell in a kind of limbo Eden which,

[3] It is possible that the key clause, "Terrific among the Sons of
Albion . . . / A Bard broke forth" (2:33–34) refers only to the
singer's lineage, not to his sole audience, but the poem never resolves
the possibility. Mary Lynn Johnson (*op. cit.*, pp. 12–13) argues that
"in each of Blake's poems about the fall it would be more accurate
to speak of a 'fallen remnant' than a saving remnant. . . . In all
three long treatments of the fall, in fact, Albion is said to be only one
unconscious member of an infinite Divine Family that keeps trying
to reawaken him. . . ." Although I believe this of *The Four Zoas*
and *Jerusalem*, in which unfallen eternals are described, I do not
think it is true of *Milton*, in which any eternals characterized are
themselves error-ridden and frightened. There are no unfallen beings
present in *Milton* except the perfection of the collective Divine
Family toward which the entire action of the poem moves. Jesus
himself appears in the poem only when Ololon is inspired to descend
and thus completes the Divine Humanity (plates 21 and 42).
Mitchell (*Sublime Allegory*, p. 285) says the eternals in *Milton*
"represent the audience in the poem and . . . define its relation to
the poem," becoming Jesus occasionally to define the audience's
potential. This may be true, but it explains only the aesthetic func-
tion of these ambiguous beings, not their role in Blake's cosmology.

having witnessed error, is susceptible to error. Thus Eden itself is defined by Albion, its human principle.[4] As he fades, so does Eden. As he returns to imaginative reality, Eden is restored to full truth. What permits that return and dictates that restoration is the portion of Eden, of Albion himself, which is not subject to error, the human imagination which can never be annihilated. That pure imagination, Jesus, is the eternal counterpart of the polypus Orc, which comprises vegetated humanity (29:29–30) as Jesus comprises eternal humanity (both Orc and Jesus are, in Blake's myth, forms of Luvah). The eight angels who together are Jesus may not always all shine brightly, but they always exist. The abode of their existence, dark or bright, is Eden.

That Eden always exists regardless of the error it embraces is what distinguishes a faded Eden, which creates itself, from the limited fallen states of Ulro and Generation, which are created from without. That Blake maintained his faith in the perpetuation of Eden, of human imagination, despite error and loss may seem to argue a naive optimism the other major poets of his age did not share. It is true that Blake does not seem to have suffered throughout his life the fears of the other Romantics that the imagination is perishable, that it can wither or be destroyed or even destroy itself. He wrote no Peele Castle stanzas, no Dejection Ode, no *Alastor*. However well he knew and described the failures of individual beings to realize their imagination, the failures of Thel and Albion and John Milton, Blake seems never to have doubted the existence and the constructive power of imagination itself. For Wordsworth and Coleridge imagination is our means of perceiving reality, and it may fail us, leaving us alone and cold and unseeing. For Keats and Shelley, it may delude and destroy us as well, luring us away from painful realities that must be faced if we are to survive. For Blake, imagination *is* reality, and we may fail

[4] Blake equates the "Universal Brotherhood of Eden" with "The Universal Man," Albion, at the beginning of *The Four Zoas* (page 3, lines 5–6).

it and obscure it, but we cannot individually extinguish it. Wordsworth the divine egoist would draw reality within him; Shelley the skeptic would reach a kind of bargain with reality, maintaining a necessary independence from its unresponsiveness; Blake would open out into reality from the caverns of his fallen perceptions. For Wordsworth and Shelley imagination is a link to external reality, which is separate from and more or less threatening to the individual; for Blake the individual and reality are joined in a continuum which is imagination.

Still, for all Blake's conviction that imagination is "the Human Existence itself" and therefore cannot be annihilated (32:32–38), his presentation of Eden in *Milton* suggests at least a possible doubt that even eternal humanity can survive an age of tyranny and despair. Imagination is for Blake a collective force of human consciousness, a union of consciousnesses which may be damaged by individual defection but which survives, damaged or not, as long as any committed beings survive to maintain it. What makes the darkness of Eden particularly ominous in *Milton* is the possibility that no such committed beings will survive the evils of the age. Thus Los, who himself has barely been saved from eternal death by a remembered prophecy of hope, must command his four remaining sons to stay with him in Golgonooza and not permit themselves to be vegetated like their twelve brothers, lest Albion die utterly (23:61–24:43).

Blake does not openly confront the possibility of the collapse of Eden; nothing in his poetry suggests that such a collapse is even theoretically possible. On the contrary, he frequently affirms, in *Milton* as elsewhere, the permanence of Eden. Yet in this poem as nowhere else in his work Eden itself is damaged and corrupt. It will be restored, presumably, as Albion will be restored, by a coalition of prophets from all stages of reality, by the union of the Bard, Milton, and Los in Blake. Its restoration is as certain as anything in Blake's poetry, because it depends only on the self-realization of the individual imagination. But the gloomy presentation of Eden in *Milton* suggests at least the urgency of the vital imaginative act at the time of Blake's conception of the poem, and perhaps even an implicit fear of the precariousness of the imagination as well.

In the critical period of the corruption of the French Revolution Blake, like his fellow English poets, recognized the possibility of the extinction of apocalyptic idealism. Like Wordsworth in *The Prelude*, he believed that a collective consciousness could be maintained by a few individuals— even by one individual—until that consciousness could be revived in all humanity. Like Wordsworth, he undertook to be that sustaining individual. Supported by Milton as Wordsworth was supported by Coleridge (and by Catherine as Wordsworth by Dorothy), he passed through a crisis of despair to a new affirmation of vision. What distinguishes Blake from Wordsworth in this psychomachia, this prophetic reawakening, is the urgency with which Blake associates his own visionary breakthrough with the literal salvation of humanity.

Wordsworth internalizes the collapse of the Revolution; it becomes for him a personal crisis of consciousness. Having passed that crisis, having known on Snowdon the sanction and the peril of his prophetic imagination, he can yet retreat at the end of his poem into a comforting friendship and a secure faith in his own contribution to the eventual achievement of, if not a new heaven, at least a new earth. For Blake, alone with his vision, there is no such comfort and no such security. The collapse of the Revolution means for him the abandonment of imagination; even he himself, painting miniatures for Hayley's vapid friends, has nearly failed the trust. Surrounded by Hayleys and even less enlightened rural gentry, threatened with execution for sedition because he threw a drunken soldier out of his garden, ridiculed by the artistic establishment and harassed even by his wife, no wonder he felt himself the last vestige of imagination in a perilously degraded collective humanity, no wonder he felt so painfully his own near defection from prophetic vision.

That in *Milton* he can reinstate his faltering vision is not only a personal triumph and a stage in the prolonged restoration of humanity to imaginative truth, it is the single pivotal act which permits that restoration. It is so not because Blake is a better prophet than the prophets of previous ages, but because he lives in the time of the farthest descent of humanity from Edenic truth. He does not even credit himself with his own purified vision; he has been wandering in Udan-Adan when Milton enters in with him, and it is not until Los joins the union that he can enter Golgonooza. Thus imagination realizes *itself* in Blake; he who has nearly failed his vision is restored to vision by vision. That self-regenerating quality of imagination is what will purify Eden of strife and error. Meanwhile we have witnessed in the degradation of Eden the degradation of imagination, of "Human Existence itself," in both the historical and the biographical circumstances in which Blake found himself when he conceived the poem.

The error we witness in Eden in this poem is presumably an abnormality determined by the extremity of Albion's fall. Even under less drastic conditions, however, Eden is a place of momentous activity. Mental strife is trying, and many succumb to its weariness. For those the Divine Family created Beulah, a place where the weak may revive:

Into this pleasant Shadow all the weak & weary
Like Women & Children were taken away as on wings
Of dovelike softness, & shadowy habitations prepared
    for them
But every Man returnd & went still going forward thro'
The Bosom of the Father in Eternity on Eternity
Neither did any lack or fall into Error without
A Shadow to repose in all the Days of happy
    Eternity. . . .

                  (31:1–7)

Beulah, which receives its fullest exposition in *Milton*, has probably commanded more critical commentary than any of the others of Blake's four states of being,[5] and consequently we may turn our attention here to the two features of it that are most clearly related to the principles by which the poem is structured, its sexual identification and its providential creation.

As the above quotation indicates, one enters Beulah from Eden weary and female, and returns from there strong and male. The identification of Beulah with femaleness has existed in Blake's poetry from the start, before Beulah even had a name. Even in the *Songs of Innocence*, generally considered a study of Beulaic existence, the sexual orientation is female: the little boy lost by his father is found by his mother, the black child who yearns hopelessly for his father-god's love is comforted by his mother, other mothers and nurses protect children from darkness and grief. The piper who sings of Innocence and the shepherd who guards it are male, but they are no more its natural inhabitants than the poet who describes Beulah and the Divine Family who created it dwell within it. Male adults act as constructive powers in the *Songs of Innocence* only from outside its boundaries; god appears to the lost boy or an angel to the chimney sweep from realms beyond their comprehension. Otherwise male adults are either helpless (weeping fathers) or pernicious (beadles with disciplinary wands and fathers who sell their children). The positive internal powers of the Innocence Songs are female.

The Book of Thel also presents its Beulah as feminine: Luvah waters his horses there and god strolls through at dusk, but the permanent human population of the place seems to be comprised only of the daughters of the seraphim. Femaleness is positive, though certainly limited,

---

[5] See especially Percival, pp. 52–59; Frye, *Fearful Symmetry*, pp. 227–235, and "Notes," pp. 125–129; Bloom, *The Visionary Company: A Reading of English Romantic Poetry* (1961; rpt. Garden City, N.Y.: Doubleday Anchor, 1963), pp. 16–29.

in the *Songs of Innocence*; in *The Book of Thel* it bears negative implications. The vales of Har are a temporary abode from which one must proceed by active determination; that only daughters inhabit the place, that the youngest of those daughters attempts to leave the place but cannot, identifies femaleness with failure. *Milton* reinforces that identification but at the same time clarifies it in such a way as to alter its prejudicial character: it is not that women fail the rigors of Eden and must retire to Beulah, but that anyone who fails appears frail and feminine. Femaleness is thus not a synonym for failure but a metaphor of it. We shall examine that metaphor more closely later in the chapter; for now, we may see the significance of Beulah's female character simply as evidence of its incompleteness, for complete existence is integrated and does not recognize gender.

Beulah is the emanation of Eden. The description of its creation parallels descriptions throughout Blake's poetry of the division of human figures into opposing genders; the female portion separates from the male in weakness and error. One could construct upon this parallel a convincing argument for the destructive significance of Beulah, claiming its creation as a corollary of the fall of humanity from wholeness just as the emanation of Enitharmon from Los is a corollary. It is precisely such a corollary in *The Four Zoas*, in which the fall of Albion is the direct cause of the emanations' plea for "a place / In which we may be hidden under the Shadow of wings" (IV, 56:7–8). But in *Milton* Blake has discarded that causality. The emanations in the later poem are terrified not by the fall of Albion from eternity, but by the very character of eternity: "because the life of Man was too exceeding unbounded / His joy became terrible to them" (30:22–23). They beg shelter not from eternal death, as they do in *The Four Zoas*, but from eternal life.[6]

---

[6] In *Jerusalem* Beulah will also have been created "To protect from the Giant blows in the sports of intellect, / Thunder in the midst of kindness, & love that kills its beloved . . ." (48:15–16).

If the creation of Beulah were a corollary of the fall, we might envision perfect Eden containing Beulah within it as unfallen Albion contains Jerusalem; imperfect Eden, damaged by the fall of Albion, creates Beulah around it, externalizing part of its own reality, drawing a circumference beyond its vital center, opening a vortex. Blake seems to encourage such a reading in *Milton* by emphasizing the created, emanative nature of Beulah and the weakness of its female inhabitants. But if he does encourage that reading, he does so only to expose its limitations. The forty lines in which he describes Beulah and its creation are not a threnody on the loss of human wholeness, but a paean to the redemptive wisdom of the "Eternal Great Humanity." Beulah does represent the vulnerability of Eden to error, but it represents as well its salvation from error. It has duration and extent (it is "a Temporal Habitation" [30:29]), and it is frequently described by that dread word "shadow"; entering it is certainly a form of failure. But it is a very mild form, and one that preserves rather than threatens Edenic reality. To enter Beulah is not to leave the Divine Family, but to rest in it. Its duration and extent are not time and space, because they cannot be measured; its shadow is merely refuge from heat and glare; it is directly contingent on Eden, and presumably, if humanity were whole, would maintain immediate and direct access to Eden. Its creation, unlike that of fallen reality, is perpetual: "Beulah is evermore Created around Eternity" (30:8). It is designed to ensure against a fall like Albion's: "Neither did any lack or fall into Error without / A Shadow to repose in all the Days of happy Eternity" (31:6–7).

But Albion did not merely rest from the rigors of eternity, he rejected them altogether. Beyond the eternal and the eternally created realms of the Divine Family, beyond the outer borders of Beulah, lies a universe created once only, in the fall of Albion. Blake has with increasing particularity throughout his prophetic poetry charted that uni-

verse, whose cosmography is at once geometrical and ana-
tomical. In *Milton* he refines his cosmography further.

The first significant map of the fallen universe in other
than anatomical or geographical terms occurs in *The Four
Zoas*, Night the Sixth, page 74. Urizen explores the deeps:

> Four Caverns rooting downwards their foundations
>   thrusting forth
> The metal rock & stone in ever painful throes of
>   vegetation
> The Cave of Orc stood to the South a furnace of
>   dire flames
> Quenchless unceasing. In the west the Cave of Urizen
> For Urizen fell as the Midday sun falls down into
>   the West
> North stood Urthonas stedfast throne a World of
>   Solid darkness
> Shut up in stifling obstruction rooted in dumb
>   despair
> The East was Void. But Tharmas rolld his billows
>   in ceaseless eddies
> Void pathless beat with Snows eternal & iron hail
>   & rain
> All thro the caverns of fire & air & Earth.

Throughout Blake's poetry the unfallen universe is the
same, and critics have assumed that the fallen universe is
the same throughout as well.[7] But the fallen universe of the
Zoas, with Luvah moved to the south and Urizen to the
west and Tharmas' chaos everywhere, is altered significant-
ly in each book of *Milton*, and altered again, less drastically,
in *Jerusalem*. In Book I we learn that compass positions are
no longer held by the Zoas themselves, who "All fell to-
wards the Center in dire ruin," but by elements that repre-
sent them:

[7] See, for example, Bloom, Commentary, p. 831.

Four Universes round the Mundane Egg remain Chaotic
One to the North, named Urthona: One to the South,
    named Urizen:
One to the East, named Luvah: One to the West,
    named Tharmas
They are the Four Zoa's that stood around the Throne
    Divine!
But when Luvah assum'd the World of Urizen to
    the South:
And Albion was slain upon his mountains, & in his tent;
All fell towards the Center in dire ruin, sinking down.
And in the South remains a burning fire; in the
    East a void.
In the West, a world of raging waters; in the North
    a solid,
Unfathomable! without end. But in the midst of these,
Is built eternally the Universe of Los and Enitharmon:
Towards which Milton went, but Urizen oppos'd his
    path.

                       (19:15–26)

Furthermore, those representative elements are not in the
positions we would expect from *The Four Zoas*: the east is
still a void, and a fire suggesting Luvah still reigns in the
south; but the west's "raging waters" suggest Tharmas in his
rightful pre-fall position, and Urizen is not explicitly repre-
sented. The eastern void suggests him in that his element
is air, the element of the void, but in the *Zoas* he is set in the
west, opposite the void. The rigidity of the northern solid
suggests his dogmatic natural religion, as well as Urthona's
earlier steadfastness, a rich suggestion in that it would unite
Urizen and Urthona as they are united in the central con-
flict of the poem; but that solid earth is just as solid in the
Zoas passage with no reference to Urizen. Urizen has no
specific domain in the fallen universe of *Milton*; his original
territory usurped by Luvah, he has extended his hegemony

throughout the fallen universe. Tharmas' chaos was the informing principle of the fallen realms of *The Four Zoas*; Urizen's dogma is their informing principle in *Milton*. It is as regent of those shadowy realms that he opposes Milton's progress through them.

The Book I passage begins and ends with the "Universe of Los and Enitharmon," the chief refinement of the *Milton* version of the fallen universe, the providential Mundane Egg poised between eternity and chaos. In Book II Blake clarifies further the focal significance of that egg-formed world through which humanity may be reborn:

> Four Universes round the Universe of Los remain
> Chaotic
> Four intersecting Globes, & the Egg form'd World of Los
> In midst; stretching from Zenith to Nadir, in midst of
> Chaos[.]
> One of these Ruind Universes is to the North named
> Urthona
> One to the South this was the glorious World of Urizen
> One to the East, of Luvah: One to the West; of Tharmas.
> But when Luvah assumed the World of Urizen in the
> South
> All fell towards the Center sinking downward in dire
> Ruin. . . .
>
> (34:32–39)

In Book I the realms of the Zoas were still marked out by qualities identified with them, even after they fell in ruin. Now there is only chaos in these realms; the only identifiable structure left is the "Egg form'd World of Los," which thus bears all hopes for the resurrection of humanity. The vision of Book II is a refinement of the vision of Book I; in it all vestigial dreams of the simple reestablishment of former reality have been abolished. There is no return to the "Four Universes" of the unfallen Zoas. The only way back to eternity now is through self-annihilation in the city of inspiration.[8]

The Mundane Shell, Generation, domain of time and space, is created out of the chaos of Ulro through the wisdom and magnanimity of Los and Enitharmon. It tends upward from the fall's nadir toward Eden, even as Beulah, also created providentially through wisdom and magnanimity, tends downward from Eden toward Generation. One might speak at least metaphorically of Generation as the eros of fallen existence and Beulah as the agape of eternal reality.

In *Jerusalem* there will also be two formulations of the fallen universe. In the first, 32:25–37, the shifts in the Zoas' positions will be a simplification of the shifts in *The Four Zoas* and *Milton* Book I: Luvah and Urizen will merely exchange positions, leaving Urthona and Tharmas as they were. Although Luvah and Urizen are thus defined as the instigators of the fall, no single Zoa will be permitted to represent in his error the entire destructive force of the fallen worlds. Each becomes, as in the *Milton* passage, one of the four elements, the "Four ravening deathlike Forms" (32:36), but here they are collectively representative of the fall. The transposition of Luvah and Urizen *is* the infection of Urthona and Tharmas. The mutuality of the Zoas' error is complete in *Jerusalem* as it is nowhere else in Blake's poetry; this complete mutuality of error may account for the mutuality of salvation toward which this poem, more certainly than any other Blakean prophecy, builds. The second *Jerusalem* map of the fallen world, 59:10–21, will re-

[8] The poem's one diagramatic illustration emphasizes this. Plate 33 contains a map of Milton's path to the Mundane Egg, which is formed at the intersection of the four unfallen realms. Because Milton cannot journey through Albion's deathly bosom until after the reorganization of the Zoas, when their realms are vacant, any graph of the location of the Mundane Egg must use the prefallen realms as its axes. The map is paradoxical in that it traces a postlapsarian event through a prelapsarian universe—but that paradox is the only means by which a map might be drawn at all.

peat with minor modifications the first *Milton* map. In *Jerusalem*, however, that map, with fire in the south, raging waters in the west, solid darkness in the north, and a void in the east, poses no critical problem: we have seen Luvah and Urizen transposed in *Jerusalem* 32, and therefore can logically identify the southern fires with Luvah and the void with Urizen. It may be that the questions we raised and the metaphysical solution we reached about that map in *Milton* Book I were caused not by Blake's deliberately puzzling us into greater perception of the fallen world, but by his oversight in incorporating into *Milton* a formulation, devised for *Jerusalem*, which does not quite fit the expectations of the earlier work.

The complex interactions of the four states of being render any reliable cartography of Blake's universe impossible. The standard diagram which I offered in the first chapter, a series of concentric circles beginning at the infinite center point of Eden, is really useful only as a rudimentary introduction. Like all diagrams of Blake's grand schemas, it distorts by its two-dimensionality. It implies precise boundaries where in fact none exist. Ulro is on "the verge of Beulah" conceptually, not physically; the difference between them is imaginative, not spatial, and it cannot be surveyed with the vegetated eye. As Bloom points out, Beulah actually becomes Ulro for those who, like Thel, will not forego its refuge: in Beulah "the Imagination sleeps, but does not die, provided it does not sleep too long. If it does it awakens in the tomb of the Ulro. Energy struggling to get out of Ulro is Generation."[9]

The relation between Ulro and Generation is as ambiguous as that between Ulro and Beulah. Each of the two fallen states is, as Percival describes them, the obverse of the other:

Ulro is the land of eternal death, Generation the means of release. The one is chaos—error in the abstract, hid-

[9] *Visionary Company*, p. 22.

den in obscurity; the other is creation—error made definite and knowable. "Error is created. Truth is eternal." In the world of Generation error is created (given a definite form) that it may be put off time after time. As creation, thus defined, is of necessity a continuous process, proceeding as long as error exists, Generation and Ulro are overlapping worlds. Both are coexistent with mortal life.[10]

The fundamental ambiguities inherent in a universe whose borders are purely conceptual are compounded by the development of Blake's exposition of that universe. His first extensive formulation of it is in *The Four Zoas*, in which Beulah is created because of Albion's fall and Generation is all but indistinguishable from Ulro. In *Milton*, Beulah's creation is independent of and in important ways contrasted with the fall, and Generation is distinguished from Ulro as an egg in the midst of formlessness; the four states of being are defined individually, however ambiguous their relations may be. In *Jerusalem* the four states are delineated even more deliberately than in *Milton*, but by a strange reversal that further delineation seems to render their borders less rather than more distinct; the proliferation of symbolic detail about each state suggests its involvement with rather than its isolation from the rest. The great description of Golgonooza in the first chapter, for instance, has enough associative data for as many documentary tables as there are Blake critics, and no two tables need agree: the data cannot be made to tabulate the universe rationally any more than Ezekiel's vision, which they recall, can. Their profusion defies Urizenic calculation, belies any two-dimensional representation. They affirm that each part of the universe contains some version of all of the universe. The paradox of Blake's cosmology is that the more distinct its divisions become, the more profoundly interinvolved they become.

[10] *Circle of Destiny*, p. 71.

That interinvolvement is perhaps a function of inchoateness of vision in *The Four Zoas*; it is a universal abstraction (built of minute particulars, to be sure) in *Jerusalem*. In *Milton*, the interinvolvement is neither accidental nor abstract; it is fully expressed in terms of the basic human conflicts and resolutions of the poem. The four units of the universe are defined in *Milton* as two contraries and a reasoning negative: Eden and its emanative state consort with Generation, which imitates their creativity, against Ulro, which negates it.

Time is not the opposite of eternity, but its contrary; each is a perpetuation of imagination in vital form, a creative state committed to the unity of the Divine Family. The chief function of the former is to create "form & beauty around the dark regions of sorrow, / Giving to airy nothing a name and a habitation / Delightful! with bounds to the Infinite putting off the Indefinite" (28:2–4), a function that imitates the providence of Jesus, who created for the fading emanations "a habitation & a place" "because the life of Man was too exceeding unbounded" (30:24, 22). The Mundane Shell even recapitulates the geography of eternity: its capital, the city Golgonooza, is built over Bowlahoola's furnaces in the midst of cultivated Allamanda just as Eden, surrounded by the pastures and gardens of Beulah, exists above Generation; each is surrounded further by an "immense hardend shadow" (17:21–22), the Mundane Shell or Ulro.

The true opposite of eternity is the opposite also of time. Whereas eternity and time are both intricately formed and at the same time freely developing, Ulro is paradoxically both formless and rigid. It is only created, never creative. When it seems to create it is only parodying in order to destroy: the Shadowy Female's embroidered robe and Tirzah's imitation body are falsifications of the providential creations of Jesus and Los. They are designed, like snowy Florimels, to lure the imagination from genuine creation.

The struggle of eternity and time against the falsehoods of Ulro is the struggle of Reprobate and Redeemed against

the errors of the Elect. Eden and Golgonooza would lib-
erate Albion from the Ulro that is his fallen form; Rintrah
and Palamabron sacrifice to liberate the individual Satan
from the state Satan. In each case the negation cannot sim-
ply be destroyed, but must be revitalized instead: to devas-
tate Ulro would be to destroy the last vestige of Albion, and
to obliterate the satanic shadow would be to destroy for-
ever a crucial third of Eden. The frozen form of Albion
maintains him in his fall as the shadowy state of Satan main-
tains him in his; because Albion and Satan are both neces-
sary to the completion of Edenic truth, their fallen realities
must be preserved until, reinformed with vision, they cease
to be fallen, cease to negate—until "Generation is swal-
lowed up in Regeneration."

As the cosmology of *Milton* reflects the necessary inter-
involvement of the Three Classes of Men, so does its moral
vision of human relationship. The contraries that are the
creative, progressive elements of the Three Classes are rep-
resented throughout the poem in terms of the most intimate
and demanding of human bonds, that of brother with
brother and husband with wife. The bond of brotherhood
is an abstraction in *Milton*; Rintrah and Palamabron are
embodiments of mythic conceptions, vast and undetailed
categories of human conduct. William Blake's own brother
Robert is introduced into the poem in a full-page illustra-
tion, but he has no explicit function in the verbal text. The
marriage bond, on the other hand, is presented throughout
the poem in particularized psychological and moral per-
spective. John Milton did not know anyone named Ololon,
but his relations with his three wives and three daughters
are much of the substance of the poem, as are Blake's own
relations with his own harassed wife. When Ololon asks in
horrified recognition, "are we Contraries O Milton, Thou &
I / O Immortal! how were we led to War the Wars of
Death" (41:35–36), she provides both the poem's fullest
definition of the relationship of the two contrary Classes,
and its most poignant expression of the necessity and pre-
cariousness of deliberately undertaken human interaction.

The male-female relationship acts throughout *Milton* as a metaphor for the dynamic union of contraries. As M. H. Abrams says, "The central type of the contrary is the severed female Emanation; but all contraries, in Blake, operate as opposing yet complementary male-female powers which, in their energetic love-hate relationship, are necessary to all modes of progression, organization, and creativity, or pro-creativity."[11] That relationship is the opposition of true friendship in Eden, the integral relationship of form and emanation as single entity. With the fall it becomes an adversary relationship, an impediment to revitalized humanity. The relationship of the sexes is thus symbolic of contraries in both ideal and fallen states. In the Bard's Song we see the division of contraries; Rintrah flames high in Satan against Palamabron, Los seals off Enitharmon from him. In the body of Book I that division begins to heal; Rintrah and Palamabron are united, Reprobate prophets and Redeemed poets are joined in vision. But the restoration of what Abrams calls the "equilibrium of opponent forces"[12] does not take place until the great consummation of Book II, in which all contraries, from lark/thyme through William/Catherine and Milton/Ololon to Rintrah/Palamabron and Los/Enitharmon, are joined in apocalyptic vision.

The mythic aspects of the male-female relationship in *Milton* are enhanced by the personal, moral dimensions of that union of contraries. It is tempting to suppose that insofar as the poem had a crystalizing biographical impetus, that impetus was as much a quarrel with Catherine Blake as a quarrel with Hayley, a quarrel that sent Blake storming into the garden but that was resolved when, turning back toward the house, he saw her coming out to him.[13]

[11] *Natural Supernaturalism: Tradition and Revolution in Romantic Literature* (New York: W. W. Norton, 1971), p. 260.

[12] *Ibid.*

[13] This idea is supported by the illumination of plate 17 of the D copy (Erdman plate 15), discussed below, p. 227–28. The homey illumination of plate 40 (Erdman plate 36), in which Blake turns toward his house as Ololon descends to him in its direction, also seems to offer some support of such an assumption. For further discussion of this illumination see below, p. 232n.

Their mutual repentance and forgiveness, through which contention with Hayley might be transcended, could conceivably have inspired the great vision of reconciliation that is *Milton*. The Blakes' arguments during their Felpham stay are as much a matter of record as William's strife with Hayley, and the reconciliation of the speaker of the poem and his "sweet shadow of delight" in Felpham is the only explicitly autobiographical reference in the poem. The supposition that a domestic quarrel inspired the poem is no more functional critically than the assumption that a quarrel with Hayley did, but it does serve to support at least metaphorically the intimate, personal character of the interrelationship of contraries.

It is perhaps the ineluctably personal nature of Blake's principal metaphor for contrariety that accounts for a subtle but disturbing inconsistency in it. Contraries are by definition equal, but the females in the poem, however crucial and powerful Blake intended them to be, are not convincingly equal to their male contraries. Throughout the poem females are either passive or pernicious. Females presented positively are passive: emanations cannot long endure the strife of Eden, Enitharmon is uncomplainingly cut off from full vision by Los, Ololon mourns by her river in Eden and only descends to Generation when she sees Milton there, Catherine is ill in her house. Active females are pernicious: Leutha, Tirzah, the Shadowy Female all create disaster by their actions, which are only imitations of the actions of males anyway, and which need the further actions of males to complete them.

There is some evidence that the passive female can be stronger in her passivity than the male in his active glory; Enitharmon's gentle love for Satan saves him by creating a space for him, and Ololon's lamentations both produce the providential appointment of the Seven Eyes and consummate Milton's act of sacrifice. The positive functions of the females of the poem are equal in rigor and importance with those of the males. The loom provides the essential material

for the hammer. Yet still the metaphoric use Blake makes
of femaleness is pejorative. As we noted earlier, he does not
say that all females are weak, but he does imply that all
weakness is female: when you enter Beulah from Eden you
are female; when, restored and strong, you return to mental
strife, you are male. A similar example is Blake's conception
of the female will, the force, epitomized in the active fe-
males of the poem, which maintains the division of the sexes
by demanding dominance. It has often been said that fe-
male will is not the quality exclusively of women, but is that
quality of any person which provokes wars between sexes
and nations in the name of the selfhood. Furthermore, fe-
male will is surely no more destructive than the acts of the
male Zoas which created the division of the sexes in the first
place. But it is still true that there is no such doctrine in
Blake's poetry as the "male will,"[14] and that he characterizes
the scourge of fallen human relationship in terms that have
been used stereotypically in Western literature to condemn
women who refuse to know their place, from Clytemnestra
and Job's wife to Edward Albee's Martha. The divine voice
in Ololon's plate 33 lamentation castigates the female will
for its—her—destructive jealousy, demanding that she
learn instead to delight in her husband's delight: symboli-
cally that means, of course, that each of us must subdue his
or her urge to dominate, subject his or her will to enlight-
ened imagination, but the force of the symbol, drawing as
it does on the imagery of millennia of male dominance, dis-
rupts the balance of contraries Blake has so elaborately de-
vised throughout the poem.[15]

Female will may be only a metaphor for the destructive

[14] There is the spectre, of course, and he is a male figure, but he
is not identified exclusively by gender, and he does have a female
counterpart in the emanation's shadow.

[15] In *Jerusalem* Blake seems to try to redress this particular im-
balance. The speech of the divine voice ("Song of the Lamb")
that corresponds to the one in Ololon's lamentation (60:10–37) is
mild and loving, not angry and accusatory. That local redress is
amplified throughout *Jerusalem*, as we shall note.

urge to dominance which knows no gender, and the female-ness of the emanations in Beulah may be only a metaphor for weakness; the metaphor in each case is surely the most immediately suggestive Blake could have chosen. But precisely because of its suggestiveness that metaphor undermines one of the major thematic balances of the poem. Palamabron is different from Rintrah, but no weaker; Ololon is different from Milton, and also no weaker—but she seems weaker because, despite Blake's constant emphasis on her commitment and courage and on her identification with Jesus himself, she is allied in the poem with those feeble creatures who cannot withstand Edenic battle. She cannot even repeat Milton's passage from Eden to Ulro, but must make her way instead through a series of emanative steps beginning with Beulah; that new passage may suggest that she is a bold pathfinder in her own right, but it suggests even more strongly that she does not have such a bold path as Milton's to find.[16]

Blake says in *Milton* that contraries are equal, and at the same time he undermines that equality by a system of imagery that must have seemed automatic to him in his pre-Women's Liberation era. He even seems to be partly conscious of the paradox, insistently correcting the damage his

---

[16] An odd twist on the roles of male and female is suggested in dissociated comments by Jean H. Hagstrum and Florence Sandler. Hagstrum notes the symbolic presence in Blake's poetry of what Freud would call the phallic woman, the imaginary masculinization of a threatening female; he cites the Rahab figure engraved on plate 14 of *America*, "her loins producing a phallic serpent," Vala's development in *The Four Zoas* II from earthworm to serpent to dragon to weeping infant, and her mature ability in Night the Third to inseminate Enitharmon ("Babylon Revisited, or the Story of Luvah and Vala," *Sublime Allegory*, pp. 101–118, esp. 108–109). For Hagstrum the phallic woman is a Blakean symbol of perversion. Sandler notes a major positive instance of the phenomenon in the description of Ololon in Eden as a "sweet River, of milk & liquid pearl" (21:15), which Sandler associates with "the spermatic stream of the Hermeticists" (*op. cit.*, p. 21). Thus even in his rare uses of this bizarre perspective on female nature, Blake's attitude is divided between positive and negative.

own metaphor does by implying that the metaphor is pro-
visional. The division into sexes was a condition of the fall
imposed by Urizen (38:1-4), and will cease to exist when
the fall is consummated in resurrection. As the existence of
sexual distinction is a condition of the fall, so is the urge for
dominance that creates sexual hierarchy. Questions about
the relationship between the sexes are thus referred to a
better life in which there are no sexes.[17]

In *Jerusalem* Blake seems more conscious still of the diffi-
culties inherent in his now firmly established metaphors of
femaleness, more determined to correct the imbalance they
imply. He introduces a masculine emanation (Shiloh, the
emanation of France as Jerusalem is of Albion [49:47 and
55:27]),[18] and asserts later that all emanations "stand both
Male & Female at the gates of each Humanity" (88:11),
emphasizing that the weakness attributed to females by
emanation is shared by males. He transfers responsibility
for the division of the sexes from Urizen to Los (58:13-20),
implying that there is constructive value in the separate
existence of the female during the course of the fall. He re-
verses the genders of the speakers of several key speeches
substantially repeated in *Jerusalem* from earlier poems,
suggesting that his conception of sexual roles is at least
partly flexible: Jerusalem speaks the tormented lines begin-
ning "Why wilt thou number every little fibre of my Soul"
(22:20-24) spoken by Tharmas in *The Four Zoas*

[17] He makes that referral explicit in *Jerusalem*, when he calls
Enitharmon "a vegetated mortal Wife of Los: / His Emanation, yet
his Wife till the sleep of Death is past" (14:13-14). "Wife" clearly
implies status inferior in the sexual relationship to that implied by
"emanation," but it is only a temporary inferiority, because wives
will disappear altogether when the fall is reversed. It is no great
comfort that only mortal, fallen women are inferior to their male
counterparts, but Blake probably meant it as comfort.

[18] David Erdman has suggested to me that the genders of the ema-
nations of France and England were probably determined by contrast
with the traditional genders of the countries, La Belle France and
John Bull. Even so, the revocation of the exclusively female identi-
fication of the emanations is new in *Jerusalem*, and insistent.

(I, 4:28–32), and Erin explains the concept of states to her
sisters in *Jerusalem* (49:1–50:17, esp. 49:65–76) as the male
angels explained it to their brother Milton in *Milton* (plate
32, esp. 22–29).

Jesus castigates the destructive nature of his emanation
fiercely in *Milton* (plate 33), demanding her conversion; in
a parallel but much milder speech in *Jerusalem* he explains
her error and consoles her and promises to lead her to re-
demption (60:10–37). The softening of Jesus' tone toward
his emanation in *Jerusalem* is echoed in Blake's expanding
in his last prophecy the redemptive faculty of the female,
most evident earlier in Ololon's identification with Jesus, by
presenting Jerusalem as the wholly positive force that Al-
bion need only recognize and embrace to return to Eden;
she is better than he is, more nearly Edenic, less perverted:
her sons are the soul whereas his are the body (71:4–5),
her sons number four times four, the perfect numbers of
Edenic existence, whereas his only number four times three
(74:23–24).

Throughout *Jerusalem* Blake seems to be redefining for
this separate female form he has conceptualized, a position
that is wholly positive. The clearest statement of that posi-
tion is lines 39:38–40: "Man is adjoined to Man by his Ema-
native portion: / Who is Jerusalem in every individual
Man: and her / Shadow is Vala, builded by the reasoning
power in Man." The positive function of the female is to
permit union among males; her negative function is to de-
stroy that union by rationalization, which numbers every
fiber of the soul. We have seen these functions operate in
Milton, although they were not explicitly defined there: the
constructive function is evident in the intermediation of
Beulah between Eden and Generation as well as in Ololon's
uniting of Milton and Jesus, and the negative function is
evident in the acts of Leutha and Rahab and the Shadowy
Female. *Jerusalem* distinguishes even more overtly than
Milton the positive and negative functions of the female,
giving Vala equal time with Jerusalem, and yet the more

clearly the female roles are defined, the more circumscribed they are by male reality: female separateness is good when it permits communication among males, bad when it corrupts that communication, good when it passively awaits embrace, bad when it actively demands embrace. The more positive Blake's female becomes, the more passive, the more male-circumscribed she becomes. Jerusalem is better than Albion, but lesser. The conflict between Blake's doctrine and the stereotypes of sexual relationship in which he expresses it remains.

Again, Jerusalem's femaleness is more metaphoric than literal. She is not womankind, but the emanative portion of all humanity regardless of gender; presumably the male emanation Shiloh is in the same position she is in. But the metaphor is a powerful one, one built on profound social discrimination, and it dominates the poem. That Blake's metaphor contradicts his doctrine of necessary equality between contraries is perhaps more a comment on the society in which he was educated and to which he addressed himself than it is upon his faculties as thinker and poet, but it is a comment on his mind and art nonetheless. Metaphors are not divorced from concepts. When they conflict with the concepts they are meant to advance, they attest to an uneasiness in their author's mind and create an uneasiness in his reader's mind. That uneasiness is probably minor for readers of *Milton* and *Jerusalem*, who are most likely able to accommodate such discrepancies comfortably in their perception of the rich and significant schemes of these two great poems. It may have been minor for Blake himself, although he tried frequently to adjust it. It is not minor in our conception of the poet Blake, who more than any other writer of his time recognized the destructive effect of received attitudes toward women, but who was nevertheless to some extent a victim of those attitudes.[19]

[19] Brian Wilkie, in "Epic Irony in *Milton*" (*Blake's Visionary Forms Dramatic*, ed. David V. Erdman and John E. Grant [Princeton, N.J.: Princeton University Press, 1970], pp. 359–372), approaches

As the cosmology and the character relations of *Milton* are organized by the doctrine of Three Classes, so is the poem's rhetorical structure. Its three basic parts reflect the Three Classes: the Bard's Song is basically the account of the fall of the satanic Elect, the rest of Book I reports the efforts to reverse that fall by the Reprobate prophets, and Book II records the participation in that reversal by the civilized Redeemed. The parallelism of the two books rep-

---

Blake's attitude toward femaleness through the perspective of epic tradition: "In different ways and depending on kaleidoscopically shifting point of view, Blake both rejects this antifeminine tradition of epic and endorses it in his inimitably ironic way" (p. 365; see his elaboration of this idea, pp. 364–367). Thomas J. J. Altizer also defines Blake's symbolic use of femaleness in *The New Apocalypse* as both negative (pp. 48–56) and positive (pp. 95–102.)

Mitchell suggests a resolution of these ambiguities in Ololon, who casts off all sexual stereotype:

> Her seeking-out of Milton reverses the traditionally passive role of the virtuous heroine in epic and romance, but she does not escape this role by becoming a female warrior, a woman in the armor of a man, "A Female hidden in a Male, religion hidden in War" (40:20). On the contrary, she sees that the stereotypes ruling the behavior of both sexes are the basis for the vicious cycle which entraps the best efforts of Milton and the Sons of Los, and that these roles must be annihilated and recreated as human relationships. . . .
>
> (*Sublime Allegory*, p. 305)

I do not think Ololon quite so liberated as Mitchell does. She comes to imperious Milton a humble, questioning bride, bearing like a good handmaiden the robes that will transform them both. There is still about her, as there is about Jerusalem though Blake seems to have tried harder to dispel it in the later poem, the dependency that Blake defined so memorably (and probably with no intention of being patronizing) in his early annotations to Lavater's *Aphorisms on Man*:

> let the men do their duty & the women will be such wonders, the female life lives from the light of the male. see a mans female dependants you know the man. . . .
>
> (p. 585)

For all Blake's protests against John Milton's attitudes toward women, his own character Milton sounds suspiciously like the austere intellectual Adam who converses with angels in *Paradise Lost*, and his Ololon, though *she* converses with Jesus, like an even meeker Eve.

resents the parallel functions of male and female, Reprobate and Redeemed, time and space, eternity, and time/space—of any two contraries in their contention with negation.[20]

That Book II parallels Book I suggests that the events the two books record are identical; in fact, it is only through the parallel actions and patterns of action that we can at all recognize the simultaneity by which those events are identified. The multiple perspectives of the poem are given order and coherence by parallelism; randomly arranged perspectives would imply, as they seem to in *The Four Zoas*, an impersonal, perhaps even arbitrary reversal of the fall, whereas in *Milton* Blake demands the very opposite, a conscious marshaling of perspective by the individual in order to recognize truth and annihilate error.

The verbal styles of the poem attain a new dimension of meaning in the parallelism of their organization. In Book I we identified three controlling styles (each comprised of variations), the bardic, disjunctive narrative, and visionary styles. In Book II we defined the controlling styles as pastoral, disjunctive narrative, and prophetic. The progress of the first book from a bardic account of history through an act of forgiveness to a vision of the continuous creation of fallen reality is a process of the renovation of the imagination. Throughout the book characters achieve new recognition of their own identities and of the true extent of fallen existence: Milton learns that he in his selfhood is Satan, Blake observes "the nether regions of the Imagination," Los proclaims himself that "Shadowy Prophet" whose fall from human wholeness circumscribes all mortal history. The progression of the second book from a pastoral account of history through an act of contrition to a prophecy of the imminent end of fallen reality is a process of the renovation of

---

[20] I have said that contraries are equal, and called Eden and Generation contraries when clearly Eden is a superior state—but these two states are equal in their function as combatants against Ulro, because in that function Generation is as vital as Eden.

sense perception. The subject of the book is the return of mortal and immortal souls to the body for the Last Judgment, the activating style of the book is the sensuous pastoral, the emblems of the book's action are the lark and thyme which together represent the five fallen senses.

As hammer and loom perform the same function, so forgiveness and contrition are necessarily the same act, for in the act of true forgiveness one embraces all reality and recognizes one's own responsibility for it. The union of Milton and Ololon is the union of forgiveness and contrition, of hammer and loom, of center and circumference, of imagination and the perception of human existence which alone can realize imagination.

✧✧

Illuminations and Structure

The thematic and rhetorical parallelisms of *Milton* are further reflected in yet a third dimension of the work, its engraved illuminations, which reflect as well many of the subsidiary verbal techniques we have identified. David Erdman has noted of the illustrations that their "major motifs are dancing, striding, and confronting. These posed actions display the separation and unity of contraries, of male and female, brother and brother, descent and ascent, wrath and pity, bread and wine."[1]

The parallelism of the two books of *Milton* is upheld by several key pairs of illustrations divided between the books. The most obvious pair is the mirrored designs "William" and "Robert" which appear respectively as plates 32 and 37 in the D copy. (All references in this appendix will be to the D copy, which is the final extant version and which has been reproduced in excellent facsimile by the Trianon Press for the William Blake Trust [London, 1967], and the pagination of which Erdman has followed in his edition of Blake's engravings of the poems, *The Illuminated Blake*; plate numbers will differ from those of the Keynes and Erdman editions of the poems, which were numbered without the full-page designs.) The design conspicuously titled "William" occurs immediately after the last plate of Book I, and looks toward Book II; "Robert," the same design reversed, faces back toward Book I from the fifth plate of the second book. In the first, William staggers backward toward three stone steps representing the threefold sexual existence of Beulaic inspiration; the star which is Milton's falling form enters his left foot. Robert (Blake's dead broth-

---

[1] *The Illuminated Blake*, p. 20.

er, with whom he claimed to communicate and who probably represents the poet's eternal portion), in the same posture, falls backward toward four steps (Edenic reality), a smaller star entering his right foot. The congruence of the designs suggests the unification of time and eternity in the instant of Milton's descent, which in turn supports the simultaneity of the events of the poem's text. Their positions as a coda to Book I and the first full-page illustration to Book II reinforce the textual parallelism. The introduction of William Blake's literal brother provides the character Blake with a brotherly contrary, a Rintrah to his Palamabron, an Orc to his Los, an eternal self to his temporal one.

Plate 1 of the poem, its frontispiece and the emblem of the first book, shows Milton striding forth into his shadow, his body shielded from the darkness by a sheath of light. The final plate of the poem, the conclusion of Book II, shows a central female figure facing forward, both hands raised, emerging from a garment that is identified in two flanking figures as a vegetable shroud; she, like Milton, is surrounded by red and gold light. Erdman suggests that in order to recognize "the state of spousal *preparation* at the end of the poem . . . we must hold the volume open to its first and last plates to see Milton striding forward in self-annihilating wrath . . . and Ololon in pity removing her garment and stepping forth to the embrace of 'Resurrection & Judgment.' "[2] Plate 16 might be seen as an intermediate step in the progression from male wrath striding away to female pity stepping forward: in it Milton approximates Ololon's position on the last plate; he faces forward, his left foot in front of his right, his face outlined exactly like hers, his arms at half-height removing his robe.

The cosmic masculine action of Book I is framed by its frontispiece, in which Milton strides forward, his hand dividing the large letters of his name, and plate 32, in which the star which is Milton descends through the letters of "William" to Blake's foot and sends him reeling backward.

[2] *Op. cit.*, p. 267.

The second book, with its sexual reunion in Blake's garden, begins on plate 33 with a male and female form at Judgment and ends with Ololon at the last harvest.

The text of each book of *Milton* is introduced by a design, covering one-third of the page and incorporating words that identify the book, of a male and female figure joined foot to foot. In the first, the star of Milton's descent illuminates the pair; in the second, the lightning flash of Ololon's descent provides a harsher light in which are seen as well three other figures who descend to or rise from the earth.

Each book contains a full-page illustration of Milton's struggle with Urizen. In the first (plate 18), Urizen stands in the Arnon, supported by stone tablets of the law, as Milton steps toward him from a position of weakness: he is smaller, shorter, and naked (Milton's position may be his next step after the frontispiece: he faces completely away from the reader and toward Urizen, his left foot is now forward, and both hands are raised). In the second (plate 45), Milton has crossed the river and he stands in a posture of calm strength above his fainting adversary. The six musicians who observe the struggle from above in the first book have vanished in the second, except insofar as the inspiration they represent is present in the fiery halo that surrounds Milton. Each full-page design of the battle on the Arnon is followed by a plate that ends in a quarter- or third-plate "analytic variant of the wrestling":[3] Milton enters an anthropomorphic forest, identified as the fibrous limbs of Los on plate 19, to confront Urizen (as disembodied head on 19, as serpent on 46). In the first, the six musicians of the previous plate are repeated at the top in the six forms of Ololon, three dancing and three facing away from the dancers. Because plate 45 contained no observers of the struggle, plate 46 has no identifiable figures except Milton and Urizen.[4] Both "analytic variants" reflect

---

[3] *Op. cit.*, p. 236.

[4] Ololon is, after all, presented primarily as observer in Book I; in Book II she has her own action, and her own plates to describe it pictorially.

their previous plates in Milton's stance (left foot forward in Book I, like "William," right foot forward in Book II, like "Robert"), and in his relative strength (he seems tentative, unguarded, on 19, whereas on 46 he is aggressive and prepared).

Like the verbal and symbolic motifs of the text (speeches ending where they started, lark and thyme, *etc.*), repeated motifs among the illustrations form richly suggestive patterns. The marginal scrollwork of birds and flowers, and of human forms in postures that recall birds and flowers, is a constant reference throughout the poem to the mutual functions of lark and thyme. Other more prominent designs provide even more detailed reflections of the verbal techniques of *Milton.* The principal pictorial motif is a union of two human forms, joined (or nearly joined) limb to limb but arching outward from the juncture so that their bodies form a cup, like two petals of a flower or the wings of a bird. Blake uses this motif to indicate the relationship of the figures: if they are united in harmony they face each other, if not, they face away. If we imagine the William and Robert plates set together, we have the perfect example of a harmonious cup: the two brothers face each other (though each staggers backward at the impact of the star), mirroring each other's posture exactly, arms outstretched in a foreshadowed embrace.

The negative instance of this brotherly relationship occurs on plate 15: one male form flees another which lies supine behind him (presumably they are Cain and Abel, or Satan and Thulloh); the outstretched arm of the recumbent figure is on a line with the back foot of the fleeing one, but the two limbs do not touch—an indication of shattered relationship.

Positive and negative relationships are similarly indicated in two other pairs of plates. The sixfold female at the top of plate 19 is divided into two groups of three, joined feet to feet but facing in opposite directions: Ololon has not yet gathered herself together to descend. By Book II she has:

on plate 48 her six members are joined not only feet to feet, but also hands to hands; the two groups are intertwined in gaze as well as in limbs; Ololon is whole now, in Blake's Felpham garden. The opening plates of the two books seem to reverse this progress: on plate two, a male and a female form, joined at their feet but floating apart, still turn to look joyously at each other; plate 33 shows them looking away from each other, he toward darkness and she toward light. Each scene is apocalyptic, but the first portrays the glories of the last harvest and vintage, whereas the second portrays the horror of Judgment. The horror forces the pair to look about them, but at the same time they are drawn closer together than in plate 2, and each is dependent on the other for equilibrium. Significantly, after the apocalyptic first plate, all the cupped unions of Book II will be wholly positive; Book II is, after all, the book of the union of contraries. It will end with a nearly full-page close-up of the illustration on the first plate of the text: from the joined feet of the joyful couple of plate two a flower or vine grows; between the vegetable forms of a male and a female on plate 50 arises Ololon, emerging from her vegetative sheath into the last harvest, her discarded garment uniting the feet of the yet mortal pair.

One plate shows a transition in the postures of the two cup figures: on plate 17 a miniature of the William figure faces, beyond a stone wall, a gowned figure which turns away weeping. Their feet do not touch, but would if the figures were closer together. Again, as in the Cain/Abel scene, the separation is a comment on the relationship. Erdman conjectures, on the basis of Blake's pun that inspiration entered through his tarsus (identifying himself thereby with Saul of Tarsus in his transformation from bloody sinner into apostle), that "William Blake has been saved, by Milton's illuminating descent, from some act of connubial persecution."[5] The design thus indicates that Blake, like Milton, has failed his emanation (who lies sick in their cot-

[5] *Illuminated Blake*, p. 233.

tage), and that Milton's sudden enlightenment, proclaimed from five lines below the illustration, precipitates Blake's own. Such, surely, is the action of the poem, by which all falsely divided couples are reunited. The illustration of Blake's enlightenment when the text describes Milton's provides a graphic version of the repeated verbal transposition of an unexpected speaker or action for an expected one (as in Los's proclaiming he is that "Shadowy Prophet" when we have been led to expect a speech by Blake [22:15ff.], or in Milton's entering Blake's foot upon Los's descent [21:4ff.]).

Blake uses the cup motif ironically several times. The illustrations of Milton's entering the forest to battle Urizen on plates 19 and 46 echo the motif first in the anthropomorphic shape of the trees, which lean toward Milton and touch his feet with their branches, and then in the curved form of the serpent, whose tail reaches almost to Milton's foot. Plate 10 provides the most illuminating ironic use of the motif: here Palamabron reaches his foot to Satan's on a stone altar, turning toward his destructive brother in the falsely placed pity that is the source of the poem's disaster; Satan, in his false wrath, looks away.

That tenth-plate full-page design exemplifies as well the second most prevalent major graphic motif of the *Milton*. Joined with Satan foot to foot, Palamabron is also joined with Rintrah loins to loins. The union of two male figures loins to loins or head to loins is the subject of four of the poem's nine full-page designs.[6] Milton is joined at the loins with Urizen, at least in the two-dimensionality of the engraving, on plate 18; on plate 45 Urizen has sunk down, his head at Milton's loins. On plate 4 the kneeling Blake turns from binding on his sandal to face the approaching Los, his face at the level of the Zoa's loins. The explicitly sexual nature of the unions on these plates has particular emphasis

[6] Four of the remaining designs are of a single male figure, two of Milton and one each of William and Robert; the fifth is of a male and female couple. Plate 50 is nearly a full-page illustration, but it contains one line of text and the word "Finis."

in that none of the male-female unions in the poem is illustrated erotically. With one major exception, heterosexual couples, if they touch at all, touch only at their feet. The exception is, of course, the great plate 42 illustration that Keynes in his annotations to the facsimile calls the "Moment of Inspiration," in which an eagle hovers over a man and woman lying side by side in partial embrace. From the inertia of the human forms and from the large penis fully apparent only in the A copy, Erdman concludes "that the lovers have been interrupted in . . . copulation."[7] Because there is no textual reference to such a sex act anywhere in the poem, I interpret the inertia and the obscuration of the penis differently. The recumbent male form has begun to lift his left arm, the thumb relaxed and the fingers beginning to extend; if he only gathers himself up on his right arm, drawing his left leg up for balance, he will reproduce Michelangelo's Adam about to be touched by a hand of God shaped remarkably like the head of Blake's eagle. The inertia of Blake's recumbent couple I interpret as the inertia of the Sistine Adam before he is awakened to life; the eagle who calls to them is the only divine inspiration Blake recognized.[8] The compositions of Blake's and Michelangelo's pictures are, though not identical, revealingly similar: both show inert mortal forms on sloping rocks (Blake, not limited by the Genesis sequence, has his Eve already formed and waiting to be awakened with her Adam to life), both show the inspiring forces as flying or hovering above, turned toward the mortals, beckoning them awake.[9] Blake's obscuration of his Adam's—Albion's—penis I take to be a recognition that overt sexual reference would be misleading here: any suggestion of erection would be inappropriate to

[7] *Illuminated Blake*, p. 258.

[8] *Jerusalem* plate 94, which is a verbal description of this *Milton* illustration, verifies this interpretation.

[9] The eagle's form is reflected on plate 49 in a female counterpart. Oothoon hovers over the last harvest, her arms and legs outstretched like the eagle's wings.

the pre-awakening inertia of the scene. That male and female lie together here and have begun to stir at the eagle's call makes this illumination an emblem for the entire poem, which is the account of the reunion of contraries as apocalypse begins. That Blake should emphasize the sexual nature of the relationships of male contraries and then deemphasize sexuality in the male-female relationship is neither abstruse nor perverse: to do so is to equate the relationships, to underscore at once the sexual relationship of all contraries and the contrary relationship of all sexuality.

The placement of the major illustrations of *Milton* is a suggestive issue. Some directly illustrate the text they adorn or follow, but some are placed far from their textual reference, in which case they operate to bring us back to an earlier point or to foreshadow a later one, much as some passages of the text operate.[10] On the whole they are progressive; we can trace, for example, the development of Ololon's unification from the divided trios of plate 19 through the six intertwined dancers of 48 to the whirling unity of 50. The backgrounds of the illustrations attain progressively more greenery as we move toward the final harvest of the last plate. (Plate 28, with its two illustrations of bedrock England, the first of the stony north and the second of the greening south, is a kind of locus of this progression.) Milton confronts a strong Urizen on plate 18, and supports a

[10] Wittreich cites the orders of the illuminations of Blake's poems as evidence that Blake intended to emphasize deliberate disjunctions in the narratives:

> It also appears that Blake, in early versions of his illuminated books, preserved his narrative line but, in later versions, subdued and all but concealed it, first, by rearranging plates so that narrative continuity is broken and then by redistributing full-page designs so that these ruptures in the narrative do not go unobserved. (The early copies of *Milton* [A and B] in comparison with the later ones [C and D] are a case in point.)
>
> (*Sublime Allegory*, p. 41)

Another "case in point" is *The Book of Urizen*, in which, according to Erdman's textual note (p. 725), the pictures are moved farther away from their corresponding texts in successive printings.

fainting Urizen on 45. We might even see the partial embrace of 42 as a culmination of the sexual union begun on 2 as the flying pair touches toes and carried further on 33 as they stand together, supporting each other, although the horror around them forces their gazes outward.

Yet the progressiveness, the linearity of the designs, is far from complete. If Milton first confronts and then defeats Urizen on 18 and 45, the suceeding plate in each case takes the action backward in time, the first to before the confrontation (Milton seems merely to happen unprepared on to Urizen in the forest of Los's limbs), and the second to its beginnings (he steels himself for battle). Milton strides forward naked to eternal death on the frontispiece, but only removes his garments on plate 16. The star of his descent hovers over the pair on 2 and then meets Blake's foot on 17—but plates 32 and 37 back up and show the star before it quite reaches anyone. Some of the major illustrations are completely out of synchronization with the text: Los joins Blake in tying on his sandal in the second third of Book I, but after copies A and B, the illustration of the event does not occur until the end of Book II; the small design of Milton's star entering Blake's foot occurs with the appropriate text, half-way through Book I, but the full-page design of the same act does not appear until after the book is finished, and the corresponding Robert design answers to nothing explicit in the text. Blake seems to use these instances of broken synchronization to attack the seeming linearity of the pictorial development as he uses several textual elements to attack the linearity of the verbal development. The pictures, like the text, end where they began—in the enlightenment of the twofold central character Milton/Ololon and in the approaching apocalypse that enlightenment signals.

Both illustrations and text seems to establish a linearity from inception to conclusion, but both actually undermine that linearity by doubling it back upon itself again and again. Both verbal and pictorial motifs suggest in their re-

currence and in their misplaced chronology the simul-
taneity of the actions they record; both verbal and pictorial
motifs suggest in their significant variations the multiplicity
of perspectives through which we see those actions.[11] In
both illustrations and text, simultaneity and multiple per-
spective are organized by a rigorous system of parallelism
between books and within them.

[11] The range of perspectives is represented in the illuminations by
a range of pictorial styles. W. J. T. Mitchell cites three different
styles of engraving in the *Milton* illuminations, from crude line-
drawings through sophisticated high-finished designs, which he ex-
plains according to their possible thematic functions ("Style and
Iconography in the Illustrations of Blake's *Milton*," *Blake Studies*,
6, 1 [Fall 1973], pp. 47–71). We might look to one of the crudest
of the line-drawings for support of the kind of parallelism we have
been exploring. Despite variations in engraving techniques, nearly
all the designs of the poem are set in the mythic milieu of striders
through Ulro and human sheaves; one illustration alone departs
from this setting: engraved plate 40 (36, Keynes and Erdman) rep-
resents the descent of Ololon to Blake in a simple, homey scene
rather in the manner of a Tudor woodcut. This one old-fashioned
design thus supports the progress of the text from the universal
scale of Book I with its visions of Eden and Golgonooza to the per-
sonal, individual scale of Book II with its return to the flesh in a
Felpham garden. Yet even this picture with its child-like naiveté
participates in the cosmic symbolism of the poem: Blake on his gar-
den path looks upward to Ololon in the sky; between them are two
angles, one near Blake formed by the convergence of two paths, its
apex toward Ololon, and one near her formed by the branches of a
tree, its apex toward Blake. The suggestion is of the dual vortices,
whose points will meet where Blake meets Ololon. Where those
vortices meet, eternity meets time, and time ceases to be.

✿✿✿✿✿✿✿✿✿✿✿✿✿✿✿✿✿✿✿✿✿✿✿✿✿✿✿✿✿✿✿✿✿✿✿✿✿✿✿

Revisions and Structure

The revisions we know Blake made of *Milton* support the structural inferences of this study. Because no manuscript of the poem survives, no early revisions survive, and the actual motive for the revisions we have, the six plates added after the engraving of the first two copies of the poem, are as much a matter of conjecture as motives usually are. Yet without infringing on those motives I think we can safely say that the inclusions of plates 3, 4, 10, 18, and 32 in the C copy (plates 10 and 32, David Erdman informs me, after the completion and pagination of the volume), and plate 5 in the D copy, serve to strengthen and tighten the system of parallels we have extrapolated. We noted in Chapter Two some of the thematic contributions of the late incorporations, and their disruption of the narrative order of the Bard's Song. Now let us examine their relation to other parts of the poem.

Plates 3 and 4, the opening plates of the Bard's Song, overhaul the parody of Genesis Blake first devised for the *Book of Urizen*, identifying the binding of Urizen with the fall of Satan and through that identification extending the consequences of their mutual fall from the cosmic level to the mundane, from the rocky bones of the universe to the atrocities of South Molton Street. Thus Book I begins, after its invocation, just as Book II begins, with a myth of creation. The clamorous book of the hammer begins with the anguished creation of Ulro, the gracious book of the loom with the fashioning of Beulah.

Plates 5, 10, and 18 interpolate into the largely masculine first book its crucial feminine counterpart. The parallel functions of male and female are especially strongly emphasized on plate 5, Blake's last addition to *Milton*. The plate begins and ends with Satan's fainting, in the first passage presumably because of the fiery harrow of Palamabron and in the second because of the arrows of Elynittria, which may be the harrow's flames. The rhyme of "Harrow" and "arrow" may be accidental, but the mutuality of male and female it suggests is the theme of the entire plate. The functions of the sexes are summarized in line 3, which might be an emblem for the plate or for the whole poem: "Christ took on Sin in the Virgins Womb, & put it off on the Cross." The incarnation through which humanity is saved begins with the female weaving of the fabric of flesh, and ends with the hammers of the males at the cross. (Christ is, of course, in Blake's doctrine neither male nor female, but undivided humanity.) That paradigm is realized for Blake in his own England; in plate 4 he placed calvary on South Molton Street and Stratford Place, "Where the Victims were preparing for Sacrifice their Cherubim," and now we see that preparation in terms of the sexual functions of the incarnation: "While the Females prepare the Victims. The Males at Furnaces / And Anvils dance the dance of tears & pain."

Plate 5 adds to the doctrine of the Three Classes of Men its female counterpart, the Three Heavens of Beulah, the source of the creation and sacrifice that maintains the Three Classes. Bloom sees them as temptations "cruel and deceptive" because their bliss is illusory,[1] and we know certainly

---

[1] Commentary, p. 825. He also assumes that the song which covers nearly half the plate is "the mocking of the Female Will" (*Apocalypse*, p. 346), but I find it neither mocking nor female. The pity seems to me very real; lines like "Ah weak & wide astray! Ah shut in narrow doleful form" sound sympathetic to my ear, as does the comprehension the song displays of what vegetated souls have lost. That Blake intended this passage to imply the sympathy of its chanters seems to me verified by his having it spoken in *Jerusalem* by Erin, a loving heroine (49:32–41). Also, as I read it the passage attributes the song to the males, not the females; it is the males who dance, and who "turn the whirlwinds loose upon / The Furnaces, lamenting around the Anvils & this their Song. . . ."

that at least some females do support that description in their imperfect sexuality. Furthermore, it may well be that the Three Heavens of Beulah are Alla, Al-Ulro, and Or-Ulro, the emanative realms of devastation. But it seems more likely that the heavens in this case are Beulah itself, threefold because it is not Eden, and because it is here defined as the female parallel of the Three Classes. And if that is true, then to assume that those heavens are altogether illusory is to contradict most of the allusions to Beulah in the poem: Beulah is the source of Blake's inspiration, the higher state through which he aspires to enter Eden; it is the necessary resting place of weakened Edenic souls, the place where Satan himself might rest and recover if only he would (12:49–13:2); from it "the three Classes of Men take their fix'd destinations" (5:13).

Although any description of Beulah is necessarily ambiguous because Beulah is ambiguous, this particular description seems to me to present a positive attitude toward the realm of heady pleasures. The females' taking up into their heavens "whom they please" "in intoxicating delight" certainly warns of whim and delusion, but here that act is presented in apposition to the necessary and positive act of maintaining the Three Classes: the daughters take up whom they please, "For the Elect cannot be Redeemd, but Created continually." Blake does not explicitly identify that continuous creation with the Heavens of Beulah, but his syntax suggests the identification.

Whether we see the functions of the Three Heavens as positive or negative, or as an ambiguous blending of the two, plate 5 is clearly concerned with the relation of that function to its male counterpart. If the females save their "victims" here, so do the males; if they destroy them, so do the males. The plate begins and ends with the subduing of mathematic by living proportion, an act for which the female is as responsible as the male.

Plates 10 and 18, the remaining additions to the earlier version of Book I, both deal also with the mutuality of male and female, but from a new perspective. In these plates the sexes rebel against that mutuality, rejecting responsibility and demanding power. On plate 10 we learn that the female space, created by Enitharmon to preserve Satan from annihilation (8:42–44), preserves only by shrinking and confining, and that it confines Los as well as Satan; in response to his imprisonment Los rails not only against the god of the place, but against the female treachery he thinks keeps him there. Plate 18 records the epic struggle in which the love of each for the other is perverted into jealousy and wrath.

The additions made in the C and D copies to Book I do support our inferences of structural parallelism. The first two interpolated plates align the beginning of Book I with that of Book II, and the remaining interpolations inject one of the basic parallelisms of the poem, male-female mutuality, into a book that is otherwise mostly masculine in orientation. Yet it is impossible to deduce from these observations that Blake added the extra plates to adjust the structure of Book I and balance it with Book II. His addition to Book II, on the other hand, seems designed specifically to reflect a clearly corresponding section of Book I. Plate 32 contains a central Blakean doctrine which amplifies many of the themes of the poem; its conclusion anywhere in the poem would certainly enhance the work. Its inclusion where it does appear, and in the form in which it appears, suggests that Blake used it with structural considerations at least as much in mind as thematic considerations.

Milton's conversation with the Seven Angels of the Presence interrupts the lamentations of Beulah with which Book II opens. It is neither thematically nor rhetorically related to the preceding and succeeding plates, except insofar as the doctrine of states and self-annihilation can be used to explain almost anything in the poem. One might explain its position in the work wholly by expediency—it was good material and it had to go someplace. Blake even changed his mind slightly, placing it first after and then before the plate we are calling 33.[2] But despite that minor vacillation, he does place the new plate among the opening plates of Book II, and not in what would seem its logical position, before plate 15 in Book I.[3] A conversation between Milton and the angels in Book II balances effectively the Book I description of their relationship, which may have led Blake to keep the two descriptions divided. But the later passage provides an even more significant balance by being placed exactly where it is in the last version of the poem: the construction of the plate dramatically parallels the segment that occupies the same position in the Bard's Song as plate 32 occupies in the Book II prologue. Each is the third segment of its book's prologue, each takes place around a couch of the dead (Albion's, Milton's), each is concerned primarily with judgment, sacrifice, and the salvation of Satan. That Blake consciously devised plate 32 to parallel the third part of the Bard's Song, even that he ultimately positioned it as a parallel, would be impossible to prove. That its position perfects the parallelism of the two books when it might otherwise more logically be placed elsewhere suggests that Blake did add the plate at least partly for structural purposes. Without plate 32 in its final position, the books of *Milton* are suggestively parallel; with it, they are precisely parallel. Its late inclusion in the one place in which it could have major structural significance seems to me to argue Blake's deliberate organization of his poem into two exhaustively parallel books.

There is one more revision of *Milton* that may have bearing on the poem's structure, but it is a baffling revision. Blake probably conceived and wrote much of *Milton* dur-

[2] Erdman, textual notes, p. 729.

[3] It may be that an addition fits more easily among the opening plates of Book II, which are discrete units requiring no alterations of the plates themselves to accommodate interpolations. Still, the transition between 32 and 15, both of which are about Milton and the Seven Angels, could easily be accomplished. Facility of inclusion does not seem to me a strong enough explanation of the final position of plate 32.

ing his Felpham stay (1801–1803), and he engraved its title page in 1804, promising a poem of twelve books. When he finally engraved the first two copies, on paper watermarked 1808, he wrote "Finis" after the second book and obscured the "1" in the title page "12." That much is not surprising. But in the last two copies of the work, on 1815 paper, he not only restored that "1" but emphasized it, thus adamantly describing his two-book poem as a twelve-book poem.[4]

David Wagenknecht suggests that the twelve books comprised, in Blake's mind, the two books of *Milton* and the ten of *The Four Zoas* (including both Nights the Seventh), which Blake had by 1815 decided not to engrave but could not abandon altogether.[5] That hypothesis attests to the poet's willfulness, his teasing of the reader—but so does any other hypothesis of the reasons for the change. Why should Blake deliberately call two books twelve? One could conceivably find three books in the poem by isolating the Bard's Song, or six books by separating the poem as I have done into two prologues, two action sections, and two visions; one could even be dazzlingly ingenious and find twelve books in the eight prologue subsections, two actions, and two visions. But the fact remains that Blake himself defined only two books and then called them twelve. Whether that means he was at least thinking about the structure of his poem, or whether it means he was not thinking about it at all, seems to me moot. It may be that the reason for the number game has nothing to do with the organization, or potential organization, of the poem. Perhaps Blake was merely enjoying some prophetic private joke. Do those ten unwritten books represent Blake's ten lost tribes?

[4] Erdman, textual notes, pp. 727–728. Erdman notes that Blake also described the four-book *Jerusalem* on its 1804 title page as a twenty-eight-book work, but later deleted that incongruity.
[5] *Blake's Night*, p. 216.

Index

All literary works except Blake's own are listed under their authors' names.

Library of Congress Cataloging in Publication Data
Fox, Susan, 1943-
    Poetic form in Blake's Milton.
    Includes bibliographical references and index.
    1. Blake, William, 1757-1827. Milton. I. Title.
PR4144.M63F6   821'.7   76-6461
ISBN 0-691-06300-0